D0609134

The Time Bomb

BY THE SAME AUTHOR
The Story of Peter Townsend

THE TIME BOMB

*A Veteran Journalist Assesses Today's
China from the Inside*

Norman Barrymaine

PETER DAVIES: LONDON

Printed in Great Britain by
Morrison & Gibb Ltd, London and Edinburgh

This book is dedicated to the people of China whom I have known with affection for nearly fifty years and against whom I still have no bitterness.

CONTENTS

ILLUSTRATIONS

The illustrations will be found between pages
102 and 103

Shanghai Bund
Junks going up the Whangpoo River
Red Guard statue
Workmen painting a Mao slogan
Entrance to the former British Consulate,
    Shanghai
Wall-newspapers
Petro-chemical plant in Shanghai
Red Guards
Commune houses
A Chinese woman welder
A commune
In a commune kindergarten
Chairman Mao
Watching and celebrating the hydrogen bomb
    test
The author, after his release

Part One

1 Premonition

HANDCUFFS are cold—spiritually as well as physically. It is a traumatic sensation as steel bites into flesh. In a split second you have lost mobility, freedom. Your mind focuses only on the frightening, gleaming bracelets, linked by a chain. Black misery envelops you. Momentarily you have lost hope.

I felt thus on Monday, March 4, 1968, when, after ten days' interrogation, I was finally charged with being a spy and taken to Shanghai's prison for foreign and political offenders. I was held in solitary confinement there for twenty months.

When and where does a story begin? Was it in Amoy forty-eight years ago when I first set foot on Chinese soil after sailing a tug-boat from Manila on the edge of a typhoon? China immediately fascinated me, got into my blood like passion for a woman one has bedded.

Since then I had returned to China many times, most recently in November, 1967. It was towards the end of the militant stage of the Cultural Revolution, and the walls of the grand staircase linking the two floors of the Friendship Shop in the Nanking Road (a cut-price Chinese shop for foreigners) were covered with anti-Moscow diatribes.

Britain, however, was the country against which anti-foreign feeling was mainly stimulated. Wall-newspapers lampooned

Johnson; bayonets of American G.I.s were depicted running red with the blood of Viet Cong (freedom fighters in the eyes of the Chinese) in South Vietnam, but in the ultimate it was the British whom all Chinese were daily taught with blistering propaganda to hate. It was understandable; it was credible to a Chinese urban factory worker or peasant on a commune. For it was Britain, a hundred years or so ago, that led the Big Power struggle to plunder China, beginning with the Opium War of 1840. There followed repeated and bitter humiliations, such as the burning of the Summer Palace in 1860 by an Anglo-French force, and the repression of the Boxer uprising in 1900. It is true that other powers joined in the scramble for markets, keeping the country divided by backing the competing warlords and preventing the development of industry. Germany annexed Shantung province and demanded a huge indemnity as a penalty for the murder of two German missionaries: nothing they did for their country was so great in life as in their death. There was the defeat by the Japanese, always regarded by the Chinese as petty and barbarous. The hatred remains. However, to the average Chinese, a foreigner is synonymous with an Englishman—respected perhaps for his business integrity, but not loved.

The anti-British campaign explains why the Chancery of the British mission in Peking was burned down by Red Guards; why the fanatical mob of boys and girls tried to make Donald Hopson, the Chargé d'Affaires, bow his head before a portrait of Mao; why the British Consulate in Shanghai was seized and the Consul-General paraded around the grounds with his suit plastered with oil; why Anthony Grey was held hostage in his house in Peking for more than two years; why I languished for nearly twenty months in solitary confinement in a cell of a Shanghai prison; why other Britishers are still in prison in China (even if likely to be released in time).

While on my visit in November, 1967, I felt a little of the xenophobia of the mob. I got into an ugly incident on the Bund.

On the previous day I had been to a commune with a China Travel Service guide, a Mr Cheng. Now he was trying to arrange for me to meet some Red Guards. So I went for a walk, taking my Leica which I loaded with a Kodacolour-X film.

It was a sunny, crisp morning, but there were very few people on the streets when I started along the Bund. There was a kind of tension hanging over the city.

I came up to some men busy in the middle of the broad road painting white pro-Mao characters on a huge red banner. As I took a photograph, they looked up but resumed their work. They made no protest.

The gate of the British Consulate, from which the Consul had been expelled a few months previously, was festooned with Mao slogans and there was a huge portrait of him in the garden. I took a picture.

In the Bund gardens, which incidentally once bore a sign 'No Chinese, no dogs admitted', I photographed four young workers against a portrait of Mao.

I continued my walk over Soochow Creek bridge, passing what was once the plush Astor House Hotel where in the bar you could eat a free snack lunch for the price of a beer, while outside starving urchins, probably the victims of flood or famine in the valley of the Yellow River—the River of Sorrow, as the Chinese call it—begged for coppers.

Today, the hotel appears to be a disused building, its windows grimed with dirt. Hongkew had not much changed since I lived there in the 'twenties. Its small, red-brick Edwardian-type houses were depressing. They are now even more so for want of paint. In fact, all Shanghai exudes a state of dilapidation, though the streets may be cleaner: there are no beggars to pester you; no prostitutes.

I retraced my steps to the Bund. Near the Peace Hotel on the corner of Nanking Road, Shanghai's main shopping street, which once vied with Bond Street in the elegance of its shops, a small crowd was gathered round a man selling hand-made bradawls. They were very crude. Just a rough wooden handle with a sharp pointed piece of steel stuck in it. The man was doing a brisk trade. At the time it struck me as incongruous. Here was a monolithic State, which during two years of the Cultural Revolution aimed at wiping out individualism, but a

3

man could still have the courage to practise private enterprise. In Shanghai there is a degree of private business, however. There are many small shops, tea houses and restaurants. Of course, they come under government control. The shops buy their goods from state factories.

Anyway, I thought it was worth taking a photograph of this man. He was standing in front of a wall-newspaper with a hideous caricature of President Johnson. I took out my Weston light meter, measured the light, set the shutter speed and aperture of the camera. I had just raised the view-finder to eye-level when a man with upraised arms and a grim scowl on his face jumped in front of the lens. I thought at first that he wanted to be photographed but he shouted aggressively in English, 'No photographs! No photographs!'

I tried to explain that I had official permission to take photographs. But he merely repeated more vehemently, 'No photographs! No photographs!' And then without warning he snatched the camera out of my hand, unscrewed it from the leather case and stuffed it in his pocket. He handed me back the case.

By now the crowd had swollen to about 200 men, youths and children. They appeared as if by magic. Before the incident the Bund had seemed comparatively deserted. There was no retreat. My accuser was addressing the crowd; whipping up hostility. They began to jostle me.

A hostile Chinese crowd is terrifying. My mind went back to June 1, 1925—forty-eight hours after British police opened fire on demonstrating Chinese students in the Nanking Road. A number of students were killed and wounded. On Monday, June 1, about 20,000 indignant Chinese, shouting 'People of China, unite!' and 'Down with imperialism!', congregated in the four roads that lead into Nanking Road. I found myself, with two police officers and a fire engine and half a dozen firemen, trapped in the centre of the junction of the five roads. Those in the front ranks began pulling up granite stones between the tramlines and throwing them at us. We should certainly have all been killed if a contingent of Sikh police had not fought their way through to us. After firing warning shots

4

over the heads of the crowds, who refused to disperse, they opened up at point-blank range. There were more dead, more wounded, and the crowds fell back before the onslaught.

At that time I was only twenty-four and very idealistic. The affair made me sad at heart. But I recognised that there is no crowd in the world more frightening than a Chinese mob. They can easily be whipped up into mass hysteria. And they have a strong sadistic streak, which found an outlet in the excesses of the Cultural Revolution.

On this occasion I tried to reason with the self-appointed accuser. I knew I must not show fear or lose my temper. It was an exercise in patience.

'Whom do you represent?' I asked.

'The People,' he shouted. He meant people with a capital P. 'You are an imperialist spy. You are taking photographs to use in propaganda against China.'

It seemed futile to argue this piece of Cultural Revolution rhetoric. In fact, before I got a chance to say anything further, he demanded: 'What is your nationality? Show me your passport.'

'By what authority do you make the request?'

'The People.'

'Swiss,' I replied. In a sense this was subterfuge. I have lived in Lugano, Switzerland, for many years. It is given in my passport as my place of residence. To have confessed to being an Englishman would have probably aggravated my position.

I took the passport from my pocket, opened it to the appropriate page and showed him. I did not let the passport out of my hand. He made no comment.

Some of the heat had now gone out of the atmosphere. I felt the moment had come to try and settle the matter amicably. I didn't want to lose my Leica which I had had for nearly forty years.

I began by explaining that I was visiting China under the auspices of the China Travel Service. I said that the offices were on the ground floor of the Peace Hotel, only a few yards away. Would it not be better to go there to clear the matter up?

My accuser pondered this proposal. The crowd were silent. Having gained the initiative, I didn't give him too long to think. 'Come along,' I said, grabbing him by the arm and propelling him through the crowd that was now 300 or more.

The crowd—I suppose I should say the People—seemed a little taken aback by my surprise move; they parted to let us enter the Peace Hotel, then followed us into the offices. No one tried to stop them. I asked an official to send for Mr Cheng. My accuser took the Leica from his pocket and put it on the counter.

Mr Cheng came down from his upstairs office. As he listened to my accuser he became embarrassed.

I asked him: 'What is this man's authority?'

'The People,' he replied.

The People, who were crowding the foyer, were jabbering like magpies. It was a public trial in miniature. Mao, I suppose, would call it 'Dictatorship of the Proletariat'.

Cheng disappeared upstairs 'to fetch someone who spoke English more fluently' (this, obviously, was an excuse for he had spent five years studying English at the Shanghai Institute of Languages). In a few minutes he returned with another official who took immediate command. His attitude towards me was hostile. When I tried to say something, he shouted: 'Don't argue.'

There was a further long discussion with my accuser. There were appeals to the crowd. I could not understand if they were witnesses or jury. Then, turning to me, this official said: 'The People tell me you have two cameras. One is a small spy camera.'

I was puzzled by the accusation. It then occurred to me that they might be mistaking my Weston light meter for a camera. I took it from my overcoat pocket; held it high so that all could see.

There was a chorus of shouts: 'There it is! That's it!'

'This is only a light meter,' I explained. I demonstrated how it worked.

Cheng was still looking embarrassed. I said: 'Mr Cheng, if

6

I have committed an offence, I apologise. If I have
interpreted your instructions, I am sorry. But I understood th
I was free to take what pictures I liked. You did not even
request my negatives to be developed before I left China. Can
we settle this problem by having my film developed? It is a
colour film. Can you process it?'

Cheng's superior cut in indignantly: 'The People demand
that the film be developed.'

'It is a new kind of Kodak film,' I replied. 'That is why I
was very worried about the processing.'

'Of course we can develop a colour film. If China can make
an atom bomb, we can do anything.'

I had nothing to fear by the film being developed. I had
made only five exposures.

At the photographic shop I told the elderly man behind the
counter the speed of the film. He nodded without comment.
He got a black bag and put the camera inside and unloaded
it. He gave me a receipt. Cheng explained that the developed
film would be sent to his office and that I could have it the
next day.

We walked back to the Peace Hotel in silence. We then had
a maddening, almost Alice-in-Wonderland conversation. It
went like this:

'Will you please define what photographs I can take?'

'Before the Cultural Revolution tourists could photograph
freely. Now there are some restrictions.'

'What restrictions? Yesterday I understood there were none.
This morning I photographed only people reading a wall-
newspaper, some men painting a sign, the entrance to the
former British Consulate, a group of workers in the Bund
gardens, a man selling bradawls to mend shoes. Such photographs are surely not a breach of security?'

'We want you better to understand the Cultural Revolution
in China.'

'That's fine. It's why I'm here.'

'Since the Cultural Revolution it is forbidden to photograph
wall-newspapers.'

I refrained from saying: 'Why didn't you tell me yesterday?'

It's difficult to avoid including wall-newspapers. ... few yards.'

... ard statue* on the Bund must not be photo-

... not proud of the Red Guards? The statue ... ant youth of China.'

... Red Guard statue is on the waterfront. No photographs are allowed of the river and the ships.'

'Are these all the restrictions?'

Cheng's superior cut in: 'You must not photograph people without their permission. Nor must you photograph soldiers.'

Cheng resumed: 'We wish you to talk freely in the city; to travel in the country. I hope you will come with me to Hangchow. It is very beautiful.'

'You are implying that I shouldn't take photographs when alone.'

'The People may misunderstand if you do. They may regard you as an enemy. Chairman Mao says: "Our enemies are all those in league with imperialism."'

'Do you believe I may experience similar incidents to this morning's if I go on photographing alone in the streets?'

This question was too blunt for a Chinese Communist. It required a simple 'Yes' or 'No' answer. So Cheng and his superior just remained silent. Cheng glanced at his stainless-steel wrist-watch. It was noon.

'I suggest you go and eat,' he said. 'We can meet again at two o'clock. I hope I shall then know when you can meet the Red Guards.'

The Chinese people are being subjected to intense anti-foreign propaganda. During that visit in November, 1967, I was all the time conscious of a simmering malevolence towards me. There were no smiles. It seemed pointless to take unnecessary risks. The incident that morning had flared up like a tropical storm. I had been fortunate that I was near Cheng's office. I decided for the future not to carry a camera when alone. On another occasion I might be in greater danger.

* The statue was removed while I was in prison.

2   Armed with Mao Thought

THE official Chinese date for the start of the Cultural Revolution is September, 1965, when, at an enlarged meeting of the Politburo Standing Committee, Mao called for a struggle against 'bourgeois reactionary thinking'. To trace its real origin, however, you have to go back nine years, to Krushchev's de-Stalinisation speech in October, 1956—a traumatic shock for Mao in the autumn of his life. It was then that he suddenly realised what could happen to his cherished policies after he died.

Possibly a ranging shot in the Cultural Revolution was fired by Mao himself on July 14, 1964, in an article he wrote entitled *On Krushchev's Phoney Communism and Its Historical Lessons for the World*. A portion of the article is quoted in the Mao Thought book, in the chapter on cadres. The first sentence reads: 'In order to guarantee that our Party and the country do not change their colour, we must not only have a correct line and correct policies but must train and bring up millions of successors who will carry on the cause of proletarian revolution. . . . In the final analysis, it is whether or not the leadership of our Party and State will remain in the hands of proletarian revolutionaries, whether or not our descendants will continue to march along the correct road laid down by Marxism-Leninism, or, in other words, whether or not we can successfully prevent the emergence of Krushchev's revisionism in China.'

This admonition explains the mass recruiting of 2,000,000 university and middle school students into the Red Guards. These young Chinese were the first generation of the Communist takeover of China. They knew nothing of the hardships and sacrifices endured by the old-line Communists like Mao and his contemporaries—the men who led the Long March of 7,500 miles across China to Yenan in which, of the original force of about 90,000, 82,000 perished. Only the young could carry on the banner of revolution, preaching Mao's gospel.

When I was in prison in Shanghai, I once asked my young interpreter, a fervent Maoist: 'What happens to your country when Chairman Mao dies? It will be a terrible shock for the people, from which they may not ever fully recover.'

He answered me in a single sentence: 'We are *armed* with Mao Tse-tung Thought.'

Mao is a compelling personality, a ruthless idealist, supremely confident of his personal ability to surmount China's immense domestic problems. He has immense pride in China and its future. In 1958 he observed: 'Our country is so populous, it has such vast territory and abundant resources, a history of more than 4,000 years, and culture. But what a boast! We are not even as far advanced as Belgium. Our steel production is so low. So few people are literate. But now our nation is all ardour; there is a fervent tide. Our nation is like an atom. After the atom's nuclear fission, the thermal energy released will be so formidable that we will be able to accomplish all that we cannot do.'

By the 'sixties he had become increasingly worried that the party had developed into an élite, bureaucratic conglomeration of mortals, no longer keeping itself pure by contact with the masses. 'At present some comrades fear mass discussion very much,' he warned in 1962. 'They fear that the masses put forward views different from the leaders. This attitude is extremely bad. Comrades, we are revolutionaries.'

From the secret political history of China, you can almost see the Cultural Revolution taking shape in Mao's mind, growing out of the vision of the ideal society and China's slowness to achieve it. There are two key themes in Mao's Thoughts that culminated in the Cultural Revolution: his strong egalitarian bent, with his belief in the necessity of keeping close to the masses and his contempt for intellectuals; and a feeling that conflict is inherently beneficial, in keeping with the Marxist dialectic.

In 1966 he said in a speech: 'I have spent much time in the rural areas with the peasants and was deeply moved by the many things they knew. Their knowledge was rich. I was no match for them.'

In a directive on public health work, just before the Cultural Revolution began, Mao displayed hostility to intellectuals who he felt were divorced from the masses, and consequently useless to society. Asserting that the Ministry of Public Health had not done enough for the peasants, he suggested it be re-named 'the "Lords" Ministry'.

To the Central Committee of the Chinese Communist Party in 1966, the Chairman said: 'The final test of whether or not socialism will make it, will be decided by your putting politics in command and your going among the masses where, together with them, you will carry out the great Cultural Revolution.'

So, in large part, the future depends on whether Mao's successors will be able to achieve the lifelong dream of harnessing the fervent tides of China to build a modern society.

However, the people cannot expect a placid life, for Mao has predicted that there must be other 'cultural revolutions'—at regular intervals, one assumes—which will be necessary to ensure that China continues to follow the pure ideological road of Marxism-Leninism-Mao Tse-tung Thought, which is how Peking now puts it. For Mao and his fanatical cohorts are bent on changing the ingrained money-making characteristics of the Chinese people—turning them into a faceless, selfless, non-acquisitive race. In truth, these men would like to make us all the same. It can be done in China only by periodic upheaval like the Cultural Revolution that convulsed the country for nearly three years. Even today, the tremors have not completely subsided. We see Maoist students clashing with neo-Fascists in countries all over the world.

The Great Proletarian Cultural Revolution was obviously the brain-child of Chairman Mao, the only man in China with the necessary imagination and political flair. But the red book of *Quotations from Chairman Mao Tse-tung* was compiled by Chen Po-ta, Mao's former political secretary and a fanatical revolutionary. Today, it is believed that his power and influence have given way to the pragmatism of the army leaders who are really ruling the country (although Mao, in reasonably good health for his age, remains the unchallenged spiritual leader). There is a dampening down of 'the cult of personality'. Many big portraits of Mao have disappeared in the cities and it is no longer ideologically fashionable to wear a Mao badge. The year 1970 has given birth to the Era of Ideas.

On November 10, 1965, a Shanghai newspaper called *Wen Hui Pao* published a seemingly trifling piece of literary criticism. It was written, with the help of Mao's wife Chiang Ching, by a young Shanghai journalist named Yao Wen-yuan, on the direct instructions of Mao, and comprised a devastating analysis of a historical play entitled *The Dismissal of Hai Jui* written four years earlier by Wu Han, Vice-Mayor of Peking. This marked the real beginning of the Cultural Revolution. It is difficult to think of any country in the world where a play about a man who lived 400 years ago could provoke such tremendous political and social upheaval. Workers, peasants, students in every country in the world have been made aware of the clarion call 'Rebellion is justified!'. And from it has sprung guerilla movements in Asia, Africa and South America. Shanghai was chosen as the city to launch the Cultural Revolution because of its strong Maoist pressure groups and its revolutionary traditions.

The previous January Mao had appointed Peng Chen, Peking's Mayor and First Secretary, then regarded as his heir, as head of a five-man 'cultural revolution group'. Their task was to work out a new-style rectification drive to eliminate the revisionist danger, especially among the intellectuals. But Peng didn't sense the true scope of Mao's ambition and wasn't to last long. He was outspoken and eventually he ran up against Mao's wife (a former cinema actress and drama instructor now in charge of Chinese culture), who hated him for blocking her cultural reforms.

In February, 1966, Peng Chen issued a memorandum on behalf of the Cultural Revolution Group putting forward a programme for a new 'rectification' of China's intellectuals. It was not what Mao wanted. He called upon his wife to draw one up under the imprimatur of the army. Immediately afterwards the army newspaper began publishing a series of editorials setting out the principles of a cultural purge. With the increasing prominence given to the Minister of Defence, Lin Piao, these leading articles indicated that the army would have a new political role in the great revolutionary movement that was to come. Another of Mao's chosen instruments was his wife Chiang Ching, whose long-festering resentments were vital catalysts in his planning.

On May 16 Mao presided over an enlarged session of the Politburo. It cancelled Peng Chen's February memorandum, dissolved his Cultural Revolution Group and appointed a new group under Chen Po-ta. Two weeks later Peng Cheng was dismissed as Mayor of Peking and the first secretary of the Municipal Party Committee.

The purge of Peng Chen, the highest-ranking Communist to fall from power since Peng Teh-huai was dismissed as Defence Minister in 1959, precipitated a major upheaval in Peking.

That same day the first big 'character poster' was put up by seven young teachers and students at Peking University. The poster denounced the President of the University and the university's party secretary for 'falling into the pit of revisionism'. These 'bourgeois royalists' were fired by the new Peking Party committee at midnight on June 23. The next day the purge began to spread through the country.

Everywhere the movement followed a common pattern. An official would be attacked, first in isolated posters, then, as attackers gathered strength, in a blitzkrieg of posters and at a succession of mass meetings.

Often the victim would try to organise his defence, as the President of Peking University did, by counter-attacking his critics and attempting to use his authority to silence them. But at this point a 'work team' from the high-level Party committee would arrive to decide the case, usually putting the official seal on the purge.

Shanghai's six major campuses got a 'work team'—usually about thirty members headed by a senior Party official.

Most of the hundreds of men who fell during June and July, 1966, were educators or Party workers concerned with ideology and propaganda. A professor in Shanghai, a friend of mine for over forty years, was a victim of this purge. (He was not saved from imprisonment by the fact that his grown-up children were important to China in the field of nuclear research.)

Those who fell were from the circles which Mao had pinpointed as the breeding grounds of revisionism. In mid-June, after a number of university presidents had been dismissed, all China's schools and universities were shut down. It was promised that by the time they re-opened—originally intended to be six months—China's educational system would have been completely revolutionised.

Early in July, 1966, the next major purges were announced. Chou Yang, the man who had been Mao's literary czar and the leading champion of literary orthodoxy since the 'thirties, was denounced as 'a big umbrella' covering up 'demons and monsters' in the literary field. Shortly afterwards, Chou's boss, the Party propaganda director and Minister of Culture, Lu Ting-yi, also lost his job. He was replaced as propaganda director by an up-and-coming Party leader from the central south region, Tao Chu.

And it was in July, 1966 that Mao made his famous Yangtse River swim, marking his emergence from six months' retreat —probably for contemplation. Immediately afterwards he returned to Peking to prepare for the first plenary session of the Central Committee of the Communist Party of China in four years. He took over the management of the Cultural Revolution from the men who had been directing it since his retreat in November, 1965: his second-in-command, Liu Shao-chi, and the head of the Party secretariat, Teng Hsiao-ping. Months later, attacks on these two men revealed that Mao felt they had betrayed his revolutionary purposes in this period by

organising the purge so as to suppress the genuine leftist
protect the revisionists. This alleged mishandling of the
phase of the Cultural Revolution was probably used as
immediate pretext for the demotion of Liu, the Head of St
and Teng at the momentous meeting of the Central Committee
from August 1 to 12.

On the eve of the Central Committee session, Lo Jui-ching,
the Chief of Staff of the army, was dismissed from his post.
The dismissal had probably taken place some months before
because he had been out of public sight since the previous
November. Yang Cheng-wu was appointed acting Chief of
Staff. Yang's speech at the Peking celebration of the army
anniversary indicated the reason for Lo's fall: he had opposed
the ever-increasing emphasis on Maoist indoctrination of the
army at the expense of specialist training and the acquisition
of modern weapons.

Army Day, August, 1966, was also made the occasion for the
publication of the first of two important Maoist documents.
The Army Day message called for nothing less than the
immediate implementation of the project dearest to Mao's
heart: transformation of the Chinese people into a new breed
of Renaissance men: 'By acting in accordance with what
Comrade Mao Tse-tung has said, the 700 million people of our
country will all become critics of the old world as well as
builders and defenders of the new world. With hammer in hand
they will be able to do factory work; with hoe, plough or harrow
they will be able to do farming; with the gun they will be able
to fight the enemy and with the pen they will be able to express
themselves in writing. In this way, the whole country will be a
great school of Mao Tse-tung Thought, a great school of
Communism.' This extraordinary transformation was to begin
with the army. The rest of the country was expected to follow
'where conditions permit'.

The second major cultural revolutionary document was a
sixteen-point decision by the Central Committee issued a week
later on August 8. It acknowledged that the Cultural Revolution had met a formidable resistance, chiefly from within the
Communist Party. But it reminded over-zealous revolutionaries

that the struggle should be conducted by reasoning and not by force. And it continued to regard the Party as the rightful leader of the new mass movement.

If the sixteen-point decision had been put into effect, the Cultural Revolution would have been a different movement from what it turned out to be. But only ten days after this sober-worded document, Mao's true intentions were revealed at a million-strong rally in Peking. First, the rally confirmed that the Cultural Revolution was no ordinary rectification drive; the rank order of the top leaders on the reviewing stand revealed the most important Party shake-up since Mao assumed the Party leadership thirty-one years before. And, second, the rally unveiled the new youth organisation which was to lead the movement into a terror wave lasting a year—the Red Guards. These young students were fanatic nationalists—as students in China have been for fifty years—puritanically devoted to the singleminded pursuit of the aims of the Great Proletarian Cultural Revolution under their beloved Chairman Mao.

The chief casualty of the realignment of the leadership was Liu Shao-chi. After twenty-one years as Mao's second-in-command, he was pushed down to number eight in party rankings. In his former place at Mao's side was Lin Piao, the Minister of Defence—since confirmed as Mao's heir in the new constitution adopted at the 9th Congress. Premier Chou En-lai remained in third place (he still does), but after him came two newcomers to the top ranks: Tao Chu, the new propaganda director, in fourth place, and Chen Po-ta, the head of the Cultural Revolution Group, at number five. The other significant change in the rankings was the promotion of Mao's wife, Chiang Ching, into the top Party lists for the first time at number twenty-eight. (Soon she was to rank as number six, with Chen Po-ta and Kang Sheng as numbers four and five.)*

* Kang, a shadowy figure who has called himself 'the Beria of China', is reputed to be the head of the Secret Police. It is likely that very much more will be heard of him in future. (He could be appointed Chairman of the People's Congress to be held in 1971.)

It is difficult to determine whether Lin Piao or his Chief of Staff, General

Peking had scarcely recovered from the impact of the August 18 rally when the Red Guards began to show their stuff. Brandishing their talisman—the little red breviary of Mao quotations—the roving bands of boys and girls came out on the streets on August 20. City walls were covered with big character posters. The residents were presented with an ultimatum: all remnants of bourgeois society must be destroyed within the week.

Shopkeepers were ordered to stop selling cosmetics to women and 'outlandish' western fashions. Red Guards lopped off girls' braids. Short hair was a sign of female emancipation. Restaurants were ordered to simplify menus. Signs were ripped down from shop fronts and 'odious imperial street names' like Eternal Peace Boulevard and Street of the Prince's Well were changed to East is Red Boulevard and Prevent Revisionism Street. The Russian Embassy ironically found itself on the road called Struggle Against Revisionism. Students held a massive demonstration shouting anti-Russian slogans around portraits of Stalin and Mao.

The slogan was 'Smash the old; build the new!' Yet, the smashing was selective, symbolic. Stone lions were broken with sledge hammers, wooden motifs chiselled off old house walls, statues of Buddha carted away in trucks, Christian emblems replaced by red flags.

The tension was lessened by an air of carnival. In spite of rampaging Red Guards in the initial phases of the Cultural Revolution in Peking there was no feeling that people would be killed. It was rather like a huge Chinese opera, the students acting out the triumph of the revolution.

Huang Yung-sheng, is the real power in the army. Huang now appears more prominently on state occasions, often in the company of Chou En-lai. But Chou is still, it is understood, working in harmony with Lin. So if Chou is repairing the 'international face' of China ravaged by the Cultural Revolution—twenty-five ambassadors, including those to Russia and Yugoslavia, were appointed in the summer of 1970—he is doing so with the support of the army which is controlling the country through the provincial revolutionary committees. If these men do not accept whole-heartedly Mao's thesis, at least they recognise his dictum—'political power comes out of the barrel of a gun'.

But violence mounted day by day. Riots spread to other cities. Targets changed from 'bourgeois' names, possessions and habits to 'counter-revolutionary' Party officials. Bands of young vigilantes invaded Party headquarters, dragged out offending officials and paraded them through the streets in the traditional symbol of humiliation—the dunce's cap.

The official press confirmed that the Red Guards had the full backing of the Maoist regime. Peking called the demonstrations 'magnificent'. The *People's Daily* editorial declared that 'opposing the revolutionary actions of the revolutionary students constitutes a direct opposition to Chairman Mao's teachings'.

At a second massive Red Guard rally on August 31, Premier Chou En-lai endorsed the increasingly popular pastime of Red Guard migrations throughout the country to 'exchange revolutionary experiences'. But two weeks later, at a third million man-and-woman rally, he sounded a note of caution: Red Guards were not to invade factories and farms. Pragmatic Chou was apprehensive that the Red Guard movement would wreak havoc with production. It did.

Chou En-lai saved the 1966 harvest. But by mid-autumn the attack on local Party committees was having a disastrous effect on the nation's administration. Officials from twenty out of twenty-six provincial Party committees and hundreds more on lower levels had been purged or criticised. In Maoist China, more than in other Communist countries, even in Russia in the days of Stalin, the Communist Party dominated all branches and all levels of government. So paralysis of the Party meant paralysis of administration. Also, by their ruthless treatment of veteran Party workers, the Red Guards were pushing more and more Party officials into opposition. Many, where they had long associations with the local military command, organised their own battalions of supporters to battle with the Red Guards.

Since his downfall Liu Shao-chi had been ignored. This was peculiarly Chinese. Then began concerted attacks on him. Posters stated he had been required to write a self-criticism. Like all subsequent ones, it was rejected as inadequate. Posters then demanded his dismissal. But as head of state, Mao must have felt that his case required special treatment. Even after he had been denounced in the official press, he remained somehow, mysteriously, in the background. He was never offered up to the Red Guards for public humiliation. He was never officially dismissed because this could be done legally only by the National Assembly or a Party congress. And, as we now know, three years had to pass before this happened. (He was deposed as President of China and stripped of all his other offices at the 9th Congress in April, 1969.)

But the other top purge victims were not so lucky as Liu. Early in December, 1966, Peng Chen was hauled out of his home in the middle of the night by Red Guards. A week later Peng and Lu Ting-yi, the former propaganda chief, Lo Jui-ching, the former army Chief of Staff, and Yang Shang-kun, a former high-ranking member of the Central Committee, were all forced to appear at a public rally in Peking wearing huge placards of denunciation. Lo's leg was broken, reportedly in a suicide attempt. Perhaps he was the only top-level Communist to suffer injury in the Cultural Revolution. Mao has never been a Stalin. Any of these men could re-emerge in a few years' time 'rectified' by 'recantation'.

⌈Although the Red Guards had been the main shock troops of the Revolution from the beginning, since October more and more workers and even some peasants had been drawn into the conflict, both by local Maoists and resisting Party officials. Clashes between workers and students were becoming more frequent and bloody.⌉

By December, 1966, Mao had decided that the phase of insulating the economy from the Cultural Revolution was at an end; the time had come to link the Red Guard movement with a similar revolutionary uprising by the proletariat and the peasantry. On December 26, his seventy-third birthday, the *People's Daily* gave a formal go-ahead for a full-scale extension of the Revolution into factories and farms.

January, 1967, say the Chinese today, was the high point in the history of the Cultural Revolution. It was the month of the 'January Revolution' when the 'revolutionary masses' carried out their first 'power seizure' in Shanghai.

3   Guards and Rebels, Scarlet and Red

THE militant Red Guards of Peking arrived in Shanghai at the end of August, 1966. During the whole thirty-hour journey these teenage boys and girls were utterly absorbed in studying and discussing sheaves of documents. They might have been cramming for a tough examination. But their assignment was not academic: they were to subvert a whole city of ten million people.

At this time Shanghai was much quieter than Peking. Girls were still wearing their hair long. Trousers and shoes were newly styled and would not have been tolerated in Peking. But street names had been changed, and so had titles of businesses, like the department stores Wing On and Sincere in the Nanking Road, which had kept their names from pre-liberation days. There were also detachments of Red Guards going round the city searching houses and blocks of flats in what were formerly bourgeois districts, and hauling out their victims. A prisoner might be given a shove or spoken to sternly, but no one got hurt.

These young Red Guards regarded themselves as the vanguard of a new era, entrusted with the task of cleansing away every vestige of Shanghai's humiliating imperial past. They were still unaware of the true motive of the Cultural Revolution, however. Unlike their brothers from Peking they did not realise that the real target was not only the bourgeoisie, the professors and teachers, but the Communist Party itself.

The Shanghai Municipal Party Committee, which had given the city's Red Guards every assistance in their fight against the bourgeoisie, resented any interference from Peking and

The Peking delegate was Chang Chun-chiao. He had left Shanghai for Peking in July to attend the 11th Plenum. Unlike the mayor and others who attended the conference, he did not return when it was over but stayed on to become Vice-Director of the Central Cultural Revolution Group. It meant leaving Shanghai in the hands of the enemy, but it put him right in the heart of the Mao group.

At a meeting in Culture Square in Shanghai on November 13, Chang, in his Peking capacity, signed the Rebel demands in the presence of the workers who had come back from Anting. At a single stroke, he did more harm to the mayor and his committee than the Red Guards had managed to achieve in six months.

On November 25 Chang left for Peking. There, a few days later, the Central Committee of the Party met to discuss problems created by the Cultural Revolution in industry and communications. The Shanghai representative reported back that there was a wide gap between the opinion of the Central Cultural Revolution Group and that of provincial and municipal leaders. He said a full-scale debate was unavoidable, and he demanded information on factories stopping work, and people being beaten up (what he was really after was material to show that the Workers' Headquarters had set up courts and beaten or imprisoned people).

What irked the Municipal Committee members most was Peking's interference in Shanghai's affairs. And this, from my knowledge of China, must have happened all over the country. Because of poor communications, local government has always —even since the Communist 'liberation' in 1949—enjoyed considerable autonomy.

At the Peking meeting the provincial leaders tried to combine to oppose the local Maoists. But these men miscalculated the situation if they thought that warnings about production losses would divert the course of Mao and his group. The Cultural Revolutionaries did not mind if factory production dropped by 20 per cent. China was to have a new spirit, would slough off outmoded cultural forms. Mao foresaw the *spiritual* liberation of his people, who would transmute this freedom into rapid *material* progress. Production might drop during the period of struggle. It would catch up and surge ahead as the movement went on. It was the meaning of Mao's slogan: 'Make Revolution: Increase Production.' And, as we now know, this has proved true. I saw it with my own eyes. Even my prison was better run when I left it than when I arrived.

To the young, the call to break free from administrative repression sounded good. They represented the stringent discipline, almost priestly paternalism of the Party's old cadres. But the senior, older cadres hated the situation, which threatened to destroy the discipline that had been painfully created out of the chaos the Communists inherited in 1949.

On November 30 Shanghai woke without its major daily newspaper *Liberation Daily*. The trouble had begun with a student publication *Red Guard Despatch* which had issued scathing attacks on the Mayor and the Municipal Committee. Ironically the first eight issues had been printed on the *Liberation Daily* presses, but when the Rebels demanded 650,000 copies of the ninth issue, the astounded officials wanted to know how they were going to circulate so many. They were told that the issue should be sent out with *Liberation Daily* to all subscribers. The Party Committee of the newspaper refused, and the Municipal Committee backed them. Whereupon the Rebels took over the *Liberation Daily* building.

This was the scene of a protracted siege. December 4 was the most violent day, with 140 Rebel defenders injured and 18 of the assault force hospitalised. Even fire engines with ladders, hoses and grappling hooks had been in action, but the attack was repulsed.

The siege was giving a tremendous boost to the revolutionary consciousness of the Rebel students and workers. Students in the colleges and revolutionary workers of *Liberation Daily* toiled through the night printing leaflets in support of the Rebels. Roving propaganda teams spent all their waking hours putting slogans on walls. Rebels gave concerts in factories, singing they soon made their disapproval felt by refusing the Peking Guards any equipment for a liaison centre. The Committee unjustly alleged that the leaders of the proposed centre were 'doubtful characters', unorthodox, politically unsound, who 'upset normal relations between the sexes'.

In the face of this opposition, the Peking Red Guards demonstrated outside the Committee's headquarters on the Bund, and followed this up with a two-day sit-in beginning on September 2. Meanwhile from Peking the 'official' line had been laid down by Lin Piao at a rally in Tien An Men Square: Red Guards were not to resort to physical violence but at the same time they must oppose any attempts to suppress them.

On September 4, the Peking Red Guards decided to force their way into the building. Those who did were almost immediately expelled, but they plastered the walls with posters.

That evening, however, the anti-Maoist mayor, Tsao Ti-chiu, delivered a short speech from the steps at the entrance to the building (formerly the Hong Kong and Shanghai Bank). The Peking Red Guards had forced his hand, but had betrayed their code by resorting to violence in the process. 'Everyone has seen today's efforts with his own eyes . . . If the Peking students hit people, the Shanghai comrades are not to hit back.'

Radicals now complained that by repeatedly defending the Municipal Committee policy, Tsao was instituting 'a reign of terror' in Shanghai. He had treated Mao's emissaries as counter-revolutionaries, as terrorists. For the radicals, the mayor symbolised the revisionism of the Municipal Committee. It was not long before he was getting all the blame. Yet at that time the sympathy for the Red Guards was minimal. In a sense, the Committee had every reason to be pleased with itself. It had weathered an invasion from Peking, emerging with the vast majority of its people behind it. And it had far more power than the revolutionaries, for it controlled the mass media.

September in Shanghai was a month of great activity. Well-organised bands of local Red Guards searched houses of the middle-class and the 'rich'—people who formerly had owned factories and since 1949 had been living on interest which Mao had allowed them on their original capital investment. They were the richest men in China, as many had continued to manage their own factories at a high salary. The youths dug up gardens, drained wells, poked around the chimneys and behind walls. They found arms and ammunition, hoarded goods, old land titles, gold, silver and Kuomintang flags.

[September was also the month of student liaison, when millions of Red Guards travelled the country to 'make revolutionary contacts'.] The city's walls carried protest and counterprotest from towns near and far, describing local resistance to Red Guard incursions. Mayor Tsao maintained that the students were interfering with production in Shanghai's 300 factories.

However, as National Day (October 1) drew near, the Peking Red Guards went home. Tsao said they had returned because they were in trouble with the Central Committee, and he called on Shanghai to 'clean out the noxious influence' they had left behind.

National Day was a boon for the Municipal Committee. The whole city was decorated with huge red slogans reading 'Long Live Chairman Mao'. For the big parade in the People's Square, formerly the racecourse, there were more Red Guards than workers.

But on October 5 an 'Urgent Directive from the Central Military Committee' was issued, which introduced a new dimension into the struggle. Its military origin suggested that Lin Piao was behind it, and it made it clear that the Cultural Revolution was a fight to the death between two distinct Party lines: the 'proletarian and revolutionary line of Chairman Mao' and 'the bourgeois line of Party authorities taking the capital road' (later to be called 'Liu Shao-chi's line'). It certainly increased the vulnerability of *all* Party members, even the members of the Central Committee.

There followed a month of bitter confrontation behind the walls of the centres of government. The Party officials were under attack. The Shanghai Municipal Committee building on the waterfront was plastered with posters, but they were fairly cautious, such as 'Something is Rotten in the Municipal Committee'.

With November came a distinct change of mood. On the walls characters three feet high blared 'Bombard the Municipal Committee!' and 'Burn Mayor Tsao'. Soon it was common to see threats like 'Any Rat that Dares to Try and Shift the Revolutionary Peacemakers Half a Hair's Breadth off Course will be Smashed to a Pulp!'

This escalation coincided with the return of powerful Red Guard groups from cities in the North. The Shanghai authorities had weathered the onslaught in August, but the November invaders were now armed with the Mao thesis, 'It is Right to Rebel'. Their new tactics reinvigorated the radicals, who immediately joined forces with the newcomers. The Rebel policy was to abandon the idea of a purely student movement and take advantage of the growing restlessness of the workers and of the Press.

The Municipal Committee managed to keep the journalists quiet for another month, but the ferment among the workers could not be contained. Rebel students were now making the rounds of the factories, urging a coalition against the authorities. A Shanghai-wide organisation of Rebel workers was formed, holding an inaugural rally in Culture Square on November 9, and this was attended by 20,000. The organisation called itself the Shanghai Workers' Revolutionary Rebel Headquarters—immediately abbreviated into Workers' Headquarters—and from its inception it was opposed by the Municipal Committee which had spies in Culture Square phoning in hourly reports.

It was no milk-sop organisation. The next day November 10, 2,500 of its members descended on the Shanghai railway station, commandeered a Peking-bound train, and steamed out of the city. They were going, they said, to see Chairman Mao in the capital.

To hijack a train in Shanghai railway station is not easy at the best of times, and on this morning the station was packed with Red Guards seeking to 'make liaison' with other parts of the country. Yet the rebel workers cleared a whole train of

Red Guards, took their places, and set off for Peking. And they did *not* provoke any violence.

For the authorities it was an emergency and they responded in a typically Chinese way. The Municipal Committee ordered the train to be stopped at Anting East, a small siding a few miles beyond the city limits, and an Assistant Director of the Political Bureau of the Department of Industry mobilised 'trustworthy' people—relatives and workmates of the Rebels—to go to Anting, ostensibly to look after their friends, but actually to divide and weaken them. More than half the hijack workers went back to their jobs, but 1,000 hard-core Rebels refused to leave the train and settled in for a siege.

Wall-newspapers described their sufferings—three days in packed carriages without provisions or water. Food was given to them but they threw it out of the windows with the cry: 'This is revisionist! We won't eat it!'

Every minute the Rebels remained in the train, the prestige of the Shanghai authorities drained away. Desperately, they telephoned the Peking Central Cultural Revolution Group headed by Chen Po-ta—then the most powerful man in China. He sent a telegram saying he understood the enthusiasm of the 1,000 Rebels. It was right for them to join the Cultural Revolution. (Chen knew that Mao, a month later, was going to give the go-ahead for the revolution to be extended to factories and farms. The moment had not yet come, however, to crush the anti-Maoist Shanghai Municipal Committee.) But the Rebels should go back to work and devote their leisure hours to the Cultural Revolution. The mildness of the telegram seemed remarkable. Here were 1,000 workmen leaving their jobs, stealing a train, snarling up the whole railway system of East China, yet Chen reasoned with them with paternal affection.

It looked as if the Municipal Committee had won another round, except that the Mayor of Shanghai never got to Anting to read the telegram. Another member of the Central Cultural Revolution Group arrived from Peking by plane on November 12, went straight to Anting and told the workers that he supported their action and would sign their demands.

The Peking delegate was Chang Chun-chiao. He had left Shanghai for Peking in July to attend the 11th Plenum. Unlike the mayor and others who attended the conference, he did not return when it was over but stayed on to become Vice-Director of the Central Cultural Revolution Group. It meant leaving Shanghai in the hands of the enemy, but it put him right in the heart of the Mao group.

At a meeting in Culture Square in Shanghai on November 13, Chang, in his Peking capacity, signed the Rebel demands in the presence of the workers who had come back from Anting. At a single stroke, he did more harm to the mayor and his committee than the Red Guards had managed to achieve in six months.

On November 25 Chang left for Peking. There, a few days later, the Central Committee of the Party met to discuss problems created by the Cultural Revolution in industry and communications. The Shanghai representative reported back that there was a wide gap between the opinion of the Central Cultural Revolution Group and that of provincial and municipal leaders. He said a full-scale debate was unavoidable, and he demanded information on factories stopping work, and people being beaten up (what he was really after was material to show that the Workers' Headquarters had set up courts and beaten or imprisoned people).

What irked the Municipal Committee members most was Peking's interference in Shanghai's affairs. And this, from my knowledge of China, must have happened all over the country. Because of poor communications, local government has always —even since the Communist 'liberation' in 1949—enjoyed considerable autonomy.

At the Peking meeting the provincial leaders tried to combine to oppose the local Maoists. But these men miscalculated the situation if they thought that warnings about production losses would divert the course of Mao and his group. The Cultural Revolutionaries did not mind if factory production dropped by 20 per cent. China was to have a new spirit, would slough off outmoded cultural forms. Mao foresaw the *spiritual* liberation of his people, who would transmute this freedom into rapid *material* progress. Production might drop during the period of struggle. It would catch up and surge ahead as the movement went on. It was the meaning of Mao's slogan: 'Make Revolution: Increase Production.' And, as we now know, this has proved true. I saw it with my own eyes. Even my prison was better run when I left it than when I arrived.

To the young, the call to break free from administrative repression sounded good. They represented the stringent discipline, almost priestly paternalism of the Party's old cadres. But the senior, older cadres hated the situation, which threatened to destroy the discipline that had been painfully created out of the chaos the Communists inherited in 1949.

On November 30 Shanghai woke without its major daily newspaper *Liberation Daily*. The trouble had begun with a student publication *Red Guard Despatch* which had issued scathing attacks on the Mayor and the Municipal Committee. Ironically the first eight issues had been printed on the *Liberation Daily* presses, but when the Rebels demanded 650,000 copies of the ninth issue, the astounded officials wanted to know how they were going to circulate so many. They were told that the issue should be sent out with *Liberation Daily* to all subscribers. The Party Committee of the newspaper refused, and the Municipal Committee backed them. Whereupon the Rebels took over the *Liberation Daily* building.

This was the scene of a protracted siege. December 4 was the most violent day, with 140 Rebel defenders injured and 18 of the assault force hospitalised. Even fire engines with ladders, hoses and grappling hooks had been in action, but the attack was repulsed.

The siege was giving a tremendous boost to the revolutionary consciousness of the Rebel students and workers. Students in the colleges and revolutionary workers of *Liberation Daily* toiled through the night printing leaflets in support of the Rebels. Roving propaganda teams spent all their waking hours putting slogans on walls. Rebels gave concerts in factories, singing revolutionary songs. Often their lives were in danger, but they made many converts.

Behind the scenes negotiations were going on to settle the dispute, both sides manoeuvring to extricate themselves with honour. The demands of the students were far beyond the original aim of mailing their paper with *Liberation Daily*. They insisted that the Party Committee of the newspaper make a 'profound self-criticism to the revolutionary masses'. They also demanded access to original drafts and revised versions of editorials written during the Cultural Revolution.

It would have been political suicide for the Party authorities to have acceded to this last demand. There is not a newspaper in the world that would care to have a bunch of angry students pore over its records. And *Liberation Daily* was particularly vulnerable for it was the organ of the Shanghai branch of the Communist Party of China, and had printed what the Municipal Committee had told it to print. If it was disgraced, the Party leaders were disgraced, too.

To worsen the situation, the Workers' Headquarters now added some demands of its own. It insisted that when the workers returned to their jobs the Party authorities and Work Teams must not make life more difficult for them. It also demanded that 'other mass organisations do not interfere with the revolutionary actions of the Rebels'.

This was the more important demand for among the 'other mass organisations' referred to was one that was gaining strength as the siege of *Liberation Daily* progressed. It was a moderate, small workers' group which grew into the largest organisation in Shanghai and the Rebels' main enemy.

The Scarlet Guards were formally founded on December 6. The previous evening the Municipal Committee had suddenly capitulated and agreed to the Rebel demands. When the Rebels eventually evacuated the *Liberation Daily* offices, the site was promptly taken over by the new organisation. A blistering propaganda battle ensued. As December wore on a minor civil war seemed inevitable.

The Scarlet Guards were the creation of the Party authorities and, to confuse matters further, were also opposed to the Municipal Committee. On December 23 they presented Mayor Tsao with a number of demands which he obligingly signed. Not to be outdone, the Rebels then forced him on the 25th to admit to 'grave error' in signing the demands! The Mayor had gone about as far as he could go without abdicating.

The main clash between the Rebels and the Scarlet Guards took place at the end of the month, thirty miles from Shanghai. The Guards had decided to stage a mass exodus from the city following a defeat at the hands of the Rebels outside the East China Bureau Secretariat on the 28th. The Rebels caught up with them at Kunshan.

The Scarlet Guards painted themselves as victims of aggression: 'On December 30 and 31, some 70,000 Scarlet Guards set off on foot and in trucks for Peking. When they reached Kunshan, they were subjected to the most brutal treatment.'

The Rebels had their own version: 'A few Scarlet Guard leaders, in an effort to regain the initiative, plotted to cut off Shanghai's water and electricity and to paralyse communications. They also organised more than 100,000 unenlightened Scarlet Guards to lay down their tools and head for Peking. The men were told it was a mission of protest, whereas, in fact, it was a direct attack on the Central Committee of the Communist Party of China—a blow at the headquarters of the proletariat.'

Certainly there was fighting throughout the afternoon and night of the 31st and during it the Rebels gained the upper hand. Word got through to Peking and Chou En-lai ordered both sides to return to Shanghai, but the affair went on for many days, and its repercussions for many months. By January 6 most of the Scarlet Guards had returned to Shanghai.

Another major disturbance rocked the city at this time. At the junction of the Tibet and Nanking roads—the busiest intersection of the city—there was a sit-in. It caused traffic chaos for a week. It started when 117 organisations, composed mainly of Shanghai students who had been sent to work in the surrounding countryside after graduation, held a mass rally in People's Square. They claimed to represent every major province and town of East China. They demanded to return to the city of their birth. The East China Bureau refused to receive their petition. After their rally they took non-violent revolutionary action by simply sitting in the heart of the city. Red silk banners flew from the elevated police traffic-control box. There were straw mats everywhere. Some students were sleeping in broad daylight. Wooden buckets were used as latrines. The streets were like a camping site.

Mayor Tsao spoke to them without success. The sit-in began on December 27 and did not end until January 6. The Scarlet Guards treated the participants as Rebels—one of their last acts before going off to Kunshan had been to march a column through the demonstration.

Whether they were Rebels is open to question. But they were rebelling against a policy of the Party siphoning urban youth off to surrounding districts to relieve the population pressure on Shanghai. (This is also the policy of the Mao group. For a year since the end of the Cultural Revolution city youths—boys and girls graduating from middle schools—have been encouraged to 'volunteer' for service in the country to 'learn from the masses'. Apart from working as farm labourers on the communes, these youths are also serving as teachers or helping in clinics. Mao's plan, which is definitely meeting with resistance, is that these boys and girls should settle in the country for life and raise the level of intelligence among the country folk. A higher standard of education will make the peasants more amenable to the scientific methods of farming needed if agricultural production is to keep pace with a rise in the population of between 15 and 20 millions annually.) The sit-in group in Shanghai were probably merely taking advantage of the current disorder to air their desire to return to Shanghai. The Rebels accused them of causing chaos in the city in an effort to support the Establishment. But the resulting paralysis of Shanghai's transport system hastened the fall of the old guard of the Municipal Committee.

Another contributing factor was the editorial in Peking's newspaper *Red Flag*, the theoretical organ of the Party, on January 1. It warned that the people who said the Cultural Revolution would interfere with production were 'muddle-headed' and would be 'swept on to the rubbish heap of history by the revolutionary masses'. The Shanghai Party authorities and all the moderate organisations supporting them had constantly warned of the need to maintain the quantity and quality of industrial production. Thus the *Red Flag* editorial left them idealogically defenceless.

Shanghai was ripe for change. As the city was virtually paralysed, the Party was vulnerable. And with the Scarlet Guards discredited, the authorities had no one to hide behind.

The climax came on January 3. Mayor Tsao Ti-chi was arraigned before a mass rally in Culture Square and humiliated. To the right of a huge portrait of Mao, six student 'judges' sat. On the left the 'defendants', heads bowed. They were members of the university's Party Committee. To a red-covered witness-box in the centre of the stage came witnesses from the audience. Any attempt by the 'defendants' to answer the charges was shouted down by the audience. It was a highly theatrical performance.

The 'trials' went on for days. There were no lawyers for defence, no constitutional rights, no judge, no body of law, no court of appeal. This was justice of emotion. And yet a form of democracy was in action. It was the people—the audience in the 'court'—who demanded the answers. Even if mass sentiments prevailed over individual opinions, all felt that they had participated.

On January 5 the Shanghai newspaper *Wen Hui Pao* published a strong condemnation of the Scarlet Guards, referring for the first time to the Kunshan affair. It was the famous 'Message to All the People of Shanghai', and it was signed by eleven Rebel groups, allies, if not all instruments of Chang Chun-chiao. The Message charged that the Scarlet Guards had (1) disrupted production and threatened people's livelihood; (2) plotted to cut the city's water and electricity; (3) thrown the transportation into chaos.

The stage was set for the triumph of the Left. Chang Chun-chiao made a dramatic entrance by flying from Peking on January 6. He met the Rebel groups and assured them that Chairman Mao personally approved their actions.

The next day a massive rally was held in People's Square. It was a grim scene. The first winter snow was falling, flakes swirling in the icy air. Dressed in heavy cotton-padded winter overcoats, the old-guard Party leaders looked dejected. They were led on to the stage to a roar of denunciatory slogans. Then they listened to speech after speech exposing their crimes, the charges ranging from degeneracy to high treason.

The rally ended with an order to Shanghai's leading officials to prepare full confessions of their crimes. The mayor was also informed that the Rebels would no longer recognise his authority and that the Central Committee in Peking would be asked to dismiss him from his posts and to reorganise the Shanghai Municipal Committee completely.

However, all minor officials of the Municipal Committee and the Party's Standing Committee were permitted to do their usual work and 'if they contribute to the welfare of the Party and the people, it will mitigate their crimes'. In a word, they were merely required to change their attitude.

Throughout the Cultural Revolution, confession and change of attitude were the keynotes of forgiveness. I had learned this on my visit to Shanghai in 1967. I was to remember it when arrested and charged with being a spy. I knew that denials of guilt were useless. I was not likely to face a public trial— although I was threatened with such legal procedure, even confrontation with Red Guards. I had to confess. But confession was a question of finding a form of words (a loophole whereby I could save face) acceptable to my accusers. Also, I had to appear to change my 'attitude'. That was the more difficult proposition, because changing 'attitude' goes beyond 'confession' and seeking 'leniency'.

On January 7, the day after his return from Peking, Chang

Chun-chiao was resorting to threats. The police, he warned, would support the 'revolutionary left' against anyone who tried to sabotage the Cultural Revolution. It was in part bluff, since the police were split from top to bottom, but Chang knew that people would accept his administration only if he restored order in Shanghai. He kept his propaganda machine at full blast, and intensified Rebel infiltration in factories. But deployment of students in the factories and at the docks, where work was almost at a standstill, did not in itself bring peace. Transport remained in chaos, which led to a shortage of coal, Shanghai's main source of power in the factories.

Having at first welcomed the Shanghai upsurge as a model revolutionary action, Peking was almost immediately making frantic attempts to stop the economic and political chaos which accompanied the 'power seizure', for it had spread to other cities. Mao was now serious about stopping violence among the workers. The Central Committee issued a new set of public security regulations. And on January 23 Mao ordered the People's Liberation Army to 'send troops to help any genuine revolutionary body which seeks help' and to 'attack any counter-revolutionary elements which resort to arms'. From this moment the army became the dominant power in China. It is still so today.

The army played a crucial role in supporting all subsequent revolutionary 'power seizures' and also assumed gradually most of the administrative functions previously performed by the Government and the Party. It was not, however, altogether free of ideological problems. Its Cultural Revolution Group was reorganised in early January, 1967, and again in March. Its political department was dissolved some months later. A considerable number of leading military figures were purged. But because of its increasingly important responsibilities as the only nation-wide organisation still intact and functioning, the army was spared the full brunt of a revolutionary struggle within its own ranks.

Mobilisation of the army for administrative purposes is regarded by some western political analysts as Mao's first major compromise with his idea of a 'spontaneous popular revolution'. The second, it is claimed, was the reintroduction, from February 1967, of rehabilitated Party officials into the new organs of power, to stabilise the revolutionary elements.

I do not think that Mao ever envisaged the Red Guards and the workers becoming an effective political force. In fact, perhaps one of his hidden motives for the Cultural Revolution was to bring about a military dictatorship in China. The choice by Mao of Lin Piao, the Defence Minister since 1959, as his heir bears this out. Through all his chequered political career—and Mao has often been 'put in the dog-house' by the Party—he has never once divorced himself from the army, and he has used it to support his comebacks.

The fanaticism of the Red Guards made it easy for Mao to call in the army. In Shanghai there were 111 separate groups of them within a week of the seizure of power, and the same thing happened in other major cities like Canton, Nanking and Wuhan.

In Shanghai there was a brief flirtation with a nebulous structure modelled on the Paris commune of 1871, but by mid-February Mao had fixed the final pattern for the new revolutionary organs.

Peking plumped for a 'revolutionary committee' for the province consisting of a 'three-way alliance' of representatives of revolutionary mass organisations, Party cadres and the army.

By March the tempo of the Cultural Revolution was moderate. Red Guards were told to stop exchanging revolutionary experiences and get back to school where the army would put them through 'a painful process of protracted ideological struggle'. Peasants were told to suspend the Cultural Revolution in order to devote their full attention to spring planting. And workers were reminded that the time for carrying out revolutionary activities was after they had worked a full eight-hour day.

This effort to steer China back to normality was short-lived. By early April 1967 the Leftists in the leadership had regained the upper hand—or so it appeared to outside observers. A powerful general offensive was launched against the 'top party leader who is taking the capital road': Liu Shao-chi. Again, one can only deduce that Mao, perhaps with continuous prodding from his militant wife, was the inspiration behind this new move.

A directive from the Military Affairs Committee on April 6 limited the army's powers in dealing with feuding revolutionaries: troops were forbidden to open fire on mass organisations, to label them counter-revolutionary or to make mass arrests without specific authorisation from Peking.

A new wave of 'anarchism' and 'unprincipled civil wars' broke out. The army's hands were tied by the prohibition to use force. Posters reported lurid stories of mass murders by rival factions. The masses were fighting among themselves.

Why did Mao agree to limit the army's authority? The reasons were probably twofold: (1) he could not permit the army to shoot at the proletariat because the army had always enjoyed the respect of the people, even from the early days of the formation of the Red Army. Mao, writing in 1938 'On Protracted War', said: 'The army must become one with the people so that they see it as their own army. Such an army will be invincible . . .'; (2) Mao may have felt that the 'purging' had to go on a little longer. Screws were tightened on all local military leaders and weapons were distributed to selected Red Guard units to serve as a balancing force for the Left. But this had the effect of extreme Leftists taking advantage of the prevailing radical sentiment. Some seized control of the Foreign Ministry. Others burned down the Chancery of the British Mission in Peking, and took over the British Consulate in Shanghai. In Wuhan, both Mao's public security chief and his propaganda director were arrested; Peking retaliated by dismissing the entire Wuhan military command.

'This extremely serious state of anarchy', as one leader in Peking put it, was used to convince Mao finally that there must be a slowing down in the Revolution. In an important speech on September 5, Chiang Ching, Mao's wife, repudiated armed struggle and the widespread attacks on the army that had followed the Wuhan incident. And on the same day, the Central Committee ordered the confiscation of all weapons seized from the armed forces and authorised them to hit back in self-defence.

Just before I arrived in East China in November, 1967, Mao undertook his first provincial tour—of Shanghai and five provinces in the Yangtse valley—since he went to investigate the problems raised by the Great Leap Forward in 1958. I have to accept that he actually made this tour, but there was some mystery about it. It was claimed that he stayed in Shanghai for a month. But while I was there I could not find one person who had actually seen him. A high-level but unquotable source finally told me categorically: 'I know Mao was not here.'

However, whether or not Mao actually toured the Yangtse valley provinces did not stop this euphoric conclusion: 'The situation of the great proletarian cultural revolution throughout the country is not just good but excellent . . . The important sign of this excellent situation is that the masses of the people have been fully aroused. Never before in any mass movement have the masses been mobilised so widely and in such a deep-going manner as this.'

But his 'great strategic plan' for carrying out the next phase of the revolution showed somewhat more realism. He acknowledged that bitter factional struggles divided his revolutionary forces and demanded an effort to heal them. He re-stated the need to rehabilitate party cadres and bring them into the revolutionary alliance. He called for a national spiritual revival through an intensification of the cult of his thoughts. He sanctioned a purge of several members of the Cultural Revolution Group who were made the scapegoats for the extremist 'terror' of the summer.

When I was in Shanghai in November the city was quiet, although the people looked as though they were emerging from a traumatic experience.

When I returned in February, 1968, the Red Guards were going back to the universities and schools. Workers were at their factory benches. The tall chimneys of Shanghai's factories were once again belching smoke round the clock.

Part Two

4 Spy-ship Piracy—*Pueblo*

MY visit to Shanghai in February, 1968, was unintentional. The story began on Thursday, January 25, 1968.

On that evening I was sitting in the lounge of the Orchard Road, Singapore, apartment of Ian Ward, the Far Eastern correspondent of the London *Daily Telegraph*. We were listening to the nine o'clock news. Over the radio came sensational details of the daring piracy by the North Korean navy of the *Pueblo*.

A few minutes later Ian's telephone rang. The call was from London; from his Foreign Editor, Ricky Marsh, whom I have known for many years. Ian was to fly to Seoul to cover the *Pueblo* affair.

After seeing him off the next day, I drove back to my hotel apartment and listened to every news broadcast. In Washington and Moscow the tension was mounting. The nuclear-powered aircraft carrier, *Enterprise*, on which I had been only a few months earlier in the Gulf of Tonkin, was ordered to the Sea of Japan with an escort of destroyers. Moscow radio was trying to play the incident down, claiming it should be treated as a ship 'inadvertently' infringing territorial waters.

At 9.00 p.m. I put in a call to Ricky Marsh, suggesting I try to gatecrash into North Korea itself, as I had done once before to cover the American bombings of oil installations in Haiphong. It would be a great scoop if I could get the story on the spot, though I stressed that even if I got there, I might have difficulty covering the story and cabling it.

He promised a definite reply in two hours.

I also spoke on the telephone at his home to Mr de Suza, the passenger manager of the Polish Ocean Line on which I had travelled to North Korea in 1966. I arranged to meet him at his office early the next morning. I had already made up my mind to make the journey even if Marsh finally rejected the idea. It was a story too important not to be investigated at first-hand if entry to the country could be achieved. I recognised that I might not be permitted to land without a visa. But on previous visits to Chungjin, the North Korean port near the Soviet Russian frontier, I was given a shore pass, and I had contacts in the port to help me.

Shortly before midnight Marsh called me back. I was commissioned to go to North Korea. I put in a call to Bob Moskin, Foreign Editor of *Look*, and told him my plans; *Look*, too, like the *Weekend Telegraph*, was publishing my China articles. I also informed Garry Barker, Far Eastern correspondent of the *Melbourne Herald*, that I was 'off to North Korea'.

The last call was to prove important. For it was Garry who broke the story to the world of my arrest in Shanghai, wringing the news out of the captain of the *Hanoi* when it arrived ten days late in Singapore.

It was three more days before I heard from Mr de Suza that a cabin would be available on the *Hanoi*, a 10,000-ton freighter sailing from Kobe on February 1. No reply had yet been received from the shipping line's head office in Gdynia, Poland, to whom Mr de Suza had sent a telex, but, as it turned out, Japan cleared the passage over the telephone. I stress the point because of what happened when I arrived in Kobe.

I was overjoyed with the apparent smoothness of the operation. To obtain exclusive news may require forethought, planning, but you must have luck, too.

I was not so pleased to learn, however, that after the ship left Chungjin, where it would be unloading and loading cargo for at least fifteen days, it was calling at Shanghai for about five days and then proceeding to Hong Kong. If I had difficulty in getting a story out of North Korea, I should have to cable it from Hong Kong; by calling at Shanghai, it would mean a further delay.

At 9.00 a.m. on Thursday, February 1, I was waiting in the Kobe office of the Japanese agents of the Polish Ocean Line. The passenger manager came in at nine-fifteen. A clerk handed him a yellow slip of paper with two lines of typing on it. He read it thoughtfully and turned to me apologetically.

'I am sorry,' he said, 'but I'm afraid you cannot sail on the *Hanoi*. Our head office in Gdynia informs us that reservations have been made for four passengers in Shanghai. They are travelling to Europe and will occupy the three cabins.'

I protested that he had informed me the day before yesterday on the telephone to Singapore that a cabin was available. He had even reserved my room in the New Port Hotel, Kobe, for the previous night. The Polish ships were the only ones with passenger accommodation which sailed to North Korea, and the next ship, which was sailing in a month's time, would be too late.

It was a situation which required patience and tact. The Japanese agent had lost face. I had had too much experience with Orientals over the past fifty years not to know that this was my main strength. But would I have been so tenacious if I had known that it would land me in a Chinese prison? With the knowledge of hindsight, the answer would be 'Yes'. I say this because nearly twenty months in prison, living in intimate association with Mao's Chinese, was a unique experience—an experience that a person like myself with an insatiable curiosity would not reject lightly. (I suppose I am a born spy, a seeker out of weak spots. Anyway, I understood what my colleague on *Epoca* of Milan meant when, having flown to Hong Kong immediately I was released, he commented, 'I envy you your experience'. But then Ricci Lazzero is a unique reporter.)

Appearing to sympathise with the unenviable position in which the Japanese passenger manager found himself, I persuaded him to take me to see the captain of the *Hanoi*. He might let me sleep in the pilot's cabin or in the lounge from Shanghai to Hong Kong. It would be for only two nights.

At first the captain was reluctant to agree to my proposal,

but finally he consented to carry me and to my sleeping on a sofa for two nights if his head office in Gdynia approved, and if I could not get permission from the Chinese authorities in Shanghai to travel by train to Hong Kong.

The passenger manager was confident that Gdynia would agree to my sailing, and at 6.00 p.m. a clerk handed him the telex reply from Gdynia. He read it aloud: 'Permission granted subject to the captain's agreement for Captain Bruno Neroni and Norman Barrymaine to travel on the *Hanoi* to Hong Kong.'

It was the first time I had heard the name of my fellow passenger.

After paying for my ticket, I went to the port immigration office to have the exit visa stamped in my passport. The immigration officer enquired when the *Hanoi* was leaving. I informed him it was scheduled to sail at 7.00 the next day.

'Cargo ships are often delayed,' he replied. 'I had better date the exit visa February 3 instead of tomorrow.'

It is a small point. But my Chinese interrogators could not understand it. The bureaucratic Communist Chinese entangled in red tape would never date an exit visa a day ahead of a traveller's actual departure. They suspected a trick. It took me a whole afternoon to convince them (well, I assume I did) that I was speaking the truth when I said that the ship sailed from Kobe on February 2 and not February 3 as stated in my passport. I pointed out that my statement was simple to verify by examining the ship's log book.

I then spoke to the *Telegraph* correspondent in Tokyo, requesting him to advise London that I was sailing the next morning and that as there was a possibility I might travel by train from Shanghai to Hong Kong, to ask London to cable £50 to me care of the Bank of China, Shanghai. An hour later confirmation came from London that this would be done.

At 11.30 p.m. I went up the gangway of the ship. The chief steward was waiting to show me to my cabin. It was on the starboard side, a well-furnished cabin with bathroom, more comfortable and spacious than on many modern passenger liners.

I unpacked my suitcases immediately—the habit of a lifetime

of travelling. I like my surroundings to be orderly. The cabin on a ship must be, to use a sailor's phrase, 'ship-shape'. Then I went to bed, falling immediately into a dreamless sleep. It had been a busy day.

I did not meet Bruno Neroni until lunchtime the following day. Over coffee, I chatted to him for an hour. Like all Southern Italians, he was voluble, finding it difficult to dissimulate. His life-story poured out in a torrent of words accompanied by demonstrative hand gesticulations. And yet I had the feeling that he was being frank almost to the point of wishing to deceive me. There was probably nothing untrue in his story but it was not the whole story.

Neroni's father was in the judiciary in Bari. Neroni himself had obviously been well educated. He had served as an officer in the Italian navy, later becoming a merchant service captain, presumably because it meant more money. He had commanded an Israeli tanker and later a freighter plying between North America and Yokohama. In Tokyo he had met a Japanese girl; they fell in love and in spite of opposition from the father, formerly a colonel in the Japanese army and a traditionalist, the couple married. For a year the wife went to sea with Neroni —for both, idyllic days. Then the wife became pregnant, necessitating her living ashore in Japan. Neroni continued to go to sea. Enforced separation caused the wife to become very jealous, often accusing him of infidelity. In a fit of temper and accusation she one day ripped three new suits with a knife.

After the baby—a boy—was born the wife persuaded Neroni to forsake the sea. Like all Italians, he adored children. So it was not emotionally a difficult decision to make. He wanted to see his son grow up. But the decision presented him with a financial problem because as a ship's captain he was earning probably $1,000 a month.

The Japanese Immigration authorities gave him a visa for 180 days but he was not permitted to work. His story was that he was now on his way to Hong Kong to negotiate with the Japanese Consul-General for a permanent labour permit. He was hoping to be employed by the American mutual funds organisation, Investors Overseas Services. He was carrying a good deal of I.O.S. literature and tried on repeated occasions to interest me in investing in one of the funds. He also solicited business among the ship's officers, which struck me as ironic in trying to turn Communist sailors into capitalists.

That he was taking such a 'slow boat' to Hong Kong also surprised me. I could only reconcile this decision on the grounds of economy as Communist ships are much cheaper than other lines.

In his sea career, Neroni had never been to North Korea or China ports. He was excited at the prospect of visiting these two countries. He questioned me interminably when I told him that I had been to Chungjin and Shanghai in recent months. He was immediately anxious to know if we should be allowed ashore.

I replied that I did not anticipate trouble in Shanghai but in Chungjin it might be more difficult because of the recent *Pueblo* incident.

I did not reveal to him that I was a journalist and had a particular interest in the *Pueblo*. To strangers I am reluctant to reveal that I am a journalist. Not because I am ashamed of my profession, but immediately you disclose it, you spend your time defending newspapers. For some unaccountable reason, journalists are regarded as dishonest, and everyone feels he could produce a better newspaper than professionals. In fact, after fifty years' experience I have found reporters on the whole more honest than many doctors, lawyers or chartered accountants who specialise in tax 'avoidance'. And journalism is certainly a less sleazy occupation than the spy trade.

At 3.00 p.m. on Monday, February 5, 1968, we dropped anchor seven miles off Chungjin. The white cliffs to the right of the small town, once a fishing village, now sprawling up the hillside, reminded me of Dover.

The sea was covered with thin, broken sheets of ice. The sun was shining from a clear, cobalt sky; the air exhilarating like champagne. But it would not be so pleasant when we entered the harbour, artificially created by a long breakwater when North Korea was Japanese territory. On the landward side of the docks is a coke furnace, belching sulphur fumes. At night it is ablaze with red flame—a foretaste of Hades. Behind this plant is a steel mill.

Chungjin is an uninviting town; its people dour. You never see a smile. Their lot is hard, made even more so by the rigours of a suppressive Communist regime.

The pilot, the Immigration officials, security police and the shipping agent finally arrived two hours later, and the ship was moved through a tortuous, zig-zag channel to two miles off the entrance to the docks. There would be no berthing space available inside until the next morning. There is docking accommodation for only about five ships.

The chief officer was depressed because we were to load 5,000 tons of cargo. As North Korean stevedores are slow workers (and there is no incentive for them to put their backs into the job) he estimated it would take at least fourteen days. However, this news pleased me. North Korean democracy is the most difficult to grapple with in the world. They have inherited the worst features of pre-war Japan, their former overlords, and modern-day Communism. I was fully aware that I should require plenty of time to secure permission to travel to Pyongyang, the capital, or Wonsan, where the *Pueblo* was lying, being dismantled, no doubt, by Russian electronic experts.

At 7.00 p.m. we were told to assemble in the saloon.

The Immigration officer requested my passport. I handed it to him, together with two letters which I wished to present. One was addressed to Kim Il Sung, the Prime Minister in Pyongyang; the second to the head of the Press Section of the Foreign Ministry. I also gave copies to the captain as a matter of courtesy, appreciating that in a Communist port he would be held responsible for my conduct.

The following morning customs officers made a toothcomb

search of my cabin. My photographic equipment was locked and sealed in a cupboard by the customs authorities until the ship sailed. (I had anticipated this regulation and secreted one loaded camera in my jacket pocket with a light meter.)

At lunch I was glad to see that the Polish representative from Pyongyang had joined us. I was shocked by his appearance, however. He was thin, looked very unwell and worried. He told me that things were very difficult, and quite different from when I was last there. It was partly because of the *Pueblo* affair, but there was also a lot of tension in Pyongyang. There was constant talk of war. He could not predict whether I should be able to go to Pyongyang.

I asked him whether he could use his influence on my behalf, but he said there was nothing he could do. It was obvious that he wished to change the subject.

I returned to my cabin after lunch. At 2.30 p.m. there was a knock on the door. The captain entered with two officers whom I immediately assessed as secret police.

'I apologise for disturbing your siesta,' began the captain, who was obviously disliking his mission. 'I am instructed that you must remain in your cabin.'

In answer to my questions, the security officers reiterated that I must remain in my cabin until they received instructions from Pyongyang regarding my request for a landing permit. I would be allowed to go to the dining saloon for meals, though I must return to my cabin immediately afterwards. And I could exercise on the deck twice a day, accompanied by a North Korean officer. My cabin would not be locked if I obeyed their instructions.

When I asked if I might talk to the representative of the Polish line, the security officer told me it was not permitted. At the time I thought this stupid since the Polish representative would be present at mealtimes. I did not know that after this intervention by the North Korean authorities he would eat only three meals in the dining saloon during our fourteen-day stay. The captain, too, seldom joined us at lunch or dinner. He ate with the Polish representative in his cabin. Presumably he wished the minimum contact with myself and perhaps Neroni too.

At the evening meal Neroni told me that his movements on the ship had not been restricted but he had not yet been permitted to go ashore. Although he was a sailor the security police refused him permission to visit the Seamen's Club, which, situated in the dock area, was under continuous guard.

The next morning, a soldier carrying a rifle came to my cabin for my exercise on deck. I walked round the deck for an hour, the soldier following a few paces behind. At the foot of the gangway another armed sentry was standing guard on the dock. He inspected all passes of persons boarding or leaving the ship, including North Korean stevedores.

A few days after our arrival in Chungjin, I noticed during an afternoon exercise on deck that a Russian cargo ship had docked astern of us. And I learned that no one was allowed to leave or board that ship either. Even our captain, who wished to go aboard to pay his respects to the Russian captain, was not permitted to do so. Nor were the Russian crew allowed ashore to visit the Seamen's Club. It reflected a change in attitude by the North Koreans towards the Soviet Union.

Precariously situated between Communist China and the U.S.S.R., North Korea for many years had been careful to avoid involvement in their ideological quarrels and conflicts. But according to Mao Tse-tung's definition, there can be no such thing as genuine neutrality. By striving to be neutral in the Sino-Soviet dispute, North Korea was accused of leaning to the 'revisionist' side, and during the xenophobia which marked the Great Proletarian Cultural Revolution in China Red Guard wall-newspapers singled out tough Kim Il Sung as the person who allegedly sabotaged the struggle of the Vietnamese people and dissuaded other countries from sending volunteers to Vietnamese battlefields.

Yet, in spite of these polemics, relationships between the two countries were diplomatically correct.

Since I began writing this narrative of my captivity in China, there has been a dramatic improvement in the relationship between the two countries, inspired no doubt by the change in the Indo-China situation.

In April, 1970, Premier Chou En-lai, who had left Peking only once since 1966 to attend the memorial service in Hanoi for the late Ho Chi-minh, made a two-day visit to Pyongyang. The mission of Chou was obviously to wean North Korea away from the Communist ideological bloc led by the Soviet Union. It was, therefore, significant that a 3,000-word communiqué issued at the end of the talks contained no reference to either the Soviet Union or the Sino-Russian border dispute, which had led to fighting between Chinese and Russian soldiers in 1969. It is not credible that this 'hot' subject was avoided. For a worsening of relations between China and Russia could lead to war.

But when I was in Chungjin on the *Hanoi* in February, 1968, this apparent *détente* with the People's Republic of China was more than two years away. It was, therefore, puzzling why the North Koreans who were ostensibly in the Russian camp should 'put in quarantine' all the crew of the Russian cargo ship, which I understood had arrived from Vladivostok. And it was even more intriguing to me a few days before the *Hanoi* sailed for Shanghai.

During my imprisonment on the ship no North Korean official came to see me, except the armed soldier who collected me twice a day for exercise on the deck. A request which I made through the chief steward to send postcards to my daughter, Anne, and friends and a telegram to Mr Marsh in London, was rejected by the North Korean shipping agent. I was not permitted to communicate with the outside world. Nor was there any response to my letter to Premier Kim and the North Korean Foreign Ministry.

I was very depressed after nine days of this because I had obviously failed in my journalistic mission to investigate the

45

Pueblo affair. It was puzzling that the North Koreans were not more co-operative because I should have thought that in terms of propaganda it was to their advantage to present me with their version of the incident.

But the North Koreans are unpredictable people, and not in my experience a friendly people.

Returning to my cabin from breakfast that morning, I found, lying on the circular table beside my typewriter, a large, thick brown envelope, sealed. There was no name written on it. As I was about to open it, my steward came in to tidy up the cabin. I asked him if he had put the envelope on my table. He disclaimed all responsibility.

When he had finished his work and left the cabin, I extracted the contents of the envelope. It contained photographs of Commander Lloyd M. Bucher, the forty-year-old captain of the *Pueblo*, and his eighty-three-man crew. One photograph, which was released to the world, showed them walking through the streets of Wonsan under armed guard. They all had their hands raised above their heads. Other photographs showed them signing 'confessions'. There were also photostat copies of every page of the 'confession' of Commander Bucher, his navigating officer and the officer responsible for the electronic espionage equipment, and other members of the crew.

As I read the 'confessions' I noted that they were all written to a formula, which obviously meant they had been extracted under duress. In the light of my own experience with the Chinese, I am not inferring that they were written under the threat of physical violence. The carrot held out was probably that if they wrote a 'confession' they would be treated more leniently. In fact, if my memory serves me correctly, all the 'confessions' ended with a plea for leniency because they had 'confessed their crimes'.

But the photographs and the 'confessions' were not the most dramatic part of the contents of the envelope that had mysteriously arrived in my cabin.

There was a single sheet of paper filled in single-space typing. It was headed and underlined: 'Please Destroy Immediately You Have Read It.' I cannot recall the exact wording of the document but the most startling revelation was that the seizure of the *Pueblo* was inspired and organised by the Soviet navy.

Apparently the reason that the Russian Government permitted its navy to help the North Korean navy carry out the act of piracy which brought the world to the brink of war, was because the *Pueblo* was not only spying along the coast of North Korea but had also been operating off the Russian naval port of Vladivostok. Nor was the *Pueblo* the first American spy-ship to operate in these waters.

If the *Pueblo* was seized, the Russians argued that it might stop this type of American electronic espionage. Further, the Russian navy, if the operation was successful, would have an opportunity to examine the ship's valuable scientific equipment. This information threw a completely different light on the affair and partially explained why the North Koreans had carried it out so smoothly. It also explained why Moscow immediately urged that the affair should be treated as a ship 'inadvertently infringing territorial waters'. In a word, they wanted to play the whole affair down.

War, however, may have been avoided only because of a breakdown in American communications and other pieces of unexplained inefficiency. By the time the President and the Pentagon had got into top gear, the damage was done. It did not matter whether North Korea succumbed to Moscow's line and allowed the *Pueblo* and its crew to leave. My mysterious informant said that Russian naval experts had already stripped the ship of its equipment.

What was the 906-ton *Pueblo* really doing? Apart from plotting North Korean radar stations, she was taking samples of the water, and mapping the bottom of the ocean by depth soundings.

All ships, including the American navy, use British Admiralty charts. But within North Korean territorial waters the charts are out of date because the Koreans, since control of the country reverted to them at the end of the war after a long period of Japanese occupation, have refused permission for coastal surveys by hydrographic units of other nations.

That the old charts are often valueless close in to shore was demonstrated when we arrived at Chungjin and anchored seven miles off the port. I took careful note of the pilot's zig-zag course when he brought the *Hanoi* into harbour. It did not seem to agree with what appeared to be the obvious channel on the British Admiralty chart. Even when we sailed, the pilot took us more than seven miles off shore before leaving the ship.

The necessity for a pilot so far out might be explained perhaps by minefields. But accurate information of the ocean bed is vitally necessary for the operation of nuclear-armed submarines.

The capture of the *Pueblo* was cleverly planned and carried out. But American navy men will argue in wardrooms for years to come whether Commander Bucher could have evaded capture, or fought it out, or deliberately sunk his ship. At the United States Navy Court of Inquiry, Commander Bucher stated he rejected the idea of scuttling because it would have taken $2\frac{1}{2}$ hours and the sea was only 180 feet deep. Divers, therefore, could have recovered the *Pueblo*'s secret gear.

The *Pueblo* was armed with only two .50-cal. machine guns which were covered with tarpaulin and according to high-level instructions given to Commander Bucher were not to be uncovered 'unless absolutely necessary'. The tarpaulin covers were frozen and would have taken some time to remove.

The document secretly passed to me stated that the *Pueblo* was about sixteen miles off shore when intercepted.* The weather was just above freezing and the sea calm. The position I was given of the ship agrees with that plotted by Commander Bucher and passed in a radio message to Sasebo, the U.S. naval base in Japan.

* Under international law, 'territorial waters' are the belt of sea adjacent to their shores which states regard as being under their immediate territorial jurisdiction. But there is much controversy about the breadth of the belt. The three-mile limit practised by the majority of states seems to have derived from the cannon range of the period when it was adopted. The line is drawn at low water from headland to headland.

The North Koreans arbitrarily claim a twelve-mile limit, but the *Pueblo* was outside Korean jurisdiction even if the twelve-mile limit is accepted.

It was noon Korean time when a Soviet-built North Korean submarine chaser with a top speed of 28 knots bore down on the *Pueblo*. Its 75-mm deck guns were manned. Among the dozen officers and men on the bridge was a Russian naval officer who directed the whole operation.

Circling the *Pueblo* at a distance of about half a mile, the submarine chaser, using international signals, requested the U.S. warship, which was not flying a flag, to state her nationality. Commander Bucher immediately identified his ship as American by hoisting the United States ensign and stating that they were carrying out oceanographic survey work. For purposes of realism, he ordered that a bottle used to collect water samples be dropped over the *Pueblo*'s side. The North Koreans were well aware of the identity of this ship painted battleship grey. They had been shadowing it with the aid of radar for many days.

Immediately Bucher had replied to the first message, the submarine chaser signalled back: 'Heave to or I will fire.'

Commander Bucher replied: 'I am in international waters.'*

My source stated that the *Pueblo* continued on an unaltered southerly course at dead slow speed. The North Korean warship did *not* open fire but circled the *Pueblo* for an hour awaiting the arrival at the scene of the action of three 50-knot 60-feet torpedo boats from the south-west.

It was now about one o'clock.

'Follow in my wake,' signalled the submarine chaser. 'I have a pilot aboard.'

The torpedo boats with guns trained on the *Pueblo* took up stations on the beam and astern. They were only about a hundred yards away, manoeuvring the *Pueblo* closer to the shore. Two MiG jets screamed in and began circling the *Pueblo*'s starboard bow.

By now the *Pueblo* had been out-manoeuvred and was inside

---

* A few years ago when I was aboard a Dutch cargo ship in the Straits of Taiwan a destroyer of Chiang Kai-shek's navy ordered my captain to 'heave to'. He slightly altered course and ignored the signal. The destroyer commander took no further action, shadowed us for an hour and then sheered off.

territorial waters. More important, it was also within range of shore batteries and guns on the island of Ung.

For the North Koreans, the operation was proceeding without a hitch. One of the torpedo boats rigged fenders—rubber tubes and rope mats—at its stern to cushion the impact when it came alongside the *Pueblo*. It began backing towards the *Pueblo*'s starboard quarter. Soldiers armed with rifles and fixed bayonets were preparing to board. Bucher ordered the engine room to increase speed to two-thirds of the top speed of thirteen knots. To the court, Bucher said he did not signal full speed ahead 'in order to present as dignified a departure as possible'. He added: 'I did not think there was any point in going to war. I was completely outgunned.'

It was five minutes past two in the afternoon—two hours and five minutes after the *Pueblo* was first intercepted sixteen miles out at sea—when the submarine chaser opened fire from 2,000 yards, a shell hitting the radar mast and fragments wounding Commander Bucher and two men on the bridge. One of the MiGs fired four rockets into the water several miles ahead of the *Pueblo*.

The sub-chaser went on firing, one shell passing through the pilot house. In Commander Bucher's presence, Chief Warrant Officer Gene Lacy signalled 'Stop' to the engine room. Commander Bucher did not reverse the order. As the ship slowed down, he has said, 'I decided that I would surrender. Any further resistance on our part would result in complete slaughter of the crew.'

Armed North Korean soldiers boarded the *Pueblo*. The crew did not put up any resistance. Actually, Commander Bucher's instructions for his mission covered everything except being boarded. But Article 0730, U.S. Navy Regulations, states: 'The commanding officer shall not permit his command to be searched by any person representing a foreign state nor permit any of the personnel under his command to be removed from the command by such person, so long as he has the power to resist.'

From the information that came into my possession in Chungjin, neither the Russians nor North Koreans were interested in sinking the *Pueblo*, even in comparatively shallow water. The whole object of the mission was to capture the ship intact so that its electronic equipment could be examined by Soviet experts.

All available precedents indicate that Bucher was justified in the initial stages of the action in playing it cool. In the game of sea-spying, the main rule has been that these ships could be harassed but never shot. Both American and Russian spy-ships are poking around each other's coasts, snooping on their fleets. When I was aboard the aircraft carrier *Kitty Hawk* during the bombing of North Vietnam, we were continuously under the surveillance of a Russian electronic spy-ship. At one stage it kept station so close to the carrier that it hazarded strike operations. An American warship was detailed to escort it. When an air strike was to be launched the American warship shepherded it away. It was all done in a very gentlemanly way.

That the North Koreans were annoyed with U.S. spy-ships operating off their coast was indicated clearly in two broadcasts before the *Pueblo* sailed from Japan. Commander Bucher was unaware of these broadcasts and so, for some mysterious reason, was the chief of U.S. naval intelligence in Japan.

When Bucher decided to surrender his ship he knew that the electronic gear on board could not be destroyed completely although an attempt was made with sledge hammers. He had tried unavailingly to have explosive devices installed that would destroy the electronic equipment, and had even requisitioned dynamite. He was given neither.

In fairness to the Commander, the *Pueblo* was never intended to fight. Its protection lay in international law or, in a crisis, possible help from elsewhere. Bucher expected assistance if in need. One signal to Japan said: 'We need support. S.O.S. S.O.S. S.O.S. Please send assistance. Please send assistance.'

Even after Bucher reported that he had been sighted by the North Korean sub-chaser, his superiors offered neither guidance nor protection.

In his last teletyped message to Japan, Bucher said: 'Have been requested to follow into Wonsan. Have three wounded and one man with leg blown off. How about some help?' The answer came back: 'We doing all we can, Capt, here.'

So ended a rather ignoble chapter in American naval history. The *Pueblo* was the only United States warship ever captured in peacetime without returning fire.

After I had read carefully the document in the envelope and taken a shorthand note of it, I tore it up and flushed it down the lavatory. But the photographs of the *Pueblo*'s crew and the 'confessions' of Commander Bucher and his officers it was important that I kept.

To secrete something in a cabin is much more difficult than it would seem to the average person. Customs officers know every trick of smugglers. And if you have ever been on a ship suspected of carrying narcotics—as I have been on two occasions—you appreciate that hiding something in a cabin that will not be found is almost impossible.

I took a good look round the cabin and also the bathroom. There was no wall-covering in the cabin which could be removed and the envelope hidden behind it. The chairs and a semi-circular sofa in one corner also offered no protection.

I finally chose the mattress. Normally I would not regard this as very safe since security officers usually examine bedding very thoroughly. But I argued that as the cabin had been searched when the ship docked and I had been confined to my cabin all the time we had been in Chungjin, there was no reason to suspect me.

That night I opened a seam about twelve inches long and stuffed the envelope between the kapok with which the mattress was filled. I sewed it up with a needle and cotton (which I always carry to stitch on a shirt button or make a minor repair to my clothes).

Unless the mattress has been removed from the *Hanoi*, some passenger from time to time is sleeping on the envelope and its contents. So far as I am aware, it was not discovered by the Shanghai security police, although they went over the cabin with great care.

Two days later we prepared to sail. (The cargo fortunately took less time to handle than anticipated.) At lunch was the Polish representative (whom I had not seen for several days) and the captain. I wished the Polish representative good-bye and good luck.

'I hope we may meet again under more favourable circumstances,' I said.

'I hope so, too,' he replied. 'I trust your journey has not been completely wasted.' The words had, perhaps, significance.

As the engines started up, I went on deck, ignoring the order confining me to my cabin. On the boat deck, the captain's quarters had exits to the port and starboard sides of the deck. As he was on the bridge with the pilot, these secluded portions of the deck were deserted. I walked forward on the starboard side, took out my Leica which had been in my jacket pocket for the last twelve days, and surreptitiously took half a dozen shots of the harbour, the Russian ship, the coke furnaces and the steel mill.

Outside the breakwater the sea was still covered with thin ice, shimmering in the brilliant sunshine. I waited until the pilot had left the ship and then took some photographs of the broken ice which made beautiful coloured mosaic patterns, reflecting the blue of the sky. Alas, I have not been able to see the results.

It was a little over two days' voyage to Shanghai. I was faced with the problem of sending my story of the *Pueblo* affair to London. To use the ship's radio would be very costly and also not very secure. I did not know the origin of my information, although I suspected the source. But I had to recognise that this was a Communist ship, and that our next port of call was in a Communist country. I could not expect protection if I appeared hostile. And my *Pueblo* information was very 'sensitive'.

I discussed with the radio operator whether I could speak on the ship-shore telephone to the *Daily Telegraph* correspondent in Tokyo. But when we tried to establish a connection the next day we had no success. It was frustrating. I had written the story which I proposed to dictate on to the Tokyo correspondent's tape-recorder.

I now had no alternative but to file the story from Hong Kong. It would be too risky to attempt to do so from Shanghai. I did not know that it would be twenty long months of solitary confinement in a Shanghai gaol before I reached the British island colony of Hong Kong. By then, the *Pueblo* incident was almost forgotten.

5 An 'Excursion' in Shanghai

AT 11.30 p.m., Monday, February 19, I stood on the bridge with Bruno Neroni as the *Hanoi* stopped half a mile off the pilot station at the mouth of the Yangtse Kiang, the mighty ochre-coloured river which cuts China in half, but which the Communists have bridged at three points.

Earlier in the day the captain had told me that as we were to load only 750 tons of frozen mutton, we should not be in Shanghai more than forty-eight hours, if we were able to obtain a berth immediately.

As our stay was to be so short, I suggested to Neroni, in the light of my experience in the previous November, that we engage and share a guide from the China Travel Service. He would cost £10 a day. I said that I was quite happy if he chose our itinerary, because I had seen everything in Shanghai that was worth while. I was more interested on this visit in comparing the atmosphere of the present with what it had been a few months earlier. Neroni was very happy with my suggestion.

Two pilots and a security officer set out from the pilot station at the mouth of the Yangtse immediately we stopped. When they arrived on the bridge, they told me, in answer to my queries, that we should anchor at the mouth of the Whangpoo, thirty miles up the estuary, at about 4.00 a.m. and that we should continue up the Whangpoo to our berth at 8.00 a.m.

Neroni was still on the bridge as I went to bed.

By the time I had finished my toilet and dressed and entered the saloon for breakfast the next morning we were already moving up the Whangpoo. Neroni did not join me. I assumed he preferred to stay on the bridge. As a ship's captain, it was not surprising that he should be interested in the fourteen-mile journey up the river; the ship would be passing communes, factories and shipyards before reaching the dock area.

The small saloon in which we ate our meals was on the starboard side, and had a large window looking forward and three panoramic windows on the side. As we passed the Shanghai Naval Station, a short distance from Woosung Fort at the mouth of the Whangpoo, I noticed three motor torpedo boats. They were dressed overall with international signal pennants, and covered with posters of Mao slogans. I could not help thinking it would make a good photograph, showing the revolutionary fervour in the naval branch of the People's Liberation Army.

At ten o'clock we docked. I then sought out the chief steward. I explained to him that there had been so much trouble in Chungjin with the security officers over my photographs and private papers—they had spent hours examining them during searches of my cabin—that I wondered if it would be possible for him to put the valise containing these possessions into a cupboard where they would not necessarily be subjected to scrutiny by the Shanghai security officers. He said that he would put it in his cabin. He accompanied me back to my cabin to collect it. Before handing it over, I opened it to give him an idea of the contents for I did not wish him to take the responsibility for anything that might be regarded as subversive. The top file, when I opened the bag, contained the carbon copies of three articles I had written after my previous visit to China. On the cover in large black printed letters were the words: 'Report from China'. I made a point of explaining the contents to him very carefully.

The Chinese agent of the Polish Ocean Line came aboard within a few minutes of our docking. This man, of course, is a government servant as everybody else is in China. I asked him to arrange for a representative of the China Travel Service to come aboard and secure landing permits for Neroni and myself.

An hour later, the representative, a Mr Cheong, arrived aboard. He was a young, enthusiastic man, obviously anxious to please. I was to learn later that he had not long graduated from the Shanghai Institute of Foreign Languages, and that this was his first assignment of escorting foreign tourists. He had been with the Travel Service for eight months, but his career as a guide had got off to a slow start because of the confusion of the Cultural Revolution, when no tourists or foreign business-men were visiting China. I fetched Neroni and we filled in the application form to land, giving Mr Cheong our passports. He did not think there would be any difficulty over our being given landing passes.

To my enquiry whether I could travel to Hong Kong by train because of the passenger accommodation problem aboard the *Hanoi*, he replied diplomatically that the ship was not staying in port long enough to arrange a visa.

Mr Cheong went ashore.

I asked Neroni if his cabin had been inspected by the security police. He said that it had not. Nor had mine been, which seemed very curious, because in my four previous visits to Red China my cabin had been carefully searched on arrival and departure. On this occasion, the security officer, whom I assumed was still aboard, had not even given us any warning about photographing on the river. I could only assume that the photographic regulations had been eased since my previous visit in November.

I next went to my cabin and slipped the Leica into my overcoat pocket. It was loaded with Ektachrome colour film. Photography on my previous visit had been unrewarding—not only because of the security problems which I have mentioned before, but also because the weather had been cold, often raining, and the streets almost deserted in the aftermath of the upheaval of the Cultural Revolution.

I walked around the decks. Refrigerator vans were already alongside. Stevedores were removing the hatch covers to the refrigerator holds. All this bustle was very different from six months earlier when ships were often held up for six weeks or more in Shanghai because of the dislocation caused by the great Proletariat Cultural Revolution.

On the bridge I photographed a panoramic view of the

Bund with its tall, stone-faced buildings—monuments of the imperialist days of the 'twenties when I lived in Shanghai. Neroni joined me. He was wearing a very heavy white ski-type sweater with a zip fastener. His Asahi Pentax was slung around his neck under the sweater.

Coming down the river towards us was a Yangtse passenger ship, bound, I assume, for Nanking. Crowds of Chinese men, women and children lined the rails of the five decks. Their weight on one side caused the ship to list slightly. Mao slogans were painted around the bridge, and on the sides of the ship. It promised to make a good photograph in the brilliant sunshine.

I rested my Leica on the ship's rail so that no one aboard the river steamer could see me photographing them. (Although I had not been warned on this visit about photographing on the river, I felt it better to be discreet.) Neroni was intrigued with the way I took these photographs—three of the ship from different angles. He was standing behind me and had unzipped the top of his sweater; he took out his Pentax and made two photographs of the ship. The wireless operator came out of the radio room and chatted for a few minutes, but he made no comment about our taking photographs. The Polish crew, either unaware of the photographic regulations or ignoring them, were snapping every day.

Neroni and I walked round to the starboard side of the bridge. Loading of the frozen mutton had already begun. We watched, fascinated, as the women lifted the carcases from the refrigerator van and threw them on to the moving belt which carried them up to the cargo deck where the stevedores threw them into a refrigerator hold. These Chinese women, all barrel-shaped, must be exceedingly strong. They handled the carcases quite effortlessly, and they seemed to work with untiring energy —almost with enthusiasm. I had noticed on all my visits to China that the women dockworkers displayed greater zeal than the men.

Neroni tried to take a photograph, but the angle was too high. He said he would go to the deck below.

'I should be careful,' I warned him. 'Although we have not

been prohibited from taking photographs on the river and in the dock area, the regulations probably still apply. It may have been an oversight on the part of the security officer, when he boarded the ship with the pilot.'

Neroni said he would be discreet.

I remained for a while on the bridge, then went to my cabin. A few minutes later the chief steward knocked on the door. He told me that the four passengers who were embarking were a man and his wife, and two small children. He suggested that they have the single cabins occupied by Neroni and myself; he would put up cots for the children—two girls of seven and four years old. If I did not object, he felt that the best way out of the accommodation problem would be for Neroni and me to occupy the remaining double cabin with bathroom—known as the owner's cabin—which led off the saloon where we ate our meals. I told him that I was quite happy with this arrangement if Neroni did not mind sharing a cabin with me.

I spent the remaining hour before lunch moving into the new cabin. I offered Neroni the choice of bunks. He said he did not mind, so I suggested that he took the bunk which was the farthest away from the cabin door—it may appear to be a very trivial matter, but forty-eight hours later it was of tremendous significance. So was the problem of the wardrobe —too small to hold all our suits. I said that I would have a word with the chief steward to see if he could hang a few of my suits in his wardrobe. This, too, later was to be interpreted by the Chinese authorities as an effort at deception.

Before lunch, over a drink, the captain told me that the new passengers were Chilean. He said, with disgust, that they were Red Guards. In a sense he was right, but as I came to know them I would have described them as Maoist 'missionaries'. They had been acting as translators in Peking for two years, but I suspect that the real purpose of their stay in the Chinese capital was to learn the techniques of 'revolution'. Men and women of all nationalities are being so trained in Peking, and have been for many years. When their indoctrination is finished they go out into the world to preach the Maoist gospel, to be the core of the cells that are to organise armed revolt by the proletariat. It is not an idle threat. Although many of the security forces in the world might not completely agree with me, most of the demonstrations, the riots that have taken place during the past three years, are Maoist-inspired.

The captain of the *Hanoi* was obviously not very happy about having them as passengers all the way to Europe. He warned me to be circumspect in my conversation at meal times, because previously we had had many interesting discussions. Although the captain was, no doubt, a faithful Communist, he had no great love for the Chinese. He had not forgotten being 'roughed up' by the Red Guards on a trip to Shanghai the previous spring.

The new passengers were at lunch. The husband and wife were both young, speaking fluent English. The children were delightful. The four-year-old, who had been to a kindergarten in Peking, spoke only Chinese.

I enquired if they had enjoyed their sojourn in China. The wife said she was very happy to be going home, and I soon sensed that she did not like the Chinese, nor her life in Peking. For two years, she and her husband had been eye-witnesses of the Cultural Revolution. In spite of the captain's warning—I could see that he was getting a little hot under the collar—I found it impossible to curb my curiosity and asked questions about what happened in Peking during these past two convulsive years. They were both very frank, often critical by implication of the Mao regime. I felt that their Communism was more attuned to Moscow's brand than Mao's conception of a Utopia inhabited by selfless men and women.

The younger child, her sister told me, knew all the Chairman Mao songs. She was asked by her sister to sing them for me. The little girl got down from her chair and entertained us for ten minutes, singing the songs like Mao's favourite, 'The East is Red', accompanied with quaint dances.

She concluded lustily:

> We clap our hands, we are so happy!
> The communes are so powerful!
> My father works in a factory,

My brother drives a tractor,
My sister works the loom,
The electric light lights every household.

I had heard children singing this song in a commune kindergarten in November. I wonder how long it will be before this little Chilean child and her elder sister forget Mao's teaching of the collective *we*.

It was four o'clock when Mr Cheong arrived aboard with our landing permits. Neroni appeared greatly relieved. We discussed what we should do in the limited time available. Neroni expressed a desire to take a trip on the Whangpoo River, which surprised me because he had been on the bridge all the way from the Yangtse pilot station, not bothering to go to bed. He explained to Mr Cheong that as a ship's captain he was interested in shipbuilding. Everything which the Chinese are doing is supposed to be secret, so it was not surprising that Mr Cheong diplomatically replied that, unfortunately, there was insufficient time for him to arrange such a tour for Neroni. As an alternative, he suggested that we visit the Shanghai Trade Fair where Neroni could see models of all the types of merchant ship which were being built in Shanghai, as well as the other industrial activities of the city.

It was obvious that Neroni was very disappointed. At the time, I could not understand why. I suggested that on the morrow we might first make a brief tour of the city by motorcar (this would give me a chance to test the atmosphere of Shanghai) and then visit the Trade Fair. We could lunch at the Peace Hotel on the Bund.* In the afternoon I thought it might interest Neroni if we visited a commune. I had been to two in November, but I was not averse to seeing a third.

Mr Cheong agreed to this itinerary and promised to collect

* Built by millionaire Sir Victor Sassoon in the 'thirties, and formerly called the Cathay, the Peace Hotel, like the multi-storeyed buildings on Shanghai's famous waterfront, is a monument to western imperialism. Today these buildings are plastered with golden Mao slogans and portraits. The younger Chinese who gravitate to the Bund on their day off firmly believe that they were built following the Communist takeover, and this illusion is officially fostered.

us with a motor-car at eight-thirty the following morning. He then enquired if we would like to go ashore that afternoon. I said that I would, as I had not been off the ship for nearly a month, and would like to stretch my legs. As it is only a short distance, I thought we might walk into the town, visit the Friendship Shop and the antique shop. At the latter I wished to buy a painting. I had selected one in November, but had been unable to pay for it because the Bank of China would not change my American Express dollar travellers' cheques—the only country in the world to refuse dollars.

We set off at once for the town. I did not bother to take a camera: the waning winter sun was not quite strong enough for good colour photographs. Neroni, however, took his Pentax. Immediately we had gone through dock gates he began snapping pictures.

I sensed a change in the atmosphere of the city. The people looked more relaxed; there were more goods in the shops. Work on the docks was going smoothly, and there appeared to be no shortage of labour.

After we had crossed Soochow Creek bridge and were walking along the Bund, Neroni found himself surrounded by children and grownups every time he took a picture. They were all laughing and joking and seemed delighted when he took photographs of them. Neroni asked me to take a picture of himself with the crowd. Everybody enjoyed this. There was not the slightest sign of anti-foreign feeling, so violently displayed to me a few months earlier. The militant side of the Cultural Revolution had apparently been forgotten.

I noticed that the Mao slogans and a portrait of him which surmounted the large double wrought-iron gates of the former British Consulate had been removed. But there was still a larger-than-life picture of him in the gardens of the Consulate.

At the Friendship Shop, the anti-Soviet and foreign slogans had also disappeared. The shop was better stocked. I examined a grand piano for tone: it could hardly be compared with a Steinway. The case was very poorly finished; the cover over the keys had not even been sandpapered smooth before

French polishing. But the bicycles—there was a wide variety to choose from at low prices—were well-finished. There were suits of clothes which might have been acceptable to the sartorial taste of Mr Krushchev, but would certainly have caused comment if worn in a Pall Mall club.

From the Friendship Shop we walked to the antique shop in the Foochow Road. The Red Chinese are preserving what antiquities are left in the country after the spoliation and moving to Taiwan of China's cultural heritage, so, although there are some nice curios to be bought in the antique shop, none is more than a hundred years old. They all have a special seal which permits you to take them from the country, but even so, the Chinese customs officials scrutinise everything with care.

When I was leaving China by ship in 1960 I had bought four very beautiful Chinese scroll paintings. They were obviously more than one hundred years old, although I had bought them through an official channel. The customs authorities held up the ship for four hours while they consulted superiors to decide whether I could take them with me. I think they only permitted me to do so because as I had bought them officially it would have been an admission, if they had stopped me taking them out, of Communist inefficiency. In a word, a tremendous loss of face.

On this occasion, I bought in the antique shop one painting reputed to be eighty years old. It was rather unique in that there were three paintings on one scroll, two executed by a father and the third by his daughter. It cost only £8.

By now it was dark and I personally had no wish to remain in the town. But Neroni said that he would like to visit the Seamen's Club on the Bund, which was once the Shanghai Club, and boasted the longest bar in the world. The bar still remains. Today, a foreign sailor can get drunk there at any hour of the day that he wishes. But in a city where there used to be thousands of street prostitutes—euphemistically known as 'Flying Pheasants'—the sailor today cannot buy a girl as in Bangkok, Taipei or Hong Kong. And he certainly won't be suffering from venereal disease forty-eight hours after his ship has sailed. A doctor informed me while I was a prisoner that all forms of V.D. had been virtually eliminated in Mao's China. This is understandable because one of the first acts of the Peking Government after China came under Communist rule in 1949 was to move all the prostitutes out to work as agricultural labourers. And they received intensive medical treatment.

Although a sailor can drink in the Seamen's Club, there is really very little other form of entertainment. There are two table tennis tables—usually occupied by Chinese sailors from foreign ships. The seaman can also buy himself a well-cooked Chinese-style or European meal. And there is plenty of opportunity for him to acquire, free of charge, Maoist literature and photographs. As a club, it is a pretty dull place—certainly not as gay as the Seamen's Club in Haiphong where there were dances for the sailors even at the height of the American bombing. (It was interesting that in Haiphong the authorities provided hand-picked hostesses, but the dances ended promptly at midnight and the girls went home alone.)

Neroni said that he had a rendezvous at the club with some of the officers of the *Hanoi*, so I left him and took a taxi back to the ship.

Mr Cheong arrived punctually aboard at eight-thirty the next morning. We called first at the Bank of China so that I could collect the £50 which had been transferred by telegraph from London. I was surprised how speedily the transaction was completed. There was the minimum of form-filling and after I had explained that as I was only going to be in Shanghai for another twenty-four hours or so I did not wish all this money in Chinese currency, I was permitted to draw £30 in sterling.

Before driving round the town and visiting the Trade Fair, we walked the full length of the Bund so that Neroni could take some more photographs. Although his Asahi Pentax was new, he was having difficulties with the winding mechanism. Mr Cheong suggested that we went to the camera shop in the Nanking Road. Fortunately, it was only a minor fault and the shop fixed it. Neroni had been very perturbed and was delighted when the fault was corrected. He bought a half-dozen, Chinese-manufactured, black-and-white rolls of film.

Throughout our drive around the city and during a ninety-minute stay at the Trade Fair, Neroni continuously took photographs, even from the car window. I thought this strange for a man who was obviously an inexperienced photographer.

I had brought my Leica with me, loaded with colour film, but during the morning I took only a few shots—one of the school building where the Communist Party was formed and the first congress was held in 1921. This secret meeting place was discovered by the French police—the building was in the French concession of Shanghai—and all the dozen or so delegates, including Mao, disappeared to Hangchow and finished the congress aboard a boat on the beautiful lake on which the city stands.

A few months later my prison interrogator could not understand why I should have photographed this historic building, which the Chinese have gone to great lengths to preserve. They also accused me of taking, for intelligence purposes, a photograph of crowds outside a state store in the Nanking Road which had in the background the tall tower of the radio building.

Neroni and I ate lunch alone at the Peace Hotel, Mr Cheong promising to collect us at two o'clock to go to a commune. The dining room of the hotel is at the top of the building. Some panoramic photographs which I took with a wide-angle and telephoto lens also got me into trouble, although I was taking the last photographs when Mr Cheong arrived and he saw what I was doing. He made no objection. When we got down to the street, to enter our car, a long procession was forming up on the Bund of gaily decorated floats all with coloured pictures or plaster effigies of Mao Tse-tung. Mr Cheong informed me that the floats represented individual factories in Shanghai, and the workers were celebrating the setting-up of 'three-in-one Cultural Revolution committees'. It was all very colourful, the workers enjoying beating their drums and clashing their cymbals.

I took a number of photographs, but Neroni seemed quite

uninterested. During the drive to the commune, about twenty-five miles outside of Shanghai, we passed a number of other demonstrations of workers and teachers, all carrying portraits of Mao and red flags. I got the driver to stop the car so that I could take some more photographs. But again, Neroni did not bother.

Just before we arrived at the commune we passed about a thousand men and women ankle-deep in the alluvial mud of the Whangpoo River, digging a big irrigation canal. They had no mechanical aids, using only long-handled shovels. Such projects are going on every day all over China—digging canals, either to irrigate the land or to carry away flood waters. These people are working with the method and industry of ants. Because of the large labour force available, these projects are being completed probably as quickly as if mechanical shovels and bulldozers were used. Western civil engineers might criticise on the basis of the waste of manpower, but if the Chinese do not have mechanical aids they have no alternative. They are pulling themselves up by their own boot-straps.

The commune which we visited was interesting because it surrounded a very old, picturesque village—extremely photogenic. I exposed a whole roll of colour film in this village, taking photographs of the streets and the insides of the tiny shops. It had two clinics—one western-style medicine, and the other Chinese. In the western clinic there seemed no shortage of modern medicines, such as antibiotics. In the Chinese clinic a woman patient was being given acupuncture—the traditional Chinese treatment of ailments by inserting into the skin long gold and silver needles. Because China is short of doctors, this method of treating illness has, in the past year, been given very wide publicity. Claims have been made of curing deaf-mutes. When I was in the prison hospital, an aged man who was paralysed on one side as a result of a cerebral stroke was also being treated with acupuncture, but it made no difference to his condition. It is a rather painful method of treatment, but in the case of the old man it didn't matter, because he had no feeling in the arm and leg where the needles were being stuck into him.

66

Again, my interrogators later criticised me for taking photographs in this village, accusing me of intending to use them for propaganda purposes to show China as a poor country. I replied: 'I had no ulterior motive in taking these photographs. The village was one aspect of the Chinese way of life. Are you ashamed of it?'

Another photograph taken on a commune was of workers cycling home. It was claimed that in the distance was a 'sensitive building'. I said that I was not conscious of any building being included in the photograph when I took it, but it was the responsibility of Mr Cheong, the guide, to stop me if he felt that I was contravening some obscure regulation. It was all part of the paranoic attitude of the Chinese towards photography.

It was a very large commune of at least 50,000 people, was completely self-contained in that it had its own workshop for repairing tractors, and even a foundry for making simple farm implements. It had a sawmill. The man who was sharpening the teeth of a large band-saw and hammering it into shape so that it did not fly off the spinning wheels when operating, was both very impressed and pleased when I complimented him and said that he was carrying out a very difficult job. He asked, through Mr Cheong, how I knew. I explained that when I was nineteen years old I worked on a lumber camp, and that the man who was responsible for the maintenance of these band-saws—they are about forty feet long—was one of the highest-paid men in the organisation.

Typically Chinese, the workman on this commune asked: 'How much was he paid?'

I replied: 'Five hundred American dollars a month which, in your currency, is about one thousand yuan.'

It was obvious that Mr Cheong was a little embarrassed at having to interpret a figure which showed the high wages of an American craftsman.

'How much do you earn?' I asked.

Mr Cheong interpreted. The Chinese muttered a few words. Mr Cheong said in English: 'Forty yuan a month.'

I did not make any comment, but I felt that in the space of

half a minute I had perhaps done more propaganda for western free enterprise than, say, the daily outpouring of the Voice of America, which very few Chinese listen to anyway.

I dropped Neroni off at the Seamen's Club on my way back to the *Hanoi*. He told me the next morning that he did not get back to the ship until 4.00 a.m.

I spent that evening as the previous one, chatting after dinner to the Chilean and his wife about China under the Cultural Revolution. They had a fascinating story to tell, and some of the details I have included earlier about those two politically passionate years came from their lips.

But I did not feel that they understood the motive of Mao as well as I do, and I found myself in the rather odd role of often defending Mao's position. I have no sympathy for Communism, but I recognise that a country which has embraced a Communist way of life can only avoid drifting back—as Russia has done—into a semi-capitalist system by perpetual revolution. This is Mao's thesis, too.

We prepared to sail for Hong Kong immediately after breakfast the next morning. As I came out of the dining saloon, I ran into the chief steward; I explained to him the problem of the wardrobe in the cabin which Neroni and I were sharing, and asked him if I could hang three of my suits in the wardrobe in his cabin. He apologised that this was not possible, because he too had a very small wardrobe, and it was full. A moment later, I met the captain coming from the chief engineer's cabin; I explained to him again the problem of my suits, and asked him if he could look after them for me. He said he would have a word with the chief steward. As he was obviously busy preparing to sail, I did not bother him further.

I returned to our cabin. Neroni asked me if I had any spare film. I offered him colour or black-and-white; he chose the black-and-white. I gave him two rolls of Kodak Verichrome. I assumed he wanted to take some photographs as we went down the Whangpoo River.

In Shanghai the previous day I had exposed two rolls of colour film. As one roll was of processions of workers celebrating the setting-up of Cultural Revolution committees, I decided to take two more photographs on the river—the motor torpedo boats if they were still dressed from stem to stern with flags, and a commune at the mouth of the Whangpoo. This very large commune can be seen without interruption for several miles; it is dotted with ancient cottages, tiled roofs and curved eaves. At this point of the river, too, is the anchorage for the majestic Shanghai junks with large brown sails flapping like the wings of a flying dragon. With the junks in the foreground I thought it would make a fine panoramic photograph. And it was a beautiful crisp February morning with the sun shining from an almost cloudless sky.

As the ship's siren indicated that we were about to sail there had still been no inspection of the cabin by either a customs officer or a security officer. There had been no prohibition of photography on the river since we arrived at the mouth of the Yangtse a little over forty-eight hours earlier.

I went up to the bridge. There was only one pilot, and he was chatting to the security officer, a rather tough, unpleasant-looking Chinese. I was obviously not very welcome. After a few minutes, the pilot informed the captain that we could sail. I went to the deck below. As the *Hanoi* reached mid-stream I took one wide-angle panoramic photograph of the Bund and the river.

I saw no sign of Neroni. I went down to the cargo deck and walked aft to reconnoitre for the best place to take some photographs of the warships and the commune on the opposite bank when we reached them in an hour's time. I found that it would be possible to photograph both sides of the river without moving from the stern of the ship. Also, I should be shielded from view by a deck-house with a companion-way below to cabins for cadets. Although I had not been warned about photography, I felt it wiser to take precautions. On my return to the bridge I passed Neroni on the cargo deck. I could see from the bulge in his blue topcoat that he had his camera slung round his neck. I told him to be careful.

From the bridge I noticed that the security officer was snooping around the ship. We were about four miles from Woosung Fort at the mouth of the river. In a few minutes we should be abreast of the motor torpedo boats. I went to the stern in readiness to take my pictures, carefully looking around to ensure that I was not being watched by the security officer. With my Weston meter I took a light reading, set the speed and aperture of the lens. I replaced my Leica in my overcoat pocket out of sight. I walked about for half a minute. I could see Neroni on the boat deck. We were now coming up to the warship. I moved behind the shelter of the deck-house. The warships were still beflagged, still covered with Mao slogans. I took two pictures in rapid succession, just varying the aperture half a stop to ensure that at least one of them would be colour-accurate. I turned round and took one shot of the commune. Fortunately, there was a large number of junks anchored, making a very good foreground setting.

When I returned to my cabin before lunch, my steward told me that if I would give him my suits, he would put them in the wardrobe of the pilot's cabin after lunch. (I thought this a little ironic because in Kobe the captain had told me that there was no pilot's cabin on the ship. I was to learn a few hours later that it had a communicating door with his own cabin, which was presumably the reason he did not wish me to occupy it between Shanghai and Hong Kong.)

At lunch, there was only the Chilean and his wife and two children, Neroni and the ship's doctor. As we neared the end of the meal, I noticed through the window that although we were out in the Yangtse, the ship was not moving. I think we all have an inbuilt sense of danger. I cannot explain why, but my hackles rose slightly. I made no comment during the meal that the ship had obviously anchored.

After coffee, I left the saloon to investigate. I discovered the pilot and the security officer sitting in the officers' lounge. To the pilot I commented: 'I thought we were due at the pilot station at three. We shall be late.'

The security officer replied: 'We are anchored to await instructions from Shanghai.'

I was immediately alert. I returned to my cabin, which led off the dining saloon. Neroni was there. I explained to him what had happened, adding: 'It is very curious. Rather suspicious. Did you take any photographs as we came down the river?'

Neroni was evasive, not giving a direct answer. He seemed embarrassed, almost nervous.

'If you have taken any photographs,' I said, 'I think you might be well advised to throw the rolls overboard.'

He left the cabin without comment. The two rolls of film which I had exposed in Shanghai I had already put in the jacket pocket of one of my suits, together with a black-and-white film taken in Chungjin. (This was not a security precaution. It was merely to ensure that the light did not get at them as they would not be processed for several days.) I unloaded the film in my Leica and placed it with the other rolls in the suit pocket.

I walked around the cabin and the bathroom to see if there was any evidence of photography. Two empty Kodak Verichrome cartons were in the bathroom wastepaper basket. I took them out, went on deck and threw them overboard. Neroni came up behind me as I was doing it. I returned to the cabin.

A few minutes later my steward came in and asked for the suits to put in the pilot's cabin. I gave him three suits, one of them with the films in the pocket, though I did not mention this to the steward.

There was nothing to do now but await events.

6   Under Suspicion

Thursday, February 22, 1968

I WENT out of the cabin into the small saloon which led off
it. The Chilean and his wife were still sitting there talking. I
sat down and joined them. While we were talking, Neroni
returned to our cabin. He remained there for about five
minutes. He seemed unduly worried when he came out again,
finding it difficult to participate in our conversation about the
Cultural Revolution.

At 3.00 p.m. the saloon door opened. The security officer
came in, followed by the chief steward, who pointed at me.

'May I search your cabin, please?' said the security officer,
addressing me.

'Certainly,' I replied. 'Come this way.'

I got up, walked across the saloon, opened the cabin door
and ushered the security officer in.

His first question was: 'Have you any cameras?'

'Yes,' I replied. 'Three Leicas.'

'May I see them, please?'

I took from a corner of the cabin a black leather Italian-
made valise. This bag has two compartments—upper and
lower, linked with a zip fastener. In effect, it is my office, and
I carry it wherever I go. In the upper half are research files,
correspondence and copies of articles. In the lower half I keep
my cameras, wide-angle and telephoto lens, typewriter, tape-
recorder and short-wave radio. I unzipped the lower half, the
security officer looking fascinated at the contents. I suppose
he had never seen a bag like this one, and was surprised by my
equipment. I took out the three cameras, and laid them on
my bunk.

'Are the cameras loaded?' enquired the security officer.

'No.'

I picked up one camera and started to open it to show him that there was no film inside. He immediately stopped me, presumably to ensure that if there was a film, it would not be spoiled by allowing the light in. The officer made a search of my half of the cabin, opening drawers under my bunk, looking in the cupboard of my bedside table. He looked under the pillows of the bunk, and turned the mattress back top and bottom. He made a cursory inspection of the bathroom, and then walked across the cabin and opened the double doors of the wardrobe. It had two compartments. Suits were hanging in one compartment, and Neroni's bags in the second compartment. I pointed out to the security officer which were my clothes, and informed him that the bags belonged to Captain Neroni. There were two suitcases in a corner of the cabin. The security officer asked me if they were mine, and I said they were not. My own empty suitcase was standing in the saloon just outside the cabin door, because there was no room in the cabin to put it.

The security officer looked around, rather puzzled. I assumed he had expected to find some film. He picked up some Ektachrome and Verichrome cartons from the lower half of my bag, but satisfied himself that they were unexposed.

Over Captain Neroni's bunk was a wooden rack which held his yellow lifejacket. There was no rack over my bunk, the lifejacket lying on the floor near the bedside table.

The security officer looked up at the lifejacket in the rack. He stepped up against Neroni's bunk, and pulled it down. The jacket was rather an unusual type, designed so that it had a number of small pockets both at the front and the rear. As the officer took the jacket out of the rack, there cascaded from the pockets on to Neroni's bunk about a dozen rolls of exposed film. Some were Japanese Fuji, some Chinese-made, and two rolls were of Kodak Verichrome, similar to what I had given him in the morning.

'Are these your films?' asked the security officer.

'No,' I replied.

At that moment the cabin door opened and Neroni came in. The officer turned to him and, pointing to the films lying on his bunk, said: 'Are these your films, Captain Neroni?'

'No,' was Neroni's prompt, emphatic reply.

I knew, of course, that they must be his films because he had bought the Chinese-made films in my presence the previous day in the Nanking Road. And then there were the two rolls of Verichrome which I had given him in the morning. Obviously he must have exposed these films as we came down the river.

However, at this delicate stage, I felt it wiser not to challenge Neroni's denial of ownership. The situation might still be saved, and I had no desire to involve him in trouble, because I was obviously the person under suspicion, though I appreciated that the situation was dangerous for both of us.

Poker-faced, the security officer scooped up the films off the bunk and stuffed them into his tunic jacket pockets. He also took my three Leica cameras and, without further comment, left the cabin.

Neroni looked embarrassed, agitated. I charged him with the ownership of the films hidden in his lifejacket. The security officer now assumed that they were exposed by me. As a journalist, I was obviously under greater suspicion than he was. I told him that if I was questioned further I would not say that the films were his, but I left it to his sense of honesty as to what course he decided to follow, if the position was investigated further. And, knowing the Chinese well, it would be.

As I reminded him, I noticed that we were about the same height; that morning we had both been wearing blue topcoats. I had seen him as we came down the river taking photographs from the boat deck—a very exposed position. One could be seen on that deck from the bridge and also from the cargo deck below. It had been careless of him.

Neroni obviously did not like this brutal assessment of the situation. He made no reply.

Without a further word, I went out of the cabin, and proceeded to the deck above to see the captain. He was in his day cabin. Before I had a chance to speak to him, however, he was called to the pilot's cabin by the security officer. The door was closed, so I did not hear what transpired, but when he returned to the cabin where I was waiting, he was a very angry man. He informed me that three rolls of film had been found in the pocket of one of my suits hanging in the wardrobe of the pilot's cabin. He accused me of using this cabin to secrete my films. In the circumstances, it was not an unreasonable attitude. And I felt very sorry for him, because as we came down the river on our way to the open sea he must have been standing on the bridge pleased to be putting Red China behind him without any incident.

I apologised to him. I explained that when I had asked permission from him for my suits to be put in his cabin—it was he who had suggested the pilot's cabin—I did not know that the ship would be stopped and a search made for the photographs.

'I do not know, Captain,' I said, 'if you are aware of the present situation. Apart from the film taken from my suit, twelve rolls of exposed black-and-white film were discovered by the security officer hidden in the pockets of the lifejacket over Captain Neroni's bunk. He denies ownership. So do I. Further, it is important that you should know that some members of your own crew did take photographs on the river when we were arriving, while we were docked in Shanghai, and also after we left. If you take my advice, you will pass word around that any member of the crew who took photographs should now promptly destroy them. There are a few hours of safety while the twelve rolls of film discovered in my cabin are taken ashore and developed.

'There is another important point. If you are questioned, as I have no doubt you will be, you should point out that neither Captain Neroni nor myself was warned when the ship arrived that photography on the Whangpoo and in the dock area is prohibited. Nor did you warn us. And I assume that the members of your crew were also not warned, otherwise they would not have taken photographs. On the *Lelewel*, when we arrived in Shanghai in November last year, we were warned both by the captain and by the security officer that photography on the river was prohibited. As there was no warning on this voyage, I assumed that the regulations had been modified. Over a period of years, the photographic regulations in China have been altered many times: at one period you could not even take exposed film out of the country without its first being developed.'

The captain was not mollified by my summary of the position. All he was thinking about, no doubt, was his ship being held up; it was costing his company, the Polish Ocean Line, money. 'If you were warned in November not to take photographs on the river,' countered the captain, 'why did you risk doing so on this voyage?'

'I am a free world journalist,' I replied, 'and I have always regarded it my duty, as other western journalists do, to search out the truth. The defence of freedom involves risks for those who cherish freedom. I am involved in that defence. However, I should like you to know that I took only four photographs on the river after we left the dock. Two were "sensitive". When these negatives have been developed, I shall accept full responsibility for them. I shall also inform the Shanghai Public Security Bureau officer that I am willing to leave the ship immediately and remain in custody until the case is settled, so that your ship can sail without further delay. I assume that the films will be developed within a few hours' time. With luck, you ought to get away by midnight or, at the latest, dawn tomorrow morning.

'But there is the complication of the dozen rolls of black-and-white film hidden in Neroni's lifejacket. They were *not* my films. And Captain Neroni, too, has disclaimed responsibility for them. It is possible, of course, that they do not belong to him. We have occupied the cabin for only forty-eight hours.

'I shall now seek out the security officer, if he is still aboard, and attempt to secure the release of your ship.'

The captain agreed that of course the holding up of the ship was his prime preoccupation. As I was about to leave the cabin, he said: 'It is not difficult to prove whether the films found in the lifejacket, and for which you've disclaimed responsibility, were taken with your camera.'

'I agree,' I replied. 'But such a test might take some time. I don't know what the facilities are like here. We're not in Europe.' I was a little surprised that the captain should have sufficient knowledge of photography to know that a laboratory test can determine what lens was used to take a particular photograph. I added: 'In my case, the test should not prove difficult. I use a Leica Elmar 2.8 lens which produces the sharpest definition of any lens in the world.'

By now the captain had relaxed and appeared to be on my side. I again expressed regret for his ship being delayed and left the cabin.

My search for the security officer proved futile. From my steward I learned that he had gone ashore, presumably to report to higher authority and have the films which he had seized developed. There was nothing more that I could do but await events.

I ought to have been scared stiff. On one of my rolls of film were the photographs of the warships. They were damaging evidence. But in moments of extreme crisis, I have always had the capacity to keep my head. Often it is better to do nothing. Many problems will solve themselves by inaction. This was a case of wait and see.

At 7.30 p.m., just after the evening meal, the security officer entered the saloon and requested permission to search my cabin again. (Neroni had hardly spoken at the meal and had disappeared immediately afterwards.)

I opened the door of the cabin and ushered the security officer in in silence. He went over the cabin with a fine tooth-comb. He took out every drawer and looked at the space in the bottom to see if anything had been secreted. He searched carefully the remainder of my suits in the wardrobe, even to feeling in the lining. The heels of my shoes were examined to see if they might be false (the heels of shoes are, after all, used by smugglers, and spies too).

He turned his attention to the bathroom; looking under the bath and probing behind pipes. High up near the ceiling where three pipes were close together he spotted something. (I wondered whether it was something Neroni or a member of the crew had hidden; for there is a good deal of smuggling among crews of ships.) After five minutes' prodding, he extracted the object. It was wrapped in paper. Eagle-eyed I watched him unwrap it. Inside was more paper. He took off the next layer. I gazed, fascinated, at the look on his face. It was a mixture of puzzlement and anticipation. The process of taking off each layer of paper was rather like a nest of Chinese boxes, each one getting smaller. The last layer was finally removed. In the centre was a solitary piece of paper, tightly screwed up.

I give the officer full marks for his reaction. There was no sign of disappointment, disgust at having been thwarted. He merely tossed the pieces of paper into the wastepaper basket and returned to the cabin. Perspiration was glistening on his forehead, for the bathroom was very hot.

He stood in the middle of the cabin for a moment, deep in thought. Then he glanced down at my black valise. He stooped and unzipped the upper half; took out a file. It contained letters and carbon copies of my own correspondence. He sat down on the bunk and began diligently to read through the folder.

One letter had a Pentagon-embossed heading. He remarked on my high officer friends in the American navy. Then he turned up a letter also with a blue-embossed United States Navy heading.

'Who is Jig?' he asked.

'It is the nickname of Rear Admiral James Ramage,' I replied.

'What does Jig Dog mean?'

This was a complicated question to answer because it involved U.S. Navy callsigns. I tried to explain. 'The initials of Admiral Ramage's first two names are J and D.'

The officer looked puzzled. I suppose to a Chinese police official it must sound improbable that an admiral should have such an absurd nickname. In fact, I suppose, in Communist China no senior officer of the People's Liberation Army ever has an irreverent name.

'In what circumstances did you meet him?'

This was a slightly sensitive question. But I felt that an honest answer was the best policy.

'Before being promoted to Rear Admiral he was Chief of

Staff to 77 Task Force of the United States Navy in the Gulf of Tonkin. I met him aboard the aircraft carrier *Kitty Hawk*, the Flagship of Admiral David Richardson, Commander of the Task Force.'

'Was the *Kitty Hawk* engaged in air operations against North Vietnam?'

'Yes.'

'Why were you permitted to visit this ship when it was engaged in operations?'

'I was researching to write an article for *Epoca*, my magazine in Milan, Italy, on the American bombing of North Vietnam.'

Useless not be frank. In another file in my valise were the carbon copies of articles which I wrote for *Epoca* about my stay aboard the *Kitty Hawk*, also an article about a week which I spent on the Australian destroyer *Hobart* on Operation Sea Dragon—seeking out and destroying North Vietnamese coastal shipping. But I was more worried about an article written after a visit to Quemoy, General Chiang Kai-shek's island bastion only a mile off the Chinese mainland near Amoy. Spies and saboteurs are always being infiltrated from Taiwan into Red China. Many are caught and executed. It would be dangerous for me if the Chinese authorities associated me with Chiang's regime.

'Do you support the American bombing of the people of North Vietnam?'

Again a sensitive, provocative question. But again useless to prevaricate. My feelings were clearly stated in my article.

'In the way it is being conducted, yes I do.'

'You agree with the unprovoked killing of thousands of innocent people?'

'That is not the answer I gave. Of course, I do not wish to see innocent people killed. To say that they are being killed in North Vietnam by the thousands is an exaggeration.'

'American bombing is indiscriminate. There must be thousands of innocent people killed.'

'American bombing is not indiscriminate. They are bombing only selected targets. It is a policy known in military terms as "interdiction". They are bombing only lines of communication which the North Vietnamese are using to carry supplies to their troops fighting in South Vietnam. The Americans are fighting in Vietnam in response to a request from the Saigon Government for military assistance made some years ago. The bombing of lines of communication in the North is in defence of American troops fighting in support of South Vietnamese soldiers.'

'You are an imperialist. Chairman Mao teaches us that all imperialists are paper tigers.'

With this last shot, the officer continued reading my correspondence file. But in the ensuing months I was to hear many times that all imperialists are paper tigers. It is a phrase spawned by Mao, and of which he seems very proud. I believe he used it for the first time to describe all 'reactionaries' in a talk with the American writer Anna Louise Strong, who died in Peking while I was writing this book.

The officer, when he had finished reading my letters, examined my other papers which included research material for two books. The files containing my research on China and articles which I wrote after my visit in the previous autumn, and a folder of my personal photographs, which included many taken in Vietnam, were not in the valise. They were in my other small briefcase which I had given to the chief steward as we arrived in Shanghai.

The security officer was with me for more than an hour before he left. He made no comment on his departure.

At 10.00 p.m. he returned with another security officer, an alert, good-looking young Chinese, brimming over with efficiency. As I was to learn in the next few days, he was what the Americans would call 'on the ball'. The young security officer asked to inspect my cabin again. He spoke impeccable English—almost without an accent. I am sure that he came from a formerly well-to-do family.

In the cabin, he wanted to see my letter file. He read it carefully, paying particular attention to the letters from Admiral Richardson and Admiral Ramage. If I was suspected of espionage, the Chinese, because of my friendship with these two officers, might link me with the Central Intelligence Agency. This was not a stupid suspicion, because C.I.A.

agents in Asia are ten a penny—today almost outnumbering the slowly diminishing western population.

After nearly an hour's reading, the two officers finally left the cabin, first returning the file to my valise.

As I was undressing to go to bed, Neroni came in. He had been drinking, looked worried, but did not speak. He went into the bathroom.

When he came out I told him: 'Bruno, I am probably in considerable trouble. There is no reason why you should in any way be involved. In fact, if we play our cards properly, only I may be the victim of this Chinese investigation.' He listened without comment. I continued: 'Let's be honest with each other. The films found in your lifejacket were obviously yours. Among them were the two rolls of Verichrome which I gave you this morning. Those films will be processed. I don't know what photographs you took. But as you have shown an intense interest in Shanghai's shipbuilding industry, I guess you took some photographs of the shipyards. And you may, too, have taken photographs of the motor torpedo boats moored at the Shanghai Naval Station.'

I paused for a few seconds to allow this to sink in. Neroni was now lying in his bunk.

'If you will tell me exactly what photographs you *did* take as we came down the river, I will decide if I can assume responsibility for them. I can't escape responsibility for the four colour photographs which I took: one of the Bund, two of the motor torpedo boats, and a fourth of the commune at the mouth of the river. I know what photographs you took in the city, because we were together. I also know that you took a photograph of the Yangtse river steamer with me, and the women stevedores loading frozen sheep. These photographs are unimportant. The "sensitive" ones are those taken on the river.'

I thought that Neroni would respond to this gesture, although I was not really taking much personal risk. I felt sorry for him. He had a wife and young baby. There was no reason why both of us should be in trouble, and for me there was probably no escape. The only 'sensitive' photographs were those of the motor torpedo boats, though they were of no real military significance.

After several minutes' silence, Neroni muttered: 'I do not wish to discuss it tonight. We will talk about it tomorrow morning. All this trouble has arisen because of your carelessness.'

'Whether I was careless is arguable.' I retorted. 'It may well have been that *you* were careless. It may be a case of mistaken identity. We were dressed almost alike. But who is to blame for this trouble is not the important point at issue. If we do not discuss the problem and settle our relationship tonight, tomorrow morning may be too late.'

'I do not wish to talk about it tonight.'

Neroni was not the first Italian I had met whose reaction when confronted with an unpleasant situation was to avoid the issue, and who lacked courage in dealing with other people when he might be in the wrong.

He pulled the curtain around his bunk and switched out his light. Almost immediately, perhaps because of exhaustion, he feel into a deep sleep, snoring very heavily. He snored all through the night, giving me disturbed rest. Everyone snores differently, almost to a determined pattern. I shall never have difficulty in identifying Neroni's snoring.

I was not too worried about my position. Even if I had infringed the port photographic regulations, it seemed unlikely that I would be detained because of the two photographs of the small warships. Photographs of similar torpedo boats— I had taken some myself—had appeared in the Hong Kong press when they demonstrated off Macao a few months previously. I could not foresee that all the photographs that I took the previous day in the city and at the commune would also be regarded as suspicious.

7   Diary of Interrogation

Friday, February 23, 1968
I⊤ is 6.00 a.m., I have just woken up. There is a knock at the cabin door. I get up and open it. Outside is the young security officer of the previous night, looking fresh, alert and immaculately dressed in a well-fitting grey wool tunic and trousers. He enters the cabin and tells me to get dressed immediately. He refuses my request to shave and take a shower.

I quickly put on my clothes, choosing a pair of dark grey flannel trousers and a dark blue blazer with buttons of the Royal Air Force. I immediately realise that this dress gives me a slightly military appearance. (In fact, whenever I was so dressed in Milan the Editor of *Epoca*, Nando Sanpietro, always addressed me as 'Admiral'.)

I am going to the bathroom to comb my ruffled hair, but the officer immediately stops me, saying: 'There is no time for that.'

Throughout this procedure, Neroni has not moved to see what is going on. The security officer ignores him. I am escorted to the large lounge on the port side of the ship, which is used by the officers. Sitting in a semi-circle of armchairs are six khaki-uniformed officers, all wearing caps with the red star of China above the peak. On the left side of their tunics gleam gold and red badges with the embossed face of Mao Tse-tung. Before them is a single chair. I am told to sit in it.

Without any preliminary opening, the presumably senior officer, his fat body slumped in the large upholstered chair, asks gruffly: 'What is your name?' (The grim look on his podgy face and his intimidating voice, I discover later, belie his true character.)

His opening question is translated by an interpreter wearing a heavily patched Mao boiler-suit—status symbol of the Cultural Revolution.

'Norman William Barrymaine,' I reply.

'What are you?'

'My passport describes me as "Independent".'

'And what does that mean?'

'Free man.'

This repartee displeases him. I guess he speaks English because a scowl clouds his face even before the interpreter has time to translate my two-word comment.

'Your files indicate that you write. Are you a writer?'

'Yes. I have been a journalist for fifty years.'

'Then why do you describe yourself as "independent"?'

'I am beholden to no one.'

'Do you describe yourself as "independent" to deceive the authorities of the countries you visit during your travels? You do travel extensively. Your passport reveals this.'

'It would be impossible to conceal my identity or my work. I am well known all over the world as a journalist. I have written books as well as articles for the world's leading newspapers and magazines. I am sure that every country has a dossier about me. Unless your security is inefficient—which I'm sure it's not—you have one, too.'

[Before I went to sleep on the previous night, I had resolved that my best line of action was not to dissemble. That only by telling the truth could I sustain my position if the interrogation went on for a long period. This proved to be a wise decision because Chinese interrogation is very repetitive. If you fabricate a story, it is difficult to remember a few days, a few weeks or even a few months later what you said at a particular point in the grilling.

But on this morning—it was not yet seven o'clock and I hadn't had even a cup of tea—I recognised that I was in a precarious position. I knew that I ran the risk of being accused of espionage, which in China carries a maximum penalty of

84

execution by firing squad in the cold, dark hours of the night.]

The senior officer continued: 'You are being taken to the Frontier Station to confess your crimes.'

The interpreter emphasised the word 'confess'. My own reaction is that I am 'guilty' in the eyes of the Chinese even before any investigation has begun. (As I discover in subsequent days, the accused has to prove his innocence, not the accusers his guilt. This poses the significant question if you are charged with being a spy: how do you prove a negative if you are *really* innocent?)

I am escorted back to my cabin. The curtains around Neroni's bunk are still drawn. The young security officer stands at the foot of the bunk, opens a chink in the curtains and says jocularly but with a slight note of cynicism in his voice: 'Did you sleep well, Captain?'

There is no reply from Neroni.

I put on my blue camel-hair overcoat, fur-felt Lock hat. I can feel the copy of Mao Thought in the overcoat pocket. I am permitted to take only a slim black leather briefcase containing my money, passport and return air ticket to Europe. I slip a comb, toothbrush and a tube of toothpaste into the case. I am not allowed to wash, shave or even brush or comb my hair which is still in disorder after a night's sleep.

A second security officer comes in and picks up my valise with files, typewriter, tape-recorder and radio. My cameras were taken the previous afternoon.

I am hustled out on deck. The chief steward is there handing the bag I had given to him for safe keeping to one of the officers. He avoids looking at me.

Two guards grab my arms and escort me down the gangway to a coal-burning tug-boat. I am put in the after compartment—a combination of galley and eating cabin. The cook is boiling water for tea over an open coal fire. The whole cabin is dirty and unkempt. The boat must be years old and nobody has bothered to maintain it. It is, I feel, typical of China, like the formerly beautiful buildings and shops of Shanghai which are all in sore need of paint. I suppose it is a question of priorities.

The water boils. The cook brews some green tea, pours it

into the cups and takes them to the forward cabin where the security officers are sitting. I am not offered a cup.

We make the short water journey to Woosung at the mouth of the Whangpoo River. Two cars are waiting. I am told to get into the back of the first—a 1948 American Oldsmobile. Contrary to the comments I have just made about maintenance, this vintage car has been well looked after. The engine is ticking over smoothly—a tribute to Detroit engineering.

The two-car cavalcade sets off on the fourteen-mile drive into Shanghai. It is forty years since I have been along this road. Once it was open country, farms. Today, it is built up, with factories and shipyards along the river.

The Frontier Station is a tall building immediately behind the Peace Hotel on the Bund. I am taken up in the lift to the fourth floor and escorted into a large, sun-lit room furnished in Edwardian style—a legacy, I assume, of the days when the building was the offices of an important foreign company. I cannot remember by whom it was owned.

Against one wall is a sofa to seat three people, upholstered in blue cloth and flanked each side with two deep armchairs covered with the same material. The walls are bare except for a colour portrait of Chairman Mao hanging above the sofa. On a low glass-top table in front of the sofa are Chinese-style handleless cups with lids.

In the centre of the room is an uncomfortable collapsible-style wooden chair. It faces the sofa and the armchairs. The security officer orders me to sit in the chair.

Five khaki-uniformed interrogating officers file into the room behind me and take up their seats on the sofa and the arm-chairs. They are not the same officers who came aboard the *Hanoi* except 'Fatsy', who sits in the centre of the sofa. I assume he is going to conduct the interrogation. The interpreter is also the same. Another officer drags up a small table on which he puts a sheaf of blank Chinese-style notepaper. He is to take the notes. All the officers are wearing cotton quilted topcoats with nylon fur collars to keep them warm in the unheated room. My own camel-hair coat is poor protection. (There is no heating in any building in Shanghai; all the radiators have long since been ripped out. It is part of the frugal life that China's millions are forced to live. Coal and electricity are precious. Everybody is taught to economise.)

An orderly enters the room with two large thermos flasks of hot water. He puts some green tea into the cups and pours hot water. I am offered a cup, and although the tea tastes bitter I welcome it, if only because it warms me up. The officers, too, immediately start drinking and warming their hands with the cups. In a few seconds, without any inhibitions, they are all belching. I am to become used to this. Nobody thinks to offer me breakfast. I am feeling a little hungry because I have had nothing to eat since a sandwich and cup of tea at about nine o'clock the previous evening.

The senior officer takes from his pocket the Mao Thought Red Book. I am to discover that no interrogation can begin without everyone being attuned to the thoughts of the Great Teacher, the Great Helmsman, the Great Leader, the Supreme Commander. To read aloud his *Quotations* is a form of homage but it also has the effect of putting everyone in the right frame of mind.

The officer flicks over the pages. Tells the interpreter which passage he is to read. The interpreter finds it in the English version. He reads: ' "Lifting a rock only to drop it on one's own feet" is a Chinese folk-saying to describe the behaviour of certain fools. The reactionaries in all countries are fools of this kind.' (He does not conclude the full quotation which says: 'In the final analysis, their persecution of the revolutionary people only serves to accelerate the people's revolutions on a broader and more intense scale. . . .')

'Fatsy' looks at me sternly, but then relaxes and in a more persuasive voice says: 'Chairman Mao shows leniency towards those who confess.' It is the first time that I have had to face up to the difficult problem of 'confession' and 'change of attitude' in the Chinese Communist sense.

The grilling begins. I am alert, tensed for a tough session. I assume it will be tricky. It is not. I soon get the impression that prints have not been made yet of the films seized the night before.

'Why did you come to China?' asks the interrogating officer.

'On this occasion, purely by accident,' I reply.

'That's a lie,' intervenes one of the other officers.

'It is the truth. I had no real desire to visit China on this occasion. I am here merely because the *Hanoi*, on which I have been to North Korea, called at Shanghai on its way to Hong Kong, Singapore and Europe.'

'Why did you go to Chungjin?'

'To investigate the seizure by the North Korean Navy of the United States Navy ship *Pueblo*. I was carrying out an assignment for the London *Daily Telegraph*.'

'Have you been to China before?'

'Yes. I was here in Shanghai last November for a month.'

'Is this the only time you have been to China?'

'No. I have been here three times before my visit in November since the Communist Revolution in 1949. But I lived in China for nearly four years when I was in my twenties.'

As the interpreter translates this reply there is an immediate response of interest from all the officers. This indicates that so far they either do not have a dossier on me in Shanghai, or if there is one in Peking it has not yet been transmitted to them. The latter is probably not surprising, because I was quickly to learn that bureaucratic communications in Red China are very slow.

'Do you speak Chinese?'

'No, I don't.'

'But if you lived here for several years as a young man, surely you must have learnt some Chinese.'

'The little that I knew I have long since forgotten. In any case, there was little advantage in those days of learning Mandarin because only the intellectuals spoke it, and if you studied the Shanghai dialect no one could understand you even twenty miles away from the city. Few foreigners in those days took the trouble to learn Chinese, except perhaps customs and police officers who found it a necessity.'

It is obvious that they do not believe me when I say I have no knowledge of their language. I notice that they watch me very closely as each question is put in Chinese to see if I understand before the translator interprets. I must be careful, because even if you do not understand a language, it is difficult not to listen intently, thus giving the impression of a knowledge of it. So I adopt a bored look whenever Chinese is spoken.

I am fascinated by the officer keeping the Chinese record of the interrogation. His calligraphy is beautiful on the lined sheets of official yellow paper. He writes so rapidly that he creates the impression of taking it down in shorthand. He never hesitates; he never has to ask for a question to be repeated.

The pace of the questioning is very slow. There is no intimidation. No hint of violence. The atmosphere is almost like being interviewed on a short list for a job. And yet even that description is not quite accurate, because the next exhortation of the senior officer is:

'You are here to confess your crimes. You cannot expect leniency unless you do.'

The interpreter has difficulty in making it sound as impressive or as strident as when spoken in Chinese. So I feel almost as though I were being addressed by a village priest who disapproves of my dissolute life, perhaps my failure to be a regular communicant.

'I am not trying to be evasive, but I have not committed, in the strict sense of the word, any crime against China. If you feel that I have done so, it can only have been because of my work and certainly not with any deliberate intention to hurt your country.

'I will be quite frank. I am opposed to the philosophy of Communism because of its restrictions on freedom—in thought, in everyday life, in movement. These things I cherish. However, in my years in China when I was a young man and travelled the country extensively, I learned to like the Chinese people, and admire their many qualities. My feelings towards you have not changed because you have chosen Communism as a way of life. I admire what you have accomplished in the eighteen years since Chairman Mao began to rule the country.'

'You are not being honest,' interrupts one officer.

It is almost like saying: 'Flattery will get you nowhere.' Actually, I am speaking sincerely, but it may not sound that way to my accusers. My line of argument may be unfamiliar to them when dealing with foreigners whom they have accused of 'crimes'.

Although this interrogation seems to be taking the form of a trial—the five security officers being the judges—the atmosphere is reasonably relaxed. Every half an hour an orderly comes in with fresh thermos flasks of hot water and tops up the cups. The tea is not changed. We are all using the cups to keep our hands warm.

The time passes very quickly, mainly because we are conducting the proceedings in two languages. So I am surprised when the senior officer, glancing at his steel-cased China-made wrist-watch, says that it is noon and that the proceedings will be adjourned until two-thirty.

I suggest that if the questioning and my case are not to be concluded today, it might be fairer to the Polish Ocean Line for my clothes to be brought ashore and the *Hanoi* allowed to sail. My proposal is received in silence.

As the officers stand up, 'Fatsy' tells me I may order food from the Peace Hotel. The interpreter adds that if I will tell him what I want to eat, he will arrange it.

I order some tomato soup, fish, fruit and coffee. The interpreter says: 'You are not permitted to have coffee.' I order black China tea. I assume they regard coffee as a stimulant.

Fifteen minutes later, a waiter arrives by rickshaw, carrying a circular wicker basket. He is dressed in blue cotton trousers, a spotless white tunic jacket, and white cotton gloves. This is my first encounter with the care taken in China over hygiene in relation to food. He spreads a white linen cloth on the table, and very professionally serves the meal. It is excellently cooked and quite as good as any one can obtain in the best Far Eastern hotels.

When I have finished the meal, I say: 'How much is it, boy?'

For an Englishman who has spent many years of his life in the Orient, it is a natural slip of the tongue to address a waiter as 'boy'. All male servants—irrespective of their age—have traditionally been called 'boy' by westerners. To the ear it

90

sounds offensive, but is not meant in a derogatory manner. In fact, by the inflexion of the voice, it can almost be a word of endearment. But the interpreter, who is keeping guard over me in the room, is shocked. He peremptorily remonstrates: 'Address the waiter as "comrade".' I apologise.

The bill for the meal is only twelve shillings. The waiter refuses to accept a tip.

The interpreter invites me to sit in one of the armchairs, suggesting that I might like to sleep until the interrogation is resumed at two-thirty. He goes off to eat his own meal, being relieved by a junior officer. I sleep for an hour.

Promptly at two-thirty, the five interrogating officers, the officer who is taking the notes and the interpreter return.

Again, there is a brief reading from the *Quotations from Chairman Mao Tse-tung*. Again I am admonished: 'Chairman Mao shows leniency towards those who confess.'

The questioning is very repetitive—covering much the same ground as during the morning, although I am asked something about my career. I mention briefly newspapers for which I have worked, my current commitments, that I served in the Royal Air Force in both the First and Second World Wars, and for three and a half years in the Foreign Office. I recognise that the latter can be interpreted as a damaging admission if they really suspect me of being a spy, but I have already decided that it is wiser not to conceal anything because I must assume that Chinese counter-espionage has some sort of record of my past. There is also the tricky problem of my having once penetrated the Russian Secret Service. However, I do not raise it at this juncture.

There is no sign of surprise on the faces of the interrogators when I say that I have worked in the British Diplomatic Service.

All through the afternoon we are drinking pints of hot tea with frequent interruptions for one or other of us to trot out to the toilet. We are all suffering from the intake of liquid and the extreme cold of the room where we are sitting.

At 6.00 p.m. the chief interrogator announces that there will be a recess until eight o'clock and that I may again order myself a meal.

I request permission to have a shave, and to brush and comb my hair. (My briefcase with my toilet things was taken away from me immediately we arrived at the Frontier Station.) My request is refused. This is deliberate, as part of a policy of making you feel dirty, unkempt. In fact, it is three days before I am able to wash myself properly, because I am given no towel or soap.

The same waiter who brought my lunch brings my evening meal. While I am eating it, he lolls comfortably in one of the armchairs. This is perhaps as near as he will ever get to 'equalitarianism'.

The interpreter is again the guard during the meal. It is obvious that he is there to prevent me from talking to the waiter, who, working in a hotel only used by foreigners, probably speaks English. The waiter seems quite accustomed to bringing food from the hotel a couple of hundred yards away. I suppose that during the Cultural Revolution many merchant service officers and seamen and businessmen visiting Shanghai may have been taken to this room for questioning.

At 8.00 p.m. the interrogation resumes. It continues until midnight. Again the pace is slow, the questions not very hostile, not even aimed at eliciting very much information. This puzzles me. Events during the next forty-eight hours perhaps provide the answer.

'Are you tired?' asks 'Fatsy', having looked at his wristwatch.

I am, but am not prepared to admit it. So I say airily: 'Not particularly. I am accustomed often to working late.'

It is not the answer that he expects, or even desires. Everybody is looking worn out, and hungry too. China is a nation of snack eaters. Rice—the staple diet—is filling, but quickly digested. Before the interrogator has made any comment on my remarks, two or three orderlies are entering the room with trays on which are bowls of rice, noodles and cooked vegetables. The officers immediately begin tucking in and invite me to join them. I am not hungry, and I am not a devotee of Chinese food, but I feel it is an act of courtesy—perhaps even policy—to accept the invitation.

The interrogators notice that I am eating sparingly. The young note-taker hurries out of the room and returns in a few minutes with a bowl of steaming soup. 'This may be more to your taste,' he says. It is an inexplicable act of thoughtfulness, and all the officers seem pleased when I start to drink it from the bowl and find it pleasant.

[There we all were, high officers of Shanghai's Public Security Bureau and the imperialist spy, sharing a midnight meal. Could this have happened anywhere else? How would I have been treated in similar circumstances in, say, Moscow? Or Athens? Or Buenos Aires?—all notorious for the physical torture of political prisoners. The sadism suffered by James Bond was not a figment of the imagination of his creator, Ian Fleming. It was based on solid evidence. I stress this point because I saw no sign of any prisoner being ill-treated while I was in China. There was ill-treatment before the Communist regime. There are some who contend that it still exists. I cannot, of course, completely refute this, but certainly nothing which happened to me, or which I saw happen to other prisoners, substantiates these allegations. I was to suffer many hardships during the ensuing twenty months. And yet I was to experience on many occasions little acts of courtesy, almost of sympathy.]

The meal over, the empty bowls cleared away, the interrogating officers leave the room. The senior one wishes me goodnight and hopes that I shall be able to sleep comfortably on the sofa. Two guards come into the room with straw mats and quilts, which they put on the floor. These are their beds. A quilt is brought for me. I lie down on the sofa, not even taking off my overcoat because it is so cold, cover myself with a quilt, pulling it round my ears, and hardly before I rest my head against the arm of the sofa, I fall into a deep sleep.

Saturday, February 24

At 7.30 a.m. I wake, completely refreshed. I get up from the sofa, stretch my limbs. The sofa is a little short, so my legs, bent up all night, ache with the feeling of a permanent kink.

The sleeping guards stir, slowly come awake. As the guards slept all night and the door of the room was unlocked, security was at a minimum. But even if I had thoughts of escape, where could I have hidden—a foreigner amid ten million Chinese? The Chinese security police knew this.

My request for toothbrush and toothpaste is granted without demur. This is understandable: these items have a medical connotation. There is even propaganda in China about the necessity for protecting teeth. And every Chinese virtually scrubs his teeth several times a day, as I notice later in the prison hospital. It is a ritual.

[But I was to discover that few Chinese use soap on their faces. The face is cleansed with steaming hot towels. The prisoner patients and prisoner nurses were amazed with curiosity when I washed my face with a flannel and soap and dried it with a towel. If you use a hot towel on the face, drying is not necessary.

The skin of a Chinese is very different to that of a westerner. Even the men are almost hairless. The skin has the softness of silk.]

My request for a comb is again denied. I was not to comb or brush my hair again for nearly twenty months, except on the few odd occasions that the warder in prison cut my hair with electric clippers.

I am escorted to the toilet. I clean my teeth; sluice my face with cold water; dry it with a handkerchief. I turn away from the mirror with disgust. I look pretty rough, bleary-eyed. I run my fingers through my hair, giving it some semblance of order.

It is 8.00 a.m. My first twenty-four hours of incarceration are over. The waiter arrives with the breakfast which I ordered the previous evening—a simple meal of fresh fruit, toast, butter, marmalade and China tea.

At nine the interpreter arrives alone. I am sitting in an armchair. He instructs me to sit on the hard-wood chair in the middle of the room. He sits on the sofa.

He tells me to write a history of my life—details of my family, schools at which I was educated (both pieces of

94

information to assess my class status) and my career. I am to state for what newspapers I have worked. I am to give dates. I am to declare what I earned. I am also to state how much is my capital; how it is invested.

Is it to check against a dossier already in the possession of the Chinese authorities? Are they awaiting a dossier from Peking? Or do they have little information about me?

It is impossible to hazard an answer to any of these three questions. I am faced with the problem: How truthful shall I be? My life has been an open book, except for the few years that I ostensibly worked for the Russian K.G.B. Shall I mention this in my written statement? It is a dangerous admission in view of the tension, the vitriolic hostility between Peking and Moscow. Might they assume that I was a Soviet agent?

If their dossier on me is fairly detailed and accurate, then they will know that I wrote a detailed account of this episode of my life for the London *Sunday Times* in 1961. It would not be credible for me to make such a public admission, which was printed in other newspapers in the world, and still be working for the Russian Secret Service.

Is my argument correct? My brain is working at high speed.

As my handwriting is very difficult to read, I ask for my typewriter which is in the black valise they brought ashore. The interpreter says he will enquire.

He goes to the door. Calls another guard. After about five minutes he returns with a portable typewriter, but not my own. He also brings paper and carbons. He does not explain why I cannot use my own typewriter. I assume it is being carefully examined. As it is a three-bank Smith Corona more than forty years old and yet in good condition, it may present something of a mystery, a piece of secret espionage equipment which they have never seen before. Even my 1932 Leica may seem strange to them.

Before I begin typing, I mention another problem. Some years ago I had a brain tumour which necessitated three operations. Since then I have had to take a grain of pheno-barbitone in the morning and again at night to prevent what are known as Jacksonian attacks—tremors of the face and limbs. These attacks are akin to epilepsy and treated medicinally in the same way. I left a small bottle containing some one-grain phenobarbitone tablets in my cabin on the *Hanoi*. Perhaps they could be brought ashore, or perhaps they might prefer me to see a doctor—but it must be a specialist. The interpreter says he will see what can be arranged.

I pick up some paper and carbons. Three copies of my statement are required. I put the paper in the machine. I decide to make it a long, detailed statement, hoping that I can word it in such a way that it will convince my accusers that I am really a journalist and not a spy.

I begin with my grandparents, explaining that my grandfather never earned more than £1 a week all his life, never had a holiday, and yet was a happy, contented man. I argue that this will establish my 'class origin'—like Mao, I stem from peasant stock. I finish the first page, take it out of the typewriter, hand it to the interpreter. Without reading it first, he immediately begins the translation.

Throughout the morning I go on writing—the translator doing his version as fast as I can get it down on paper. I am writing what is almost a profile of myself, with nuances that may help in my defence. It is a fascinating exercise in deception.

At twelve o'clock the waiter arrives with my lunch. Again a well-cooked, pleasant meal. For dessert I eat tinned peaches, ordered specially because I remember how delectable they were when I ate some in the Peace Hotel in November. They are tinned whole, unstoned.

[I had forgotten the beautiful flavour of fresh Chinese peaches. My memory was not to be revived until months later when I had them twice a day in the prison hospital. It is incongruous. What prison in the world would serve peaches to a prisoner? It was one of many illogical situations in which I was to find myself.

Handcuffs . . . white cotton gloves . . . peaches—symbols of China.]

The meal over, a guard comes in to relieve the interpreter so that he may go and eat his midday meal. The guard indicates that I may sit in an armchair. He sits in another. In a few minutes I am asleep.

It is two-thirty. The interpreter has awakened me. I get up and go back to the typewriter. I type for two more hours.

I deal in some detail with my penetration of the Russian K.G.B. arising from an introduction in the old Trocadero restaurant off Piccadilly Circus to a diplomat in the Soviet Embassy in London. I explain that the introduction came about a year or two after the defection to Russia of two British diplomats, Maclean and Burgess. I add that my motive was a purely journalistic exercise. I merely wished to unearth how Russian Intelligence operated. I had left the Foreign Office, so there was no official information I could divulge. I wrote my reports on political and economic matters purely on what appeared in the newspaper, but I couched them in diplomatic language. I feel that if the Chinese accept my story it will amuse them that I hoaxed the Russians. What I have just written follows closely, but in less detail, what I wrote for the *Sunday Times*.

The interpreter makes no comment about these revelations. In fact, his face is inscrutable the whole time he is doing the translation. He gathers up his papers, takes the typewriter and leaves the room. A guard takes over security. Without invitation I transfer myself to an armchair. I am feeling rather tired. I doze fitfully.

It is 6.00 p.m. The waiter arrives with my dinner. I immediately notice that he is carrying two wicker baskets. I am intrigued. He sets the table for me to eat. Leaves the room with the other basket. Does it mean that Bruno Neroni has been brought to the Frontier Station for questioning? It may explain why I have not been interrogated all day. Is the statement of my career unimportant? That I was asked to write it just to fill in time?

[Later I was to discover that it was regarded by the Security Police as an important document. I was closely questioned about my life. And I had to write a second version.]

I finish my dinner. Pay the waiter. Order my breakfast for the next morning.

It is 8.00 p.m. The five interrogators, the note-taker and the interpreter file into the room. They take their seats on the sofa and the armchairs. The straight-backed wooden chair is put in the centre of the room. I am ordered to sit down.

The relaxed atmosphere of the past thirty-six hours has vanished. All the interrogators look tense. What has created this new situation? There is a pause for a few minutes while an orderly brings in the thermos flask of hot water and cups with China green tea. I am again offered a cup.

The fat, senior interrogator takes his Red book of *Quotations from Chairman Mao* from his overcoat pocket. But he is reading the *Quotations* almost as a formality. The words fall on my ears without any significance. His reading ends with the normal exhortation: 'Chairman Mao shows leniency towards those who confess.'

The scene is set. The first question is fired at me. In Chinese, it sounds harsh, menacing.

'Why did you take photographs of warships?'

The question does not surprise me. I have been anticipating it ever since I came ashore, two days ago. In a conversational tone, I reply: 'To illustrate an article which I plan to write.'

'You are telling lies.'

This remark comes from a young interrogator, always trying to impress with his toughness. (Actually, he is not very impressive, and proves on the next day to be solicitous.) Tonight they are all being rough for some motive, although there is no hint that they might resort to violence. Before I can reply, the senior interrogator admonishes: 'Chairman Mao is *harsh* towards those who do *not* confess.'

'The answer which I have given is the truth,' I reply.

'How many photographs of warships did you take?'

'Two or three. I am not quite certain.'

'That is a lie. You must know how many photographs you took.'

'I am very accustomed to using a Leica camera. It is quick operating. I usually take more than one photograph of a single subject, slightly varying the aperture for each shot, to ensure that at least one will be the correct exposure. When I photographed the warships, I was using colour film. Accuracy of exposure for colour is more important than black-and-white. There were three motor torpedo boats moored near the mouth of the Whangpoo River. They were in two groups. I photographed the first warship only once, but I cannot remember whether I made one or two exposures of the other two torpedo boats.'

While I am saying this, I recognise that Neroni may, too, have photographed the warships with black-and-white film. The next question almost confirms this thought.

'Did you say to Captain Neroni after you had taken the photographs of the warships, "Those are the photographs I have been waiting for"?'

'No.'

'Did you discuss with Captain Neroni about taking the photographs of the warships?'

'No. I decided to photograph the warships only after the *Hanoi* had sailed, and we were coming down the river.'

'Why?'

'This is my second visit to Shanghai in three months. I could have photographed the warships on my visit in November. They were moored at the same place. But they were of no journalistic interest. They are small torpedo boats. I had photographed similar warships demonstrating off Macao a few months earlier. On this occasion, the warships fitted into a series of photographs which I had taken in the city the previous day, of workers celebrating the setting up of three-in-one Cultural Revolutionary Committees. The warships were decorated from stem to stern with pennants. There were Chairman Mao slogans around the bridge, and on the sides of the ships. I assumed that the crews of these ships were also celebrating the Cultural Revolution.'

'You took the photographs for espionage purposes.'

'I am not a spy.'

'What other photographs did you take on the river?'

'As the *Hanoi* pulled away from the dock, I took a panoramic photograph of the Bund. On the day we arrived, I photographed a Yangtse River steamer crammed with passengers lining the decks, bound, I suppose, for Nanking. After I had photographed the warships, I took one picture of the big commune on the opposite bank with a fleet of Chinese junks in the foreground.'

'You took many other photographs.'

'No. I exposed only two rolls of colour film, each with thirty-six negatives, in Shanghai. All these photographs were taken in the presence of my guide from the China Travel Service. On the morning we sailed, I put a new roll of colour film in my camera, and I made only four or five exposures. I am not certain about the number, because I cannot remember whether I took two photographs or only one of the second group of torpedo boats. These three rolls of colour film, and a roll of black-and-white film which I exposed off Chungjin in North Korea, were taken from my jacket pocket by the security officer on the *Hanoi*.'

'Were you permitted to take photographs in North Korea?'

'I was under armed guard throughout the whole of my stay in Chungjin.'

Questions and answers about my photographic activities in Shanghai go on until after midnight. I explain in detail what photographs I took in the city and my motives for each one. I explain that I used only Kodak Ektachrome film. I am subjected to extreme verbal pressure, being repeatedly accused of not telling the truth and of my dire peril if I do not change my 'attitude'.

It is soon apparent that the main theme of this grilling is to trick me into accepting responsibility for having taken black-and-white photographs—presumably the rolls of film found in the lifejacket over Neroni's bunk. But in over four hours of questioning, these films are never specifically mentioned.

It is after midnight. I am asked to make a written confession. A sheet of paper is laid on the table. The interpreter hands me his fountain-pen.

I state: 'I am willing to confess to having taken in colour two photographs of motor torpedo boats, a commune on the

banks of the Whangpoo River with junks in the foreground, a panoramic view of the Bund, and the Yangtse River steamer. I also accept responsibility for the colour negatives taken ashore in the presence of the China Travel Service guide.'

All the interrogators seemed to be speaking at once. The room is a babel of raucous Chinese, then silence. The interpreter says:

'You took black-and-white photographs, too.'

'I did not take any black-and-white photographs in Shanghai.'

The senior interrogator shouts: 'Sign a written confession.' The young, aggressive interrogator has got up from his chair and is standing behind me, looking over my shoulder. I have not written a word. He pushes my right shoulder and shouts, in English: 'Write!'

I lay the pen on the table, turn round, look him in the face and say: 'If you attempt to intimidate me, I shall write nothing.'

He relaxes. The other interrogators are watching me intently, presumably assessing my mood.

To the interpreter, I say: 'It must be clearly understood that I am accepting responsibility for only four rolls of film—three colour, one black-and-white, the latter being taken in North Korea.'

He interprets this statement to the interrogators.

'Write your confession,' orders the senior interrogator.

I pick up the pen and begin to write. The young English-speaking interrogator is watching over my shoulder.

'I accept responsibility for three rolls of colour film exposed in Shanghai and taken by the security officer from my suit hanging in the pilot's cabin of the *Hanoi*.'

I sign it, and put the date. I deliberately avoid reference to the black-and-white film because it is not connected with China.

The senior interrogator, in spite of his bulk, jumps up from the sofa, grabs the piece of paper and rushes out of the room. All the other interrogators follow him. The scene has all the drama of a film, because the interrogators give the impression of having scored a victory. It doesn't seem to make much sense.

I am left only with the interpreter. I feel exhausted after more than four hours of question and answer—repeating some of my statements over and over again. I recognise that I have confessed to a serious breach of Shanghai's photographic regulations, although I have stressed repeatedly that no one on this voyage had put any prohibition on my taking photographs along the river.

Ten minutes pass. The interrogators return. They all look jubilant. A couple of orderlies follow them in with trays of food—steaming rice, vegetables and meat. I am again invited to eat with them. They are almost affable.

As I peck away at the food with chopsticks (I have never become accomplished in the art of handling these two pieces of bamboo) I speculate on the changed atmosphere. Why did they only a few minutes ago rush excitedly out of the room with my confession? Was it to show to superior officers that they had broken me down? This explanation does not satisfy me. It occurs to me that when they left my room they turned to the right. So did the waiter with the second basket of food. Therefore, the only logical explanation is that Neroni is in a nearby room. The interrogators had confronted him with my confession, which by implication denied responsibility for the dozen rolls of black-and-white film.

The meal is over. The interrogators and the interpreter leave. The two night guards bring in their straw mats and quilts and put them on the floor.

One escorts me to the toilet. I brush my teeth: rinse my face. I'm looking pretty dishevelled.

Disgustedly I return to the room. Exhausted, I lie down on the sofa, pull the quilt over my chilled body, close my eyes. Before I fall asleep I wonder whether I shall ever know the truth of this night's drama.

Sunday, February 25
I awake at 8.50 a.m.—my fourth day in custody.

I again request soap and towel. It is ignored. I came to describe this attitude as 'negative response'. You are never refused a request. You just don't get an answer.

Shanghai Bund.

nks going up the Whangpoo River at dawn on the flood tide to load with food from communes.

Red Guard statue on the Shanghai Bund which the author was forbidden to photograph. The statue was removed in 1969.

Workmen painting a Mao slogan on a street banner.

Entrance to the former British Consulate in Shanghai. The Mao slogans were removed shortly before the author was released.

Wall-newspapers in China. In the foreground is the latest type of bus, made in China.

Petro-chemical plant in Shanghai.
This photograph is similar to
one on which the espionage
charge was framed.

Red Guards in Bund
Gardens.

毛主席说：
公社农民以农为主（包括林、牧、
副、渔），也要兼学军事、政治、文
化。在有条件的时候，也要由集体办
些小工厂，也要批判资产阶级。

摘自《人民日报》社论：《全国都
应该成为毛泽东思想的大学校》

Commune houses twenty miles from Shanghai.

A Chinese woman welder on a commune.

A commune.

Children in a commune kindergarten.

Mao at his desk.

People's Liberation Army men waving Mao Thought books as they watch China's first hydrogen bomb test.

The author crossing the frontier into the New Territories of Hong Kong at
Lo Wu after his release.

However, I have awoken alert and hungry. I am astonished that I do not feel more depressed. I suppose it is because as a journalist I see a news story in everything that is happening around me. If I am camping out, so are all the security officers. The building has the atmosphere of an army barracks.

I eat my breakfast with relish. When I have finished, I order my lunch and sit in an armchair studying my own copy of *Quotations from Chairman Mao* which I bought in Hong Kong some months earlier. Apart from propaganda publications thoughtfully provided, it is the only reading matter I will have for many months.

The interpreter enters the room. He tells me that they are taking me to see a doctor this morning, to examine me and decide what medicines I need. He goes out again.

An hour passes. The young security officer who speaks excellent English and who visited my cabin on the *Hanoi* the night before I was taken into custody enters the room. He will take me to the doctor.

He escorts me to the lift. In the courtyard below is a waiting taxi. We drive the short distance to the other side of Soochow Creek, to the old Shanghai General Hospital where I nearly died in 1926.

[A few weeks later, when being interrogated, I described a walk I had taken alone in Shanghai the previous November. During it I had passed the Shanghai General Hospital. The interpreter on this occasion was a young man. He could not understand where I meant. I said: 'Surely you must know the hospital which is just before you get to the post office? It has been there for more than fifty years.' There was a discussion in Chinese between him and the interrogator. Although I could not fully understand the conversation, it was obvious from the expression of surprise on the interpreter's face that he thought the hospital had been built after 1949 when China became a Communist country. I firmly believe that many of the younger generation are under the impression that the tall, granite edifices on the Bund—built in the early 'twenties—are outward signs of Communist progress. Why should they think otherwise? All Communist propaganda is directed towards convincing the people that they are better off than in the old days of neo-colonial rule. The Bund, in a sense, is a showpiece where factory workers on their day off congregate.]

The entrance hall to the hospital is a shambles. The long unpainted walls are plastered with tattered posters of the Cultural Revolution. It is milling with men and women of all ages, with mothers and children.

We push our way through the throng and up the stairs to the first floor. We walk along two or three corridors and enter a room where a young woman in a spotless white medical coat is sitting at a desk. A stethoscope is dangling professionally around her neck. The room is immaculately clean. The couch on which a patient can be examined is covered with a clean sheet. The pillow case, too, is unsoiled. The whole atmosphere of the room is in striking contrast to the confusion downstairs. I feel that the Cultural Revolution has passed by this room without interfering with it. There is an air of tranquillity. I glance around the walls. There is not even a portrait of Chairman Mao.

The young woman doctor invites me to sit by the desk on a small wooden stool. The security officer explains that she is not the doctor who is to examine me, but his assistant. However, she will take down a few details of my medical history.

She has already taken a card from the drawer of the desk. She inquires my full name, my age. Although she puts the questions in Chinese through the security officer, I notice that she is writing the answers in English. (I discover later that anyone with even a smattering of English is not allowed to talk to me direct. It has to be done through an interpreter. Even if I speak to them they never reply.)

As I detail my long, complicated medical history—three brain operations, a colon resection for cancer—she looks up from her writing and asks in Chinese: 'Did you say you were sixty-seven?'

'Yes,' I reply.

'You are very lucky to be alive.' She resumes her writing.

Another doctor—a man of about fifty-five—enters the room. He is obviously a man of forceful personality, efficient. The security officer greets him very respectfully. He invites me into his office next door. It is well furnished with a large mahogany desk, two armchairs and a sofa. I sit on the sofa. The young woman doctor follows us into the room and places her notes on the desk. While the male doctor is reading them, the security officer explains in a soft voice that he is Dr Chang, the most eminent surgeon in Shanghai.

Dr Chang finishes reading the notes. 'Who performed the brain operations?' he asks.

'Mr Wylie McKissock at the National Hospital in London.' (Mr McKissock is world-famous and will be known to Dr Chang by reputation.)

Dr Chang rises from his desk and sits beside me. He examines my head with meticulous care. I have no skull on the right side, the trepanning flap having had to be removed on the third operation because of damage to the bone by an abscess. Since my brain tumour originally caused paralysis on the left side, Dr Chang also tests the reflexes of my arm and leg and the power in these limbs.

He returns to his desk. I ask the security officer to explain to Dr Chang that on Mr McKissock's advice I have taken two grains of phenobarbitone daily since my brain surgery twenty years ago. I hope that he will agree that I can have this medicine while I am in custody.

The doctor next takes my blood pressure and listens to my heart with his stethoscope. 'You have rather high blood pressure,' he says. 'Has this been diagnosed before?'

'Yes,' I reply. 'I have had it on and off for several years but it has never been considered by my doctors to require treatment.'

'Do you sleep well?

'If you have had brain operations there is a tendency occasionally to have bad nights.

'I will prescribe some phenobarbitone tablets for you and also some sleeping pills. It would be advisable for you to take the latter every night.'

The doctor and the security officer discuss something together for several minutes, the officer listening very intently.

I am interested by the prescription for sleeping tablets he hands to the security officer: as I am still undergoing interrogation, I would have thought that the Chinese authorities would want to wear me down. But, presumably, whatever the attitude of the Public Security Bureau, the doctor has an overriding authority.

On our way out we go to the dispensary downstairs where there is a long queue. The security officer ignores it and walks to the window of the dispensary, says a few words and hands in the prescription. In five minutes the medicine is ready for us. The security officer tells me that the cost is four yuan (about twelve shillings), and I give him the money.

We drive back to the headquarters of the Public Security Bureau. The taxi fare is six yuan; I pay it. We go up in the lift to the bleak interrogation room. I am surprised when the security officer hands me the medicine because there is enough phenobarbitone for me to commit suicide. The truth, I suppose, is that he does not realise the nature of either the pheno-barbitone or the sleeping tablets. This does not speak very highly for Chinese security.

Immediately after lunch the interpreter informs me that if I wish to buy some towels and soap he will take me to the Friendship Shop in the Nanking Road. As I have not had a wash for nearly three days I accept with pleasure. We go downstairs, where the taxi which took me to the hospital in the morning is waiting. It is only a few hundred yards to the shop; there I purchase two medium-size towels and a face flannel, some perfumed toilet soap and a packet of detergent soap powder. The carton of the detergent is a copy of Daz.

I ask the interpreter if it will be possible for me to have some clean underclothes and shirts from the ship. He thinks this can be arranged.

All the items that I have purchased are quite cheap, the bill coming to about ten shillings. We drive back to the Frontier Station. Again, I have to pay for the taxi.

At 6.00 p.m. three security officers enter the room and tell me that I am to be removed to another building. They hand me back my briefcase. Hoping that I shall now be able to comb my hair, I unzip it, search inside. To my disappointment I find that the comb has been removed. All that is left in the case is my money and air ticket.

We go downstairs. The 1948 Oldsmobile is waiting for us. We drive the few yards to the Bund, along the waterfront and turn right up the Foochow Road. After a quarter of a mile, we turn left under an archway which is guarded by two People's Liberation Army soldiers. Inside is a large courtyard, buzzing with activity. Surrounding it is a complex of three buildings. (I learn later that it is the headquarters of the Shanghai Municipal Security Bureau.) I am taken in the lift to the top floor of one building and into a large, bleak, draughty, ice-cold room. At one end are stacked collapsible chairs. At the other end between two windows is a larger-than-life-size portrait of Mao Tse-tung. Against one wall is a rusty iron bed with a grimy straw-filled mattress and a couple of quilts. Against the other wall is a well-worn, leather-covered sofa, two leather-covered armchairs, a table and a wooden straight-backed chair.

The room is where members of the bureau hold Mao Thought meetings. In the next few days, I am often turned out for an hour or so while security officers sing revolutionary songs and debate Mao Thought.

A small desk and chair is brought in and stood near the door. It is for an English-speaking guard who watches over me day and night. He proves, after an initial trial of strength, to be quite friendly, and during the seven days that I am in this room we have a number of interesting political discussions.

The three security officers who have brought me from the Frontier Station have left the room. A few minutes later my waiter arrives with the wicker basket containing my evening meal. I eat it, pay the bill plus 50c for the trishaw fare.

I drink black China tea and invite the guard to join me. I am surprised when he agrees to do so, but then black tea is a luxury. The masses make do with green tea or hot water. Perhaps this gesture of friendliness on my part helped to establish a rapport between us.

A couple of hours passes.

It is 8.00 p.m. The five interrogating officers who have been quizzing me on and off for three days at the Frontier Station come into the room. They sit down on the sofa and the armchairs. The note-taker sits at the table. Two collapsible chairs are brought from the other end of the room, one for the interpreter and one for myself.

'Why did you choose to travel on a Polish ship?' asks the senior interrogator.

'Because it was the only ship sailing from Japan to North Korea,' I reply. 'As I have already explained, I was on an assignment for the London *Daily Telegraph* to investigate the seizure of the *Pueblo*.'

'Who suggested that you should sail on the Polish Ocean Line?'

'No one. I am familiar with the movements of ships, and I had sailed on the Polish Ocean Line before. It was on the *Kapitan Kosko* that I went to North Vietnam in the autumn of 1966.'

'Who told you to go to North Vietnam?'

'No one. It arose purely by accident.'

'That is a lie,' interrupted one of the officers. 'You are a spy.'

This line of questioning goes on until midnight. It is all confined to this visit to North Vietnam. The interrogators have the advantage of having read copies of the six articles which I wrote about the war in Vietnam and the effect of the American bombing. Also among my papers were two very long articles which I wrote after spending several weeks aboard the U.S. aircraft carrier *Kitty Hawk* in the Gulf of Tonkin. I must assume that the Public Security Bureau may believe I am working for American Intelligence.

[In the light of subsequent knowledge, this was a very reasonable assumption. And many weeks were to elapse before I was able to convince the Chinese authorities that I was in no way connected with the Central Intelligence Agency. I have no knowledge of C.I.A. organisation, but on the basis of normal intelligence operations by all countries, Tokyo is very likely a clearing centre. Many letters in my correspondence file and the carbon copies of my articles were circumstantial evidence of my possible association with American Intelligence.]

It is midnight. The chief interrogator informs me that the interrogation is adjourned until the next day and that I may go to bed. They leave the room. The guard does not interfere with me when I take a sleeping pill and a grain of pheno-barbitone. In a few minutes I am in a deep sleep.

Monday, February 26–Sunday, March 3

I wake at 7.30 a.m. The guard escorts me to the toilet. For the first time for four days I wash my face with soap. But my hair is still uncombed and I am not able to change my under-clothes and shirt.

As we enter the committee room the guard says: 'I wish you to stand in front of the picture of Chairman Mao, hold in your raised right hand the *Quotations from Chairman Mao Tse-tung* and say, "Long live Chairman Mao, the Great Teacher, the Great Helmsman, the Great Leader, the Supreme Commander." '

It is clear that this is to make me lose face. And I am really in no position to refuse this order. (I am afraid I do not have the courage of Donald Hopson, who was Chargé d'Affaires of the British Mission in Peking when the Red Guards burned it down. When they ordered him to bow before a portrait of Mao Hopson refused. For what it was worth, he had the might of Great Britain behind him, and so did the British Consul in Macao when he stood all day bareheaded in the boiling sun on the balcony of the Consulate during the riots.) However, I do not take this order complacently. How can I save face? Or even make the warder lose face? As I walk across the room and stand in front of the portrait I have an idea. I take my own copy of Mao Thought from my overcoat pocket. I stand at attention, raise my right hand holding the red book and say:

'Long Live Chairman Mao, the Great Teacher, the Great Helmsman, the Great Leader, the Supreme Commander.'

I have made my obeisance. The warder, who is standing in a position to watch me, looks very pleased. I pause for only a few seconds, moving only to lower my right arm and replace the Mao Thought book back in my overcoat pocket, before continuing:

'Long live Queen Elizabeth the Second of England, Queen of Canada, Queen of Australia, Queen of New Zealand.'

The security officer guard looks very disconcerted but words fail him. He walks back to his desk and sits down without speaking. I am not asked the next morning to kowtow to Chairman Mao.

It is ten o'clock. The interrogators arrive to continue their quizzing.

Immediately after the ritual of reading excerpts from the Mao Thought book, I point out that I have not been able to change my linen for four days. May I please have some clean clothes from the ship? The senior interrogator agrees to let me have some during the day, and I thank him.

The interrogation continues until noon, is resumed at two-thirty and again at eight o'clock in the evening and goes on until midnight. Altogether that day I am under questioning for eight and a half hours. The morning and afternoon sessions are spent in repeating in detail what I said the previous night about my visit to Haiphong. Some facts I am made to repeat several times as they test the truth of my story. Even the slightest deviation from a previous statement is seized upon.

The questioning continues in the headquarters of the Public Security Bureau for six more days. A great deal of it is very trivial. Some of the questions hardly seem relevant to my case. But I have to repeat over and over again what happened while I was aboard the *Hanoi*, whether I was given assistance by the captain, why the chief steward agreed to help me by storing the bag containing my report on China, written on the previous visit, and photographs. As in the case of my trip to Haiphong, they want to know why I chose to travel on the *Hanoi*. The difficulties that I experienced in Kobe in finally boarding this ship because of the four passengers that were being embarked at Shanghai, add to the confusion. My explanation of what happened seems to lead them to believe that I was given preferential treatment by the Polish Ocean Line. (Presumably the interrogators are trying to ascertain if there was collusion between the shipping company and myself.)

[This may seem an odd attitude as both China and Poland are Communist countries and they operate a joint shipping company, but Poland is in the Moscow camp. Also, as I had learned during my visit to Shanghai in the previous November, there was a good deal of friction between the Polish shipping representatives and their Chinese opposite numbers. They never met. Although working in the same building, all business was transacted over the telephone. Even the simplest problem could not be decided immediately. The minimum time for any decision was three hours while the Chinese conferred among themselves. Important decisions often took several days to reach. And during the Cultural Revolution—particularly in the summer of 1967—the situation was chaotic. The Poles were seriously considering terminating the agreement and winding up the company. In fact, I had gathered that the only thing which prevented them was the problem of how to divide the assets. Perhaps it was not surprising therefore that my interrogators should have wanted to know why the Polish Ocean Line agents in Kobe and Tokyo had gone to exceptional trouble to arrange my passage, and Captain Neroni's, too.]

Clean shirts and underwear are provided for me after two days in the Public Security Bureau. In spite of the intense cold, I strip and give myself a cold sponge-down. Not since I was in the Western Desert during the war, where water was rationed to half a pint a day, have I so welcomed a wash.

That morning there was no interrogation, so the security guard gave me permission to wash the dirty clothes which I had taken off. He strung a line in the room for me to hang them to dry.

There were many hours during the week at the Public Security Bureau Headquarters when I was left to my own devices. I was given magazines to read: *China Today*, *China Pictorial*, *China Reconstructs*, all plush, colour-illustrated, English-language productions extolling the virtues and progress of

Mao's China. One booklet contained photographs of the Hong Kong riots, with police carrying wicker shields and armed with batons. There were also photographs of the police firing, but the captions did not disclose that only wooden bullets were used.

A security officer saw me looking at this booklet and immediately took it away. I can think of no other explanation than that he did not wish me to gain the impression that China was engaged in anti-British propaganda, though it had obviously been produced for overseas distribution. But, in western eyes, the Communist Chinese are an illogical race.

Monday, March 4

Ten days since I was brought ashore, and a day I shall never forget.

This morning there is no interrogation. After lunch I doze for a couple of hours on the sofa. I am awakened by my guard.

'Would you like to buy a heavier coat?' he enquires. (Because my lightweight camel-hair overcoat is inadequate protection I am sitting with a quilt around my shoulders.)

'Yes,' I reply, 'if it is possible. And I should also like some warmer underclothes.'

He says he will accompany me to the Friendship Shop. We go downstairs. A taxi is already waiting. We drive to the Nanking Road.

In the Friendship Shop I select a grey gabardine rainproof coat with a cotton quilt lining and anorak hood lined with synthetic fur. I also buy a pair of brown cotton-fleece under-pants—what the Americans call 'long johns'. I feel that a couple of larger towels might be useful and some more toilet soap.

The security officer then suggests that I buy a large enamel bowl and an enamel cup—articles which everyone in China possesses for his or her personal use. The bowl is elaborately decorated with gaily coloured birds. It costs twenty-five shillings.

That he suggests I buy this bowl strikes me as curious: the toilet in the Public Security Headquarters has a basin with cold running water. And the cup seems unnecessary as my food with plates, cup and cutlery is brought three times a day by the waiter from the Peace Hotel. But I do not dwell on this thought.

My bill comes to £17 2s. od.—I am making a substantial contribution to China's balance of payments. My meals are already costing me about thirty shillings a day.

We return to the Public Security Bureau Headquarters at five o'clock. To my surprise the waiter soon arrives with my evening meal—an hour earlier than usual, but even so I am mentally unprepared for the drama enacted an hour later.

I have finished my meal, paid the waiter and sit relaxed in an armchair reading a magazine.

The security officer is sitting at his desk reading the Mao Thought book and sipping the cup of black China tea which I have given him. I am already wearing my new coat and I have put the 'long johns' on under my grey flannel trousers. For the first time for ten days I am thawing out.

It is 6.00 p.m. Without warning the door bursts open, and a galaxy of security officers excitedly crowd into the room. One is holding an ominous-looking vellum document with a large red 'chop' in Chinese characters at the bottom right-hand corner.

I am ordered to stand up. The officers encircle me. They all look very pleased with themselves. The senior officer, who is holding the document, begins to read in a stern voice. The interpreter translates sentence by sentence. But my mind seems dazed and I find it difficult to appreciate the full meaning of his words until I hear: 'You are charged with being a spy.'

Even then the full seriousness of these words fails to register.

Two officers who are standing each side of me grab my arms, and a third steps forward and snaps gleaming nickel handcuffs on my wrists. I have never been handcuffed before. It is a traumatic experience. It is almost the blackest moment in a long, often dangerous, often frustrating life.

But I am not given time to dwell on my new situation. Two officers hustle me down the stairs—we do not wait for the lift —and into the back of the Oldsmobile. The interpreter gets in beside the driver.

At the first intersection we turn left, and then right down the wide boulevard once called Avenue Foch, that divided the French and International concessions. It is a tortuous ride, travelling down many small streets crowded with people, children darting in and out—the driver with his hand almost constantly on the klaxon. Finally, in a broad tree-lined street, the car slows down and turns right, immediately stopping in front of two green-painted large iron gates. From nowhere, the car is surrounded by rubber-necking children, pressing their noses up against the rear windows to catch a glimpse of the prisoner. That I am a foreigner—'a long nose'—causes much excitement. A khaki-uniformed People's Liberation Army guard with a rifle opens a wicker gate, peers out, closes it and then opens the double iron gates for us to enter. Inside, I am surprised to see a large garden with grass (later I learn that the P.L.A. guard use it for physical exercises and drilling).

We drive along a typically French tree-lined road; this was once the prison of the former French concession. We turn right and under an archway into a courtyard crowded with soldiers in uniform, their wives and small children. Everybody is excited, talking animatedly.

The car stops. We get out. I am escorted across the courtyard through an archway on the far side and into another courtyard with trees, some flowering. Before me is the grim main prison block—a three-storeyed, grey brick building, iron-barred windows, green drain-pipes with the red star of the army painted at the top of each one where it joins the guttering. I am taken into a small reception room at the right of the entrance to the block. A receiving officer is sitting behind a raised desk—rather like you see the duty sergeant in a police station depicted in American films. I am told to sit in a wooden armchair in front of the desk. The handcuffs are unlocked and removed. I have an instant sense of freedom. With handcuffs on, you feel like a tethered animal; a bird in a cage. (After a few hours in a cell I could understand why animals in zoos seem to be perpetually restless, pacing up and down.) The interpreter stands behind the receiving officer. My black briefcase is taken from me again. Its contents are dumped on to the desk. The receiving officer counts my currency—English sterling, Japanese yen, American dollars. He enters the various sums on a receipt. Travellers cheques are counted and entered. My cheque books are examined and also entered on the receipt (it is immaterial whether I have any money in the bank!).

A tall, ferocious looking P.L.A. guard removes my gold wrist-watch, a gold ring on the small finger of my left hand, my gold cufflinks and tie-clip. My tie is removed. The belt supporting my trousers is taken off. With a pair of scissors he cuts the gilt Royal Air Force buttons off my blue blazer. He removes the shoe-laces from my shoes.

[It might be thought that this was done to prevent me from committing suicide by strangulation. The reason was to prevent me from stepping up behind a guard and garrotting him. I discovered this months later when I had become so thin that my trousers, without a belt, were continually slipping down. I asked for a piece of string to support them. The warder gave me a piece about six inches long. By gestures, I tried to explain that it was too short and therefore useless. Without comment he tied one end of the piece of string to a belt tag in the front of the trousers and then slipped the string through the tag on the opposite side and pulled it tight.]

I am surprised that I am not made to strip. The officer does run his hands down my arms and legs but it is a very per-functory search: in consequence, some confidential personal papers in the hip pocket of my trousers are not discovered—nor were they found when I left the prison.

I am given a number—1248. 'In future,' says the interpreter, 'you will always be addressed by your number and not your name. I will say it in Chinese. Repeat it after me.'

I do so. But this instant lesson in Chinese is unnecessary. I am never addressed by my number, the guards assuming that I shall not understand them if they do. The interpreters—I have four during my nearly twenty months' imprisonment—always call me 'Barrymaine' and two addressed me with the prefix 'Mr'.

I am ordered to sign the receipt for my belongings and thumb-print it in red ink. It is in duplicate—the receiving officer keeping one copy; I am given the other. I am also handed a sheet recording my currency. I am to note purchases I make while in prison on this sheet.

I am handed two blue cotton quilts from a pile lying on the floor. They are patched and not very clean. I am given the basin, soap, detergent powder, towels and the shirts and under-clothes which were brought to me a few days earlier from the ship.

Outside it is now dark. The only light in the reception room comes from a single bulb of not more than twenty-five candle-power.

The reception procedure is over. I am escorted out of the room and taken further into the prison block. We climb two flights of concrete stairs to the top storey. The prison seems quiet—no one talking. Every cell door is locked. Everywhere is ill-lit, gloomy. It is inhospitable. But I suppose all prisons are. Unlike institutions in England, such as hospitals, however, there is no perpetual smell of disinfectant. As we climb the stairs a bell echoes through the building—a signal of my arrival and part of an intricate security system to prevent a prisoner encountering another prisoner. This security pre-caution may not be so important for foreign prisoners as it is in the case of Chinese political prisoners. The authorities prefer no one to know which political prisoners they have arrested.

At the top of the second flight of stairs, a guard is waiting to escort me to a cell. It is completely devoid of any furniture except for a small, concrete, non-flush toilet in one corner. The floor is dusty, unswept. There is a window about three feet square at one end of the cell. It is in three sections and opens horizontally. The glass is painted brown but a former prisoner has made a few scratches. By pressing my eye close to the window I can see a panorama of Shanghai—the tall build-ings on the Bund forming a silhouette against the night sky, some illuminated with Mao slogans. There is a second window at the opposite end of the cell which looks out on to the landing, though the prisoner's view is obstructed by wooden slats, set vertically across the window. A guard can move them and look in at the prisoner.

The heavy, wooden cell door slams shut. The cell is lit by a single, low-powered bulb set high in the wall behind a piece of glass. It is left burning all night. So that it does not shine in my eyes, I decide to sleep beneath it.

I have nothing with which to clean the floor. I spread one quilt out like a kind of small carpet on which I can put my belongings and also sleep (later I am provided with a hard board bed).

Depressed, I pace the wooden floor. I notice a guard spying upon me through the Judas window. This lack of privacy takes a few days to get used to. Afterwards you completely ignore it, even if you are using the toilet. In Asia these small niceties of western civilisation are unimportant. In Asia no one suffers from inhibitions. Because of the enormity of the populations, everyone is living cheek-by-jowl. Privacy is not something to be cherished: there is no privacy in Asia.

My meditation is interrupted by an electric bell. Without my watch I can only hazard that the time is about eight o'clock. Presumably it is a signal for the prisoners to go to sleep. A six-inch square trap in the door is indeed opened by a warder who indicates by waving his arm through it that I am to go to bed.

The phenobarbitone and sleeping tablets have been taken away from me by a medical orderly in the reception office. I asked the interpreter to explain to him that I require this medicine each night before I go to sleep. But it is not until Christmas—nearly ten months later—that I get the problem of phenobarbitone finally straightened out. And then it is only because I am suffering from very high blood pressure.

I fold my camel-hair overcoat for a pillow, covering it with a towel to prevent soiling the cloth. Wearily I lie down, still wearing the coat which I bought in the afternoon. The cell is even colder than the committee room in which I have been incarcerated for the past seven days. I cover myself with the second quilt. I have opened the window. It is draughty. I pull the anorak hood over my head. The side on which I have no skull is very sensitive to cold. I say a short prayer but even before I am finished I fall into a deep sleep.

I am awakened with a start by the key grating in the padlock of the cell door. The bolt slams back. I am now fully awake, a little apprehensive. I have no knowledge of how a prisoner under investigation is treated though I have heard of the excesses by the Red Guards during the Cultural Revolution.

The door swings open. A security officer, with a P.L.A. guard in attendance, gestures me with his hands to rise. I get to my feet, still dazed with sleep. My body aches a little from the wooden floor, hardly cushioned by the thin quilt on which I have been lying. I walk across the cell to the door. The officers indicate that I follow them. We walk down the dimly lit concrete stairs.

On the ground floor we walk out into the courtyard, the guard unlocking the double iron-barred gates which now seal off the block. The clock over the archway to the outer courtyard shows it is now 9.00 p.m. I have been asleep only an hour. My wits were a little dulled, but the cold night air fully awakens me. I am alert: a little apprehensive. Fortunately, I have the capacity to sleep for short periods and awake refreshed.

We turn right, walk a little way along the courtyard and turn into a large, well-lit room. It is part of the main prison block and also has a door leading into the ground floor hall. (I am to use that door only when taken to the room for a haircut. I never discover why one always enters the room from the courtyard for interrogations. There must be a reason: the Chinese do nothing haphazardly. Puzzling.)

I later dub it 'the grand committee room'. Tonight, sitting behind the long, polished mahogany table, are the five officers. They are already sipping boiling hot, bitter green tea. Two large wicker-covered thermos flasks stand in a corner with a fresh supply of hot water. Against the wall behind the table and beneath three windows with iron bars on the outside stands a dark blue cloth-covered sofa.

Against the wall at one end of the table is a spittoon. In the centre of the room facing the table is a wooden armchair reinforced with iron. It is so heavy that it is almost impossible to move it.

I am ordered to sit down. An iron bar, hinged to one arm,

is put across the front of me and padlocked. I am denied almost any freedom of movement. It has an intimidating effect. And the fact that I have been awoken from my first, deep sleep enhances the hopelessness of my plight—but rousing a prisoner in the night is an old trick of interrogation, all part of a technique to wear you down.

All the officers facing me I have seen before during the ten days since I was brought ashore from the *Hanoi* at dawn on February 23. I have given them nicknames. In the centre is Fu Manchu, named after Sax Rohmer's famous character who delighted me as a boy. He looks fearsome. He speaks acidly, almost with venom in his voice. On his left is Poker Face, who conducts the investigation of my case for the next seven months. On Fu Manchu's right is Bully Boy, the young toughy who likes to intervene with threatening gestures, shouting: 'You are a spy!' or 'You are a liar.'

On Poker Face's left is Beau Brummel, the Chinese note-taker. He is responsible for my welfare during my time in prison. He is a young man of about twenty-eight, courteous, often helpful. I nickname him Beau Brummel after the English dandy in the Georgian era because he is always—unusual for a Chinese Communist—careful about his clothes.

Sitting next to Bully Boy is the interpreter, Roly Poly, as broad as he is tall, wearing the politically-favoured, heavily patched old tunic and trousers, status symbol of the Great Proletarian Cultural Revolution. He is in his mid-fifties and has known Shanghai since before the Mao takeover in 1949. His English is impeccable. A few weeks later he will be replaced by another interpreter, I suspect because we get on too well together. He takes some of the sting out of the questions, and gives me friendly, honest advice. He has explained to me the role of the officer conducting the investigation—he is responsible for persuading me to 'confess' and 'change my attitude' (I suppose you might say 'repent').

The proceedings open slowly. Poker Face is sipping his green tea. Bully Boy clears his throat, gets up from his chair, walks across the room and spits the phlegm into the spittoon. They are all wearing khaki military cotton-padded overcoats except

Roly Poly, but his old uniform is padded and enhances his bulk. They all wear caps to keep their heads warm. I have pulled the anorak hood over my head. I am not offered tea. My status is changed now I am formally a prisoner.

Fu Manchu takes from his overcoat pocket the red plastic-bound copy of Mao Thought quotations. He intones the familiar passage: 'All reactionaries are paper tigers. In appearance, the reactionaries are terrifying, but in reality they are not quite so terrible.' He flicks over a few pages: ' "Lifting a rock only to drop it on one's own feet" is a Chinese folk saying to describe the behaviour of certain fools. The reactionaries in all countries are fools of this kind.' He lays the book on the table. Roly Poly has extracted from his own breviary a slip of paper with the translation in English. I suppose he has had to say it to foreign prisoners so often that he has written it on a piece of paper to save him having to find the passage in the English volume. He reads the interpretation, trying to instil some authority into his voice.

Fu Manchu continues: 'Chairman Mao shows leniency towards those who confess.'

'And so does God,' I retort.

But he has the last word. 'Mao punishes severely those who do not confess their crimes.'

The interrogation is opened by Poker Face. It is immediately obvious that the inquisitors are determined tonight to take advantage of the mental shock of finding myself in prison on a charge of espionage. 'You are a paper tiger spy,' is the epithet hurled at me.

I smile. 'We are all paper tigers in certain circumstances,' I reply. 'It depends who is holding the gun. Anyway, that is what Chairman Mao teaches.'

'Why did you take two photographs of three motor torpedo boats at the mouth of the Whangpoo River?' asks Poker Face.

It is the first time that I have been accused of taking only two photographs of the warships. Has Neroni confessed to taking the black-and-white photographs?

I reply: 'The warships were dressed overall, I assume in celebration of having set up a three-in-one Cultural Revolution

Committee. The photographs fitted into a series I had taken the previous day in Shanghai. It was my intention to use them to illustrate an article.'

'You are a spy,' shouts Bully Boy.

'I am not,' I retort.

'Were you requested to take these photographs by British Intelligence?' continues Poker Face.

'No.'

'But you *are* employed by the British Secret Service.'

'I am sorry to disappoint you, but I am not. So far as I am aware British Intelligence does not, like Communist countries, use journalists as espionage agents.'

'I am not discussing with you the policy of British Intelligence.' He pauses and then to my surprise adds, 'I do not expect you to make statements treasonable to your country.' (An odd approach to a man charged with being a spy. In more than seven months' interrogation I was never to be asked a single 'sensitive' question.)

And so it goes on. More questions . . . more questions . . . more questions. They are all trying to secure from me an admission that I am a spy working for British Intelligence. If I do not sign a confession, my case may not be 'closed' for months, even years. They remind me of one spy who was shot.

I ask if I may go to the toilet. The interpreter gets up and comes across to unlock the bar across the arms of the chair. I expect to be taken back to my cell but the interpreter accompanies me outside into the courtyard. A low building further along the wall of the prison proves to be a military-type latrine. There is no privacy.

We return to the committee room. Poker Face resumes the questions but on a different tack.

'Why did you slander Chairman Mao in the article which you wrote after your visit to Shanghai in November?'

'I am not aware that I slandered him. I merely commented that your Yangtse pilots considered themselves better equipped to navigate in the fog with Mao Thought than with the ship's radar. Shanghai is the only port in the world where I have known this to happen.' I was referring to a sarcastic comment

I had made about the prohibition of radar in Shanghai harbour.

'You slandered our Chiang Ching.' (I note the use of the word 'our': Poker Face slightly emphasises it. Chinese emperors in bygone days, nearing the end of their life, raised the status of the empress. Mao has elevated his wife.)

'I wrote that Chiang Ching became Mao's third wife—although I believe she is his fourth—after being a cinema actress. Is that incorrect?'

There is no response. It is past midnight (I noticed the clock over the archway as we returned from the toilet).

'We will resume questioning again tomorrow morning,' says Poker Face. 'You must change your attitude, otherwise it will be dangerous for you.'

The padlock on the iron bar of my chair is unlocked. I stand up feeling stiff from the cold and from sitting in one position for four hours. Wearily, I walked back to my cell. The guards sitting at a desk inside the main door are eating rice and vegetables. My spirits are at a low ebb. I wonder for how many days this will go on. The cell door is slammed shut, bolted and the key turned in the padlock. In spite of my uncomfortable bed, I immediately fall into a deep sleep, awakening abruptly at 5.20 a.m. when the prison alarm bell shatters the silence.

During the following seven months the interrogation proceeds. Sessions last for about three hours—sometimes one a day, sometimes two, sometimes three a day. And occasionally a day or two may elapse without a 'confessional' session. This technique is nerve-racking. It is almost like the Chinese water torture. You never know at what hour of the day or night you will be taken from your cell to the one-storey confessional building across the courtyard from the main prison block. (I am interrogated in 'the grand committee room' on only a few occasions, for this room is also used for Mao Thought meetings and for sessions with a warder-barber every few months.

There is something rather eerie about the confessional block. It has twenty-six cells, each about three yards square, with a window high up on the wall, a small black desk with three chairs, and a single chair in front for the prisoner. As you enter, your ears are assaulted by a jumble of raucous Chinese voices coming from behind closed doors. Some of the female prisoners are near to tears as they answer interminable questions. (New prisoners are intimidated by a loudspeaker being placed near the window of their cell at night-times, and sometimes the tape-recordings are of a person in anguish. Every night for a week at one time a woman could be heard crying, always at the same hour, always with the same intensity of cries—presumably for mercy. A new woman prisoner is being softened up.)

Much of the ideological propaganda technique of the Cultural Revolution might have been stolen from the Church of Rome. The cherished red book of quotations of Chairman Mao Tse-tung suggests the breviary; the cadre the priest; the daily hour-long Mao Thought meetings before work are all in the formal religious worship, with Mao as the Pope and God and Chiang Ching almost like the Virgin Mary.

It took me a long time to understand the fine definition that the Chinese attach to the word 'confession'. I am not sure if I understand it now. I had many futile arguments with Poker Face, my interrogator. It is not enough to say that you are a 'spy', or reveal what you have learned by 'spying'. You *must* bare your soul and change your attitude by repentance. Only then will your political sins be absolved.

The onus of proving your innocence of the charges against you rests upon you. If they say you are a spy, you must prove you are not. But how? Such is the justice of the People's Republic of China. I ask for legal aid. I am told: 'There are no lawyers in China as in Europe or America who, for large sums of money, will secure the acquittal of a guilty man.'

[There did appear to be some kind of legal assistance for Chinese prisoners, however. One summer morning, I was taken to see the doctor. In the large garden before the entrance gate to the prison were men at tables piled high with books. Under the shade of the trees, they were each surrounded by groups of men and women, presumably the relatives of prisoners. I witnessed this scene on several occasions, but only during fine, warm weather. There did not appear to be any room where they could assemble in the prison in the winter months. I was never able to solve this mystery.]

Wearisome hours in the 'confessional' rooms bring on, I find, a feeling of claustrophobia. You have an intense desire to jump up from the wood-and-iron chair in which you are sitting and rush out of the room. The padlocked iron bar across the arms of the chair enhances this feeling: after all, that is why it is there—it symbolises loss of freedom. And it also prevents you, in a burst of fury, jumping up from your chair and attacking the accusers sitting behind the desk.

Every fifteen minutes or so during the questioning I need to urinate, presumably due to the intense nervous strain. I suspect that all prisoners suffer in the same way because there are wooden buckets at the end of the corridor for prisoners to relieve themselves. You are never refused permission to be excused. I suspect that even the interrogators welcome these breaks.

The nervous strain of interrogation is not caused by the fear of committing yourself. Your guilt is already established in the eyes of your interrogators. It is the frustrating triviality of the questions; the repetitiveness. At one afternoon's session I am asked to repeat about twelve times, at intervals of ten minutes, what my China Travel Service guide told me about a commune. And I underwent the same ordeal over what the security officer who boarded the *Lelewel* when I arrived in Shanghai in November had said to me on the subject of taking photographs.

The detail with which they went into my movements was extraordinary. They were interested not only in what I did in China but also my travels outside of China. I am asked to name the man in Japan who sold me the ticket for my passage aboard the *Hanoi*; what was the attitude of the captain towards me, the name of the chief steward? Were these officers helpful?

In this series of questions, the name of Captain Neroni is mentioned for the first time. I still have no definite knowledge that he has been arrested, though I deduced this from the excitement of the interrogators on the second night of my arrest when I acknowledged taking certain photographs on the Whangpoo River.

'Do you regard Captain Neroni as an honest man?' asks the interrogator one day several weeks after my arrest; the question comes out of the blue, breaking the thread of the previous questions during the session.

'My acquaintance with Captain Neroni was short,' I reply cautiously.

'When did you first meet him?'

'On the day that the *Hanoi* sailed from Kobe.'

'Is he married?'

'He told me he was. A Japanese lady carrying a baby was on the Kobe dock to bid him a tearful farewell. He said it was his wife and their first child. He showed me a photograph of them.'

'Did you like Captain Neroni?'

'I did not know him for very long. I found him a congenial fellow passenger, but I saw little of him on the ship except at mealtimes. He was friendly with the crew; he spent most of his time on the bridge—natural for a sea captain.'

'Would you trust him?'

'I do not think I can be expected to answer that question. As I have said, my acquaintance with him was brief.'

'Why do you think he was travelling on the *Hanoi* from Kobe to Hong Kong? He could have made the journey much more quickly by sea or air.'

'I understood that he had applied to the Japanese Government for a resident visa; that he was going to Hong Kong to conclude negotiations with the Japanese Consul-General. Because of their child, his wife wished him to leave the sea. He had not been to sea for many months.'

'Was he working in Japan before he sailed on the *Hanoi*?'

'I assume he wasn't as he had only a 180-day tourist visa. But he told me that he hoped to work for Investors Overseas Services.'

'What kind of organisation is that? Is it connected with the American Government?'

'No. It's a mutual fund finance company.'

I spend the next hour explaining the intricacies of this type of investment organisation. It was all Greek to Poker Face. And it seemed irrelevant to my case.

Poker Face continues: 'Did you show Neroni how to take photographs secretly?'

'No.'

'You are not telling the truth. You explained to Captain Neroni how to take photographs without being observed when you took pictures of the Yangtse River steamer.'

'Captain Neroni was standing behind me on the wing of the bridge when I took these photographs. For convenience, I placed my camera on the ship's rail.'

'You, therefore, could not be seen taking photographs?'

'Perhaps not. But if I wished to ensure complete secrecy, I could have taken the photographs from the porthole of a cabin.'

This conversation confirms my impression that Captain Neroni is in custody.

Some questions during interrogation are not without humour. Once we discuss the articles which I wrote about China after my visit in November the previous year.

'Why did you write these articles?' asks Poker Face. 'For filthy lucre?' (He says 'filthy lucre' in English although the interrogation is being conducted in Chinese through the interpreter.)

I smiled. 'Yes, I wrote the articles for money, if that is what you mean by the expression "filthy lucre",' I reply. 'It is a long time since I have heard anyone use that English colloquialism. Your command of English must be pretty good. But, I suppose you have your reasons for conducting the case in Chinese.

'I am what you would describe as a "capital roader". I see nothing dishonest in writing for money. You are paid for interrogating me. And, I am sure, you receive—if I may say so, quite rightly—a higher salary than a Shanghai factory worker. Chairman Mao has said that each is paid according to his ability and according to his work. That is also true in a capitalist country, though there there is an important difference: a man has the right to choose his work and his place of employment.'

Poker Face cannot allow this statement to go unchallenged. 'The workers in western countries are oppressed,' he says with acidity. 'Many are unemployed. If a man wishes to leave his job he cannot do so because he may not find other employment. In China there are no unemployed.'

'You are speaking in half-truths,' I retort. 'The crux of my argument is that we all work for money, whether in a Communist country or in the Free World. I use the word "free" because that is the key. In the West everyone has the right to say "No". In China this right is denied.'

Poker Face does not wish to pursue this sensitive political discussion.

'The articles you wrote about China are not honest,' he goes on. 'You did not tell the truth. And you did not tell the truth because you were writing propaganda and you did so for money. You are a typical imperialist. But like all imperialists, you are a paper tiger.'

'So far as I am aware, there was nothing untruthful in the articles which I wrote,' I reply. 'Everything I wrote was based on my visits to factories, to communes. I was always accompanied by a guide of the China Travel Service. In all the conversations I had, he was the interpreter. I also, of course, drew on my own observations. But if you read the articles carefully, I am sure that you will agree that I am sympathetic to what China is trying to achieve—to create a non-acquisitive, selfless society—though I may not agree with your methods of achieving it. Your country is a dictatorship: as I have said, the individual does not have the right to say "No".'

'You are wrong. We all have the right to criticise. We hold criticism meetings. During the Cultural Revolution, everyone was free to write critical posters and put them up on the walls.'

'But would you challenge a directive by Chairman Mao? Would you challenge his edict "Grasp revolution, increase production"?'

To these questions there is what one can only call a 'negative response'—stony silence.

For the first five months of these wearisome, often futile,

interrogation sessions, tempers on either side of the table remain unruffled. Poker Face and I gradually reach some kind of loose mutual understanding, almost respect. The sessions are often conducted on an almost conversational basis, as though two people were exchanging ideas. Our discussion is not infrequently political, ranging over a wide range of topics from 'American imperialism' to 'Soviet revisionism'. He is certainly surprised when I say that if I had to choose between the Russian brand of Communism and Maoism, I would prefer the latter, for in my opinion Russia is getting the worst of two ways of life. Either a country is capitalistic, with its advantages, or pure Communist (which is what Mao is seeking to establish in China). The fact that the vast majority of people in China are materially better off than before the 'Liberation' demonstrates the merits of the latter system but they pay a heavy price by restriction of freedom.

One very hot afternoon in early August, however, there is a sudden change in atmosphere. The theme of the questioning becomes sinister—to discover if I have Chinese contacts in Shanghai.

Poker Face is fumbling with some papers on a tiny shelf hidden underneath the top of the desk. Then, almost like a conjurer, he produces the carbon copies of my China articles written eight months before. He flips over pages. Stops. Reads for a few minutes. I sit tensely in my chair, waiting for his questions to begin.

'Who told you that the industrial output of Shanghai is ten per cent of the whole country?' snaps Poker Face. There is a slight note of triumph in his voice.

'It is the generally accepted figure in the west,' I reply, 'but it was confirmed to me by the guide at the Shanghai Trade Fair.'

He does not reveal disappointment.

'Who told you that Shanghai's shipyards build vessels up to 10,000 tons, that its factories produce lorries, cars, bicycles, electrical generators, diesel tractors, machine tools, tyres, television sets, radios, watches, cameras, pianos, refrigerators, textiles, shirts, clothing?'

'I saw exhibits of all these goods, including models of ships built in Shanghai, at the Trade Fair. I could have included medical and dental equipment and a host of other things.'

'Who told you that the Wuhan bridge was closed to all traffic for three days?'

'It was widely reported in the Hong Kong press before I visited China. But my guide confirmed it.'

'Who told you about the Anting incident—the fighting and beatings in December, 1966?'

'My China Travel Service guide. But a detailed account of the affair appeared in the August edition of *China Reconstructs*, your own propaganda magazine.'

'It mentions the word "beatings"?'

'Yes. Look at the edition. You will see for yourself.'

In fury, Poker Face gets up from the desk, walks round it and stands over me, shaking his fist in my face, shouting in English, 'I'll wipe you out.' He has lost tremendous face in front of the two other security officers.

But I am confident his threat is idle. I look calmly up at his face, saying: 'For five months we have conducted these interrogations without either of us losing our tempers. Please sit down and let us resume.'

For once I am master of the situation. Quietly he returns to his seat, turns over his papers for a moment, then speaks to the interpreter. The session is over. It has lasted less than an hour. The note-taker escorts me back to my cell.

I believe I should have been released after about seven months if the Hong Kong authorities had not been holding in detention thirteen Chinese Communist journalists who had taken part in the 1967 riots (a spill-over of the Cultural Revolution).

It is an afternoon towards the end of September, 1968.

Poker Face seems weary of the investigation. He starts the session by saying: 'If you write, briefly, in your own handwriting, a good confession with the correct attitude, your case will be settled with a few formalities.'

'What do you mean by a short confession?' I ask. 'In seven months millions of words have been spoken on both sides, they have all been duly recorded in Chinese and English. I have checked them, signed each page, thumb-printed them in red ink.'

'About twelve pages,' he replies. 'If you type a draft, I will see if it is all right.'

He sits in deep thought for a full minute and then comments: 'You are a very special spy, clever at politics, and you have the advantage of age.' And then, as an afterthought, he says with a fleeting smile, 'I'm not sure you have told all the truth'. But he speaks as though it is not of importance. He gets up from the table, an exhausted, sad man. The case has not quite turned out as he imagined at the beginning it would.

I am careful in my choice of words when drafting the 'confession'. I know I must confess to espionage but I qualify it. I acknowledge that under Chinese law I am guilty of political, economic and military spying if I am prepared to share information or photographs secured in China with a British official if he expresses interest. Even such a limited admission of guilt may lay me open to a public trial, but I am gambling on Poker Face's promise that my case can be settled with few formalities if my statement is satisfactory. Such a promise suggests my position is not too serious.

The interpreter collects the draft on the following day.

Three days later, the interpreter escorts me to the 'grand committee room'. Beau Brummel is sitting behind the long mahogany table alone. My draft confession is lying in front of him.

He looks up sternly as I sit down in the wood-and-iron chair.

'It is a very bad confession,' he says.

'I am sorry. I'm afraid I've never been able to understand quite what you mean by "confession". To me, it is a statement of fact, the truth, and that is what I have written. However, if you will indicate to what you object, I will write a new draft.'

He pushes the draft across the desk to me. I glance through

it. There are three pencilled deletions. First, a description of myself as a journalist. Second, a reference to my age and health. Third, a paragraph in which I describe my conversation with Mr Hsu, the security officer on the *Lelewel*. (This deletion indicates that even in Mao's China the old-boy network operates in the Security Police.)

I agree to accept the deletions. I am escorted back to the cell to write the confession by hand. It is collected the next day. Silence for thirteen months. I never see Poker Face again.

8   Prisoner 1248

IMMEDIATELY the cell door slammed shut behind me on the evening of March 4, 1968, I knew that the greatest challenge confronting me was the maintenance of my morale in the face of the ill-treatment I might receive and the multitude of petty prison restrictions I should certainly have to endure during what might prove to be many years of imprisonment (if they did not decide to execute me as a spy).

I thought of the courage of Francis Chichester, alone in his tiny yacht, battling with the wind and mountainous seas around the Horn. He is about my age. The thought gave me strength. I must emulate him.

What were the immediate trials confronting me? There was the problem of cleanliness. The problem of exercise and physical wellbeing. The problem of how to fill in the waking hours from 5.20 a.m. until 8.00 p.m.

It took me almost four months before I secured near-perfection of routine. Every morning, winter and summer, I stripped and sponged myself with cold water on rising. I am not an addict of cold showers, but I thought if Prince Charles could do it at Gordonstoun, I can do it in a Shanghai gaol. (I should like to know if the Prince has kept up the habit: I confess I immediately reverted to hot baths when I reached Hong Kong.) In prison, though, I enjoyed this morning ritual. In mid-winter, snow on the ground, temperature below freezing, chilling wind from the open window, my thin, starved body tingled with warmth after I had dried myself.

Foreigners by nature are fastidious about cleanliness. The Chinese know this. They try to keep you dirty, your hair long, your beard unshaved. In a normal western prison you would be allowed to shave and shower at least once a week. I had only seven proper showers and one hot bath (in hospital) during my imprisonment of nearly twenty months. During the very hot, humid summer of 1968—the temperature daily was over 100 degrees Fahrenheit and the humidity 90 degrees—I did not have a shower for eight weeks.

I once asked Poker Face for permission to shower.

'We are trying to economise on coal to heat the hot water,' he replied.

'I agree that Chairman Mao teaches frugality,' I retorted. 'But if the Chinese prisoners are averse to cold showers in summer-time, I am not.'

My appeal must have touched a chord of sympathy. The interrogation was interrupted. Beau Brummel personally escorted me to the shower room after I had collected towel and soap from the cell, and waited patiently for fifteen minutes while I luxuriated under the cool water.

Again, it was difficult to obtain clippers to cut your nails. A request for clippers was often refused for two or three weeks. Clipping my nails became an obsession. And yet I was in Hong Kong a fortnight before I bothered to cut my nails. The obsession had vanished merely because I knew that I could cut my nails whenever I wished. The Chinese authorities are fully conscious of the mental suffering caused by these petty irritations—a form of mild torture.

My morning wash was followed by thirty minutes' Swedish drill, similar to what I did as a sixteen-and-a-half-year-old midshipman in the Royal Naval Air Service in World War I. I tried to be punctilious; no slacking. I am sure these exercises did much to maintain my health; to keep my wasted, tiny muscles in condition.

I then made my bed and tidied the cell, sweeping the cement floor with a broom which I made from toilet paper. There was no provision to keep the cell clean. Only three times was I able to persuade the guards to give me a straw broom: on one occasion to sweep up the mess of plaster and wet cement left after they had repaired the cell walls, and twice to clean the wire gauze covering my window. (The gauze kept out mosquitoes and insects in summertime. But it also trapped the small particles of coal dust from the surrounding factory chimneys that around the clock belched acrid smoke, and this clogging of the wire reduced the daylight in the cell.)

My method was to write a note: 'May I have a broom, please? Chairman Mao teaches that dust, like everything reactionary, will not vanish of itself.' On occasion the appeal succeeded.

The window gauze kept out the insects but not the bugs that infested my bed for the whole of the first summer. When I first arrived in the cell I was puzzled by blood marks on the grimy, whitewashed walls. A few months later the mystery was solved: a previous prisoner must have crushed the bugs on the walls. Every night throughout the summer I was doing the same thing, as they tried to gorge themselves on my blood during the night. An appeal for DDT was ignored. It was October before they all vanished.

That winter my wooden bed was changed, and in the spring a guard washed the bed with a disinfectant.

The following summer, 1969, I was not bothered by bugs, but I was infested with a peculiar type of large ant. They did not bite me, but I found they would eat any type of food, with a preference for bread. So I trapped them with crumbs, killing them off by hundreds. I would put some crumbs on the floor after the morning meal, then wait. Soon several families (they lived in families) would arrive—perhaps a hundred ants in all—and start to tuck in. I then crushed the lot. I never completely eliminated them but I managed to keep the population down to manageable proportions. The trouble was that although they did not bite, they ran all over my body at night and disturbed my sleep.

The greatest problem was to prevent boredom during the fourteen and a half waking hours each day. I did laundry on four days a week—Monday and Tuesday, Thursday and Friday. This routine permitted a change of shirt, underclothes and socks every other day. At first laundry was complicated because I had only one bowl and cold water was delivered to the cell by a young Chinese girl only twice a day: I would wash the clothes in the first bowl of water delivered at 7.00 a.m. and rinse them in the afternoon delivery of water. This was unsatisfactory, though, because I had to use the same water for my cold morning wash.

After a few weeks I persuaded my captors to permit me to buy a second bowl, and also a second cup for the twice-daily delivery of hot water—all I had to drink. I used the newly filled cup of hot water both to iron my clothes and air them by wrapping the clothes around the cups and then enveloping them in a bath towel.

Much of the rest of the day I spent devising cross-word puzzles (I found this difficult), doing word games (making the greatest number of words from a single word), and playing patience with cards made from the thick brown toilet paper. My first pack of cards—hidden in a volume of Mao's writings —was discovered and confiscated (gambling is prohibited in Red China, and cards represent gambling although I obviously could not gamble with myself). I made a second pack. These were not found until the day I left, but I was not allowed to keep them.

For the first five months of my imprisonment, practically my only reading matter was the red book of *Quotations from Chairman Mao*, which I came to know almost by heart. Then, at my request, Poker Face arranged for me to buy the four volumes of Chairman Mao's works. They cost me six yuan (about £1). After another three months these too had palled with familiarity, and the interpreter arranged for me to get copies of the propaganda magazines *Peking Review* and *China Reconstructs*.

For the rest of my stay in prison I had the *Peking Review* almost every week. I do not know whether certain issues were denied me on security grounds. I think not, for in the January 3, 1969, issue I read of the Hong Kong press conference on Anthony Grey. It was obvious that Grey was not to be freed from house detention until all the Chinese journalists detained in Hong Kong were released: this was depressing news for me. I could not expect freedom before Grey, for I was regarded as a spy, while Grey was purely a hostage.

For a man who for fifty years has avidly read newspapers every morning at breakfast, listened to radio bulletins throughout the day, kept an eye on tape machines, to be without news of what is happening in the world is at first a real hardship. For days I felt I should never get used to this situation. And yet, after only a couple of weeks, I became unconcerned with events in the outside world. I had lost my thirst—I had always thought it insatiable—to know what was going on.

My world had become four grimy walls, a single barred window with a view of the tops of a few trees, the grey-brick building across the courtyard where the unmarried P.L.A. guards lived, and the sky.

One of the hardest restrictions for an energetic person like myself to bear is lack of regular exercise. The prison authorities were maddening. Basically, regulations provided for a prisoner to be exercised for fifteen minutes every week. But sometimes two, three or even four weeks would go by without outdoor exercise. And then, after a long lapse, you would be exercised twice or even three times in a week. The walls of the cell seemed to close in on you after two or three weeks without going out.

I was always punctilious about my dress on those rare, precious outings. I would slip off a pair of old cotton trousers and don clerical-grey well-pressed flannels, a blue blazer minus its gilt Royal Air Force buttons, give my fur-felt Lock hat a brush, polish my brown Italian moccasins, slip my sunglasses into my breast pocket. This may all sound superfluous, but an outing when in solitary confinement is an event. To dress correctly boosts morale.

There were six small exercise yards jointly overlooked by a watch tower manned by a single armed P.L.A. guard. He was there to prevent one escaping over the wall to freedom, but this would have been difficult even if unobserved. At the top of the high wall was jagged glass and six strands of barbed wire. As I walked round the small courtyard in solitude, hands behind my back to keep a good posture, I used to speculate how the Russian spy Blake or the train robbers—expert escapologists—would cope.

On the other side of the outer wall of two exercise yards were a primary and a secondary school. The latter had four storeys. Curious children used to gather at the third- and fourth-floor windows to watch the prisoners walking around. A daring young boy in the primary school one day climbed a tree to look over the wall at the 'imperialist spy'. I winked my eye. He looked a little surprised; beckoned down for another boy to join him on the branches. They chattered excitedly. Then the guard in the watch tower spotted them, and shouted an order. They promptly climbed down.

I used to like to listen to the children of the married P.L.A. guards when they came to spend Sunday with their parents after a week away at school. They would play in the courtyards, chattering like magpies. In particular, I remember an eight-year-old boy whose father was on guard in my cell block. One day, as the girl pushed my hot-water ration through the trap of the cell door, to my surprise, standing behind her, was the guard's small son, peering at me wide-eyed. I must have looked ferocious—long nose; long, straggling beard; long, uncombed hair. I gave him a smile and said: 'Hello!' He scampered away to his father, then returned for a second look. The girl had left the trap open for him to see me. I put down the filled cups; waved my hand. He was still standing watching me as his father gently closed the trap.

What could be the thoughts of such a child—educated to believe that all foreigners (white men) are enemies of their country? Within two more decades, China will be populated almost solely by such citizens indoctrinated from birth, people taught to hate, to betray their family or their friends before their country. What were the words of my China Travel Service guide once? 'We love our father, we love our mother, but we love Chairman Mao more dearly.'

During my first weeks in prison I was given three meals a day—rice porridge with bamboo shoots at 6.30 a.m.; two *man tau* (steamed bread rolls), about four spoonfuls of vegetables and half an ounce of pork at eleven-thirty, and the same meal again at 5.00 p.m. But without warning this slender diet was cut to two meals a day; no longer were we given rice porridge —presumably as a measure of economy. The first meal now came at 8.30 a.m. and it consisted of four *man tau*, vegetables and the inevitable pork. At 4.30 p.m. I was given the same quantity of food. Occasionally there was an egg in place of pork. Not to eat from four-thirty in the afternoon until eight-thirty the next morning—a break of sixteen hours—is a great hardship. And so was the eight-hour fast during the day. I circumvented it by saving two *man tau* from the previous after-noon to eat at 6.30 a.m. And I saved another two *man tau* at 8.30 a.m. to eat at one o'clock. I was not getting any more food but I had at least the illusion of four meals a day.

The guards, by contrast, were always indulging in snacks. They had no mess halls and ate around a desk (on summer days they sat on the ground in the sunshine). Even in the dead of night, as the prisoners sought oblivion in sleep, we were disturbed by the rattle of the guards' enamel food bowls and the clicking of chopsticks, the sounds magnified in the silence of the night.

And our gaolers had other irritatingly noisy habits. I found it almost impossible to resign myself to their fore and aft belchings—the result of sipping green tea or hot water all day. And all day long, all through the night, they would clear their throats with a revolting harsh noise, spitting the phlegm into a spittoon. The prison was never quiet.

I found prayer a great solace. It relieved inner tensions. Normally I pray in the morning and before going to bed only for a few minutes. After a short time in prison I was conversing with God for periods of up to half an hour. I prayed for my friends. But I did not pray for my own deliverance. I sought only for courage; for the maintenance of my health. And I sought inspiration on world problems. For many years I have been working on a manuscript which deals with the crisis of this century: the crisis of freedom. From prayer I gained new ideas, if not solutions.

Solitary confinement is compulsory rest undirected to any good purpose; useless to follow any activity except of the mind. If the solitary confinement is for a long period—as it was for me—you almost come to cherish it. You even resent the smallest intrusion on your privacy such as the twice-daily delivery of hot and cold water or even food.

I could ponder the problems confronting mankind—the population explosion, pollution of the cities, spoliation of the countryside, the 'haves' and the 'have nots', the millions of landless peasants eking out an existence at the expense of rapacious landlords, the crisis of freedom.

The basic requirements of each individual man, woman and child are simple—three meals a day, a roof, a few clothes. With education there grows a desire for luxuries. In China today it may be only a watch, a fountain-pen, a bicycle; tomorrow it will be a television set, a car. Even the most intense propaganda in favour of a frugal, non-materialistic life will not completely stifle the acquisitive urge.

And there is also the problem of freedom. Can you keep a nation perpetually mentally and physically enthralled? Man has the right to say 'No'. He has the right to enjoy freedom of speech, writing, worship and movement. How long must the world await the fulfilment of the dream of that great Foreign Minister, Mr Ernest Bevin, that a man can go to London's Victoria Station and buy a ticket for anywhere in the world *without* a passport, without even an identity card?

In China today, everything the people read in the newspapers, everything they hear on the radio, is controlled by the propaganda machine of the regime. They know nothing of the outside world except what is considered fit for the people's eyes or ears. Chinese people are still ignorant that the Americans have twice walked on the moon. When a report to this effect was recently spread in Canton it was disbelieved. How could such a fantastic thing be true? A few days later China launched her own satellite. The day will come when Chinese will walk on the moon; then the people will believe they are the first men to have achieved this feat in space.

In January, 1969, I was in hospital. A man two beds away was reading a newspaper. I whispered: 'Who is the new President of the United States?' The whispered reply was two words: No interest.' This means the Chinese have not yet been told. 'What's the news today?' 'Food riots in India.' A world in revolt—the masses rising against their capitalist oppressors. And when, a month later, I read in the *Peking Review* a translation of an editorial in the *People's Daily* on President Nixon, its main feature was a description of him delivering his inaugural address behind bullet-proof glass.

Politics are 'isms'. In my cell, I could see that they all add up to some kind of dictatorship, even if some are only in a mild form. But self-discipline is the key to the complete freedom of man.

A Roman Catholic priest, the Reverend Raymond J. de Jaegher, a great authority on Asia, visited me in hospital when I was released. He asked me: 'Did you find a solution to our problems?' I replied: 'I feel the only answer is a great revival of Christianity. This can come about if God sends on earth a new leader. Perhaps He will.'

If you come to cherish the hours that can be devoted to pure thought you miss the opportunity for conversation, for discussion of ideas. Having no one to talk to is perhaps the greatest hardship of solitary confinement. Man or woman was not born to live alone. I am sure that the strongest-willed person will talk to himself if left long enough alone. I had heard of prisoners or aged lonely people talking to themselves. I scoffed at the idea. I have changed my mind.

A Rumanian Pastor Wurmbarang preached to himself every night for three years in solitary confinement in a cell thirty feet under the ground. Within a few days of imprisonment I discovered myself talking aloud. I decided that I must ration solitary conversation. I talked to my daughter, Anne; to friends. I dictated articles to a secretary, a Miss Jones. Conversation relieves pent-up tension.

Some evenings I held imaginary dinner parties with guests drawn from men and women in high and low places whom I have known through my journalistic career. At the end of these dinners I always made a speech. The whole object of this imaginary exercise was to give me an opportunity to talk at length. Relaxed I would go to bed and sleep a dreamless sleep.

What did I miss most? Music. Only very seldom did I hear faintly a distant broadcast in which I could recognise the piano accompaniment to the famous Peking opera, *The Red Lantern*. (This composition is much boosted; it is claimed that the piano, a western instrument, has been used for a new 'revolutionary art form' inspired by Mao's wife, Chiang Ching. Today everybody is singing snatches from the revolutionary operas.)

I missed small children. I liked to hear them playing in the courtyard on Sundays. I wished that the little boy who had peeked through my trap would return for a second glimpse.

I was thrilled to awaken one morning to find on the wall a few inches above my head a small lizard. To my delight he stayed for two days. He would remain immobile on the ceiling for hours. On the third night he disappeared. I suppose he was hungry.

A spider wove an enormous web in one corner of the cell. In the autumn there were three eggs. The spider had vanished. I looked forward to their hatching in the spring. Alas, while I was in hospital my cell was swept; the cobwebs and the eggs had gone.

I found it impossible to kill two cockroaches—I assume husband and wife. I put small pieces of bread on the floor for them which they ate during the night. For a special treat I would give them a piece of paper soaked in the fat of my pork. They would eat only the paper impregnated with the fat: they would cut out a circle as neat as if done with a pair of scissors. In the daytime they hid in the darkness under my bed.

The truth is: Man must enjoy the companionship of something, even if it is only a cockroach.

9 'I Always Choose Good Doctors'

In the early hours of the morning of April 19, 1968, I awoke in agony. I could get relief only by sitting up on my wooden bed. When the guard on his half-hourly rounds saw me and indicated with his hand that I was to go to sleep, I walked slowly and in pain across to the door. In sign language I explained that I was ill, that I was suffering. He pointed with his hand to his own stomach. I moved the position of his hand to that of my bladder, but in retrospect I believe he felt I had appendicitis. He gestured me to lie down.

Five minutes later he opened the cell door. A senior officer was standing beside him. They beckoned me to follow them out of the cell block and across the courtyard. In the next court-yard was a jeep with a driver sitting at the wheel. I was helped into the back seat, and the senior officer got in beside me.

We set off across Shanghai. At first I assumed that I was being taken to the old General Hospital where I saw Dr Chang, but after we had crossed Soochow Creek we kept straight on instead of turning to the left.

The city was beginning to stir (it was just after 4.00 a.m.). We passed several big markets piled high with vegetables. I could see chickens, eggs, pork. Housewives were already buying.

I realised we were driving to Ward Road prison in Hongkew —the prison where the Japanese perpetrated so many atrocities during the war. It is a very large prison, holding probably six or seven thousand prisoners, built in multi-storey blocks, each cell housing two men. The windows are large: a prisoner can sit on a low stool and look out.

On a wall beside the huge double iron gates of the prison

was a full-length picture of Mao at least sixteen feet high. My guard conversed with the guard at the gate; showed him his identity card. One gate was opened to permit the jeep to pass in. We were now between the outer and inner gates. Again my guard explained the situation, showed his pass. The guard at the gate looked at me with curiosity in the dim light before letting us in. We drove into the prison compound, up to the prison hospital which stood on the right, between the prison and the road.

I was helped out. We went in to a large reception room with wooden benches, which reminded me of the out-patients' departments of many old London hospitals. I was told to sit down.

The guard went in to an adjoining room, re-emerging in a few minutes accompanied by a sleepy-eyed nurse, fat, rather motherly-looking. I was taken to a clinic at the end of the reception room.

I was shocked by its appearance. The walls had not been repainted for years—perhaps since the hospital was built, long before the war. In the centre stood an old desk, a wooden chair for the doctor, a stool for the patient. Against one wall was a couch covered with a red rubber sheet; it looked grimy. A metal hospital cupboard for instruments had long since lost its white paint and was now rusty. So was a table for gynaecological examinations, which looked in the gloom of the room, lit by only a single low-powered electric bulb, rather an instrument of torture than an aid to medicine.

I was told to sit by the desk. The nurse took a thermometer from the cupboard. It tasted of sterilising alcohol as she put it in my mouth. While waiting for it to 'cook' she felt my pulse.

Then she left the room, to return ten minutes later with a male doctor. He had obviously just been awakened. His eyes were still half-closed with sleep, and he was buttoning up his white coat as he entered the room and sat down on the chair by the desk. He started by asking me in Chinese if I spoke Chinese. His only other language was Russian. He laughed. My guard only spoke Chinese. (Normally an interpreter would have been secured from the Public Security Bureau.) The nurse finally revealed that she spoke a little English (I suspected she spoke it quite fluently but for her own safety did not wish to display her knowledge).

After the nurse had told him my temperature, the doctor enquired my trouble. I replied that I suspected cystitis as it was difficult and painful to urinate, and also that I had abdominal pain. I provided him with a urine specimen, which the nurse took away, and then I lay on the couch, half-naked, for the doctor's examination. His hands were ice-cold. He pressed the bladder. Did I feel pain? He looked at my wasted loins. He did not have to tell me that he thought I was in poor shape on my meagre prison diet. Seeing the scars on my stomach, he enquired what operations I had had, and I repeated the formidable list. The nurse by then had returned from the laboratory with the result of the urine test: I had an infection. She was told to admit me into the hospital. And then, looking at me with a smile, the doctor said in Chinese: 'You are lucky to be alive.' I agreed, adding: 'I always choose good doctors.' He made no comment as he filled in a long card to admit me to hospital.

The nurse took me up in the lift to the fourth floor and handed me over to another nurse. A P.L.A. guard came up from the floor below, jangling a bunch of keys. He unlocked the iron-barred door leading into a small ward of five beds, only one of which was occupied (I could not see the patient as he was surrounded by screens). Leading off the ward through another iron-barred gate was an enclosed verandah where half a dozen men were sleeping. The nurse roused one. He got up sleepily and came into the ward. The nurse gave him some directions in Chinese which I did not understand, but when she left the room, the prisoner-nurse (I later learned that this is what he was) gestured me to undress. He fussed around me; brought a hot water bottle; covered me carefully with a quilt after I had changed into unbleached cotton pyjamas and climbed into bed. The mattress was filled with hair, thin and hard, but underneath was a spring mattress which gave to the body. My aged, aching joints appreciated the comfort after the wooden bed of the cell. I wished only to sleep.

A few hours later, the doctor who was to be in charge of my case arrived at the bedside with Poker Face, Beau Brummel and Roly Poly, the interpreter. Poker Face looked concerned.

'Will you give me details of your medical history?' requested the doctor. He looked very businesslike. I have had so many illnesses that I have an instinct for doctors: I felt he knew his job.

I enumerated my many illnesses—three brain operations, a colon resection for cancer, three operations for haemorrhoids, a hernia. The doctor looked astonished, as did the doctor who had earlier admitted me to hospital. He wrote rapidly on the case card, then stopped. There was an animated discussion between him and the security officers.

'What do you like to eat?' There was a softness in the doctor's voice as he put the question.

'I do not mind,' I replied. 'However, I'm allergic to onions and garlic. And sometimes I have digestive trouble if I eat eggs.'

'I will put you on a European diet, which will include milk and fruit.'

I was surprised at this sympathetic treatment and thanked him gratefully.

'Please obey all the doctor's instructions,' ordered Poker Face. The doctor smiled at me as he heard this odd admonition.

'We want to make you fit again,' concluded Poker Face.

They all left the ward.

The prisoner-cooks lived up to the doctor's dietary promise. At lunchtime I was brought a dish of diced lean ham, and vegetables including mashed potatoes. The piping-hot *man tau* were made of white flour, a change from the coarse brown flour of the prison steamed bread. There was an apple and a banana, a bowl of milk with sugar.

I ate with relish, astonished how hungry I was even though I had a slight temperature. The milk (I had not drunk it for years) tasted like nectar. The truth was, I was half-starved.

This diet continued, with a variation at each meal of the main dish, for a fortnight until I was discharged. The prisoner-cooks seemed to enjoy trying to please my palate. (Another time, when I was in hospital on January 1—New Year's day—they cooked three special meals in celebration, taking great care with their arrangement on the plates.) They and the prisoner-nurses seemed unenvious, although their own food of rice porridge for breakfast and rice and vegetables at midday and in the evening continued monotonously. They were pleased to see me eating heartily. Is this Mao's thesis of selflessness in practice?

Only two weeks after my discharge from hospital, however, I had to inform Poker Face at the beginning of the morning interrogation that the renal infection had recurred. The proceedings were immediately suspended, and after a few minutes I was taken to see the doctor.

We drove across Shanghai in the Oldsmobile. It was a warm, sunny spring morning. The streets were filled with people. Even Roly Poly, the interpreter, was sporting a new, dark blue suit and cap, instead of his patched old boiler suit.

The doctor who had been in charge of my case when I was previously in hospital examined me. A laboratory test of my urine was 'positive'. I was admitted again to the hospital; put in the same ward. My prisoner-nurse, whom I have nicknamed 'George', greeted me like an old friend.

All the beds, except the end one against the wall, were now occupied. The next bed was occupied by a sixty-four-year-old, grey-haired Chinese prisoner. Shortly after his arrest a year earlier he had suffered a stroke, paralysing the whole of his left side. (I only learned this because I was to be admitted to the hospital on three more occasions and each time we occupied adjoining beds.) We were separated by a screen, but I used to pull the curtain back an inch or so and have a look at him, and give him a word of encouragement. His case, I assume a political offence, was still being investigated. Every morning at nine o'clock he was lifted out of bed by two prisoner-nurses, placed on a stretcher and carried off to a room for interrogation. Except for a break of two hours at noon, when he was fed by a prisoner-nurse, the 'grilling' continued until five-thirty. It meant he was questioned each day except Sundays for six and a half hours. There is little pity in China for those who are sick.

On the third day after this admission to hospital the doctor arrived at my bedside with Poker Face and the interpreter, who was carrying my old Corona typewriter.

'Do you feel well enough to type a statement of what you have confessed during the past fortnight?' asked Poker Face. (Every word that I uttered during interrogation was recorded in Chinese. It was then translated back into English. But I also had to write my own version of what I had said periodically, to see if there were any discrepancies which might give the security officers a clue as to the truth of my story.)

I replied that I thought I was well enough to type the statement, and I turned to the doctor for his confirmation. He agreed with me: of course, he had already talked it over with the security police.

A prisoner-nurse brought a small table to my bedside, and the officers left the typewriter, paper and carbons on it. My daily typing intrigued everyone in the ward. Some had obviously never seen a western typewriter before. Prisoner-nurses crowded round the bed fascinated. Even the regular female nurses, when they came to give me medicine or take my temperature, tarried for a few minutes. One, who was slightly more friendly than the others, even gestured for me to explain how it worked. I indicated that she should try it, and she did for a few seconds, though it was dangerous for her as no one was allowed to fraternise with me.

On my fifth night in hospital a patient in the next bed but one died. As the iron-barred door of the ward was locked, the prisoner-nurse who had been sitting by his bedside walked to a window looking out on to the corridor and shouted something in Chinese. The P.L.A. guard came and unlocked the door. The prisoner-nurse went out to report the death to the night-duty nurse. He returned, awakened another prisoner-nurse sleeping on the verandah, and they left the ward together to return in a few minutes with a stretcher. They had donned ankle-length blue gowns and skull caps.

There was no certifying clinical death by a doctor or nurse. There was no laying out, no washing of the body, no wrapping it in a shroud. The earthly remains of the old man were dumped on the stretcher. Eerily, in the stillness of the night, the body was carried down the dimly lit staircase to the mortuary.

The next day two more patients in the ward died. Their remains received the same macabre treatment.

A few days later an old, emaciated man was brought into one of the spare beds. He was dying of cancer of the throat. He could not swallow, nor could a rubber tube be put down his throat to feed him. He was given intravenous injections. All day he lay in a half-coma.

On the third morning after his arrival two men came into the ward and set up two arc lights on each side of his bed. A third arrived with a Rolleiflex camera. Two prisoner-nurses propped him up, bare to the waist, his ribs showing through almost transparent skin. One of the men slung a black placard around his neck on which were written some white Chinese characters. A nurse came along and insisted that his thin body be covered with a pyjama jacket. A prisoner-nurse fetched one. The placard was removed, the jacket put on, the placard again slung round the semi-conscious old man's neck. The arc lights were switched on, blinding the old man. He blinked his eyes. The photographer took three shots. Then the placard was removed, the old man laid down again, his head on the hard pillow filled with rice.

I never discovered the meaning of this extraordinary scene. The placard probably exposed his crimes.

I had little appetite for my midday meal that day, and after I had eaten it I went to sleep. When I awoke the old man's bed was empty; the mattress taken away for fumigating. There was a smell of disinfectant from under the bed where the concrete floor had been washed. The old man had passed over.

A few days later a prisoner-nurse came to the foot of my bed. With a big smile on his face, he threw his arms up in the air and pretended to collapse on the floor. I could not understand this charade until he pointed towards the next ward. Then I realised that a patient must have had a heart attack and died. A few minutes later I saw the macabre procession to the mortuary through the corridor window.

Within three days two more patients died of heart attacks.

The sick prisoners in the adjoining ward all had tuberculosis. Yet, in spite of their ill-health, for an hour each morning and afternoon they would hold Mao Thought meetings, reciting aloud long quotations from the works of the Great Leader.

Only once before in my life had I been present at the bedside of a person who died. It upset me emotionally for many days. (This perhaps was not surprising as it was someone whom I loved very much and yet she had died quite peacefully.) But in the prison hospital I became quite callous towards death. Life in China has always been cheap. Under atheist Maoism death is final.

However, I used to awaken in the night in the hospital and think that perhaps I, too, would one day be carried off on the stretcher, borne to the mortuary by the sinister-looking, long-gowned prisoner-nurses. It was not that I was afraid of death. It just seemed a lonely way to leave this world.

Soon after my arrest I presented a note to my interrogator, on which I had written that in the event of my death I should like my body to be cremated and my ashes flown to England for burial. I gave the address of my daughter and said that she in conjunction with the British Mission in Peking would defray the expenses. The interrogator seemed rather taken aback.

'Are you afraid of death?' he asked.

'No. But I am afraid that I might again have paralysis as I did before my brain tumour operation. If I die, will you carry out my request?'

'Yes.' He folded up the piece of paper and put it in his pocket.

'My testament for the disposal of my property is among my papers.'

The interrogator made no comment. The testament had been confiscated with all my other papers.

The striving to reach Mao's ideals of selflessness and the elimination of class, was revealed in the hospital routine.

The case boards of the patients—on my floor there were

nearly a hundred, mostly suffering from tuberculosis—were kept on a heavy trolley which the doctor himself pushed on his morning round of the wards. By performing physical labour, the doctor was being politically transformed. No prisoner-nurse would offer to push the trolley for him. It was the same if the doctor was a woman. I remember that my own doctor in hospital at the end of 1968 was a very short, frail-built young woman, whose head was only just above the trolley as she pushed it along the corridor. It required all her strength, and yet no one ever offered to help her.

The doctors on their rounds were never accompanied by a nurse. If the treatment was changed, the doctor would write it on the case board. The sole work of the regular nurses was to deliver medicines to the patients, give injections, take temperatures and blood pressures.

With the exception of one, all the professional nurses hated me, I assume because of the intense anti-foreign propaganda during the Cultural Revolution. To the nurses I was an imperialist spy. Every injection they gave me—at one period four a day—they made into a death of a thousand cuts. They seemed to delight in hurting me unnecessarily—either by not putting the needle sufficiently deep into the flesh or injecting the fluid too quickly. They disapproved of my special food.

Basically, I think, the women of China are more pro-Maoist than the men. The explanation probably lies in the fact that Mao has given them equality of status with men. As early as 1927, Mao wrote: 'A man in China is usually subjected to the domination of three systems of authority (political authority, clan authority and religious authority) . . . As for women, in addition to being dominated by these three systems of authority, they are also dominated by the men (the authority of the husband).' Mao called these four authorities the 'thick ropes' binding the women. But in 1955, he decreed: 'Men and women must receive equal pay for equal work in production. Genuine equality between the sexes can only be realised in the process of the socialist transformation of society as a whole.'

In the hospital all the bedpan chores, the washing of patients incapable of doing it themselves, the cleaning of the wards, was performed by the untrained prisoner-nurses. Towards me, they were always kind and considerate. A young, former ballet dancer often patted me on the leg in the morning, sympathetically whispering in English: 'How are you this morning?' He was not supposed to speak to me. Brave man.

And yet, towards the old man who was paralysed they often acted inhumanly. Because of his paralysis he often spilled on his bed urine from the bottle. The prisoner-nurses became infuriated because they had to change the bed-linen. They severely reprimanded him. One of them hit on the idea of tying his good right leg and arm to the bed. In consequence, he was completely immobilised and must have suffered much pain in the fettered limbs.

When I left the hospital the second time I went round the screen that divided us. I was taking a risk because I was not supposed to have contact with the other patients. I shook his good right hand and whispered in his ear: 'Have courage.' Tears welled up in his eyes and rolled down his cheeks: mine may have been the first soft words spoken to him since he was taken by the Secret Police from his house in the dead of night.

George, my prisoner-nurse, was serving a long sentence. He proudly showed me photographs of his wife and two daughters, whom he would not see for another two years, since they were not permitted to visit him. (I saw no evidence that prisoners ever receive visits from their families.) It makes me happy to know that George will be reunited with his family by the time this book is published. I could write a great deal more about him, his family, where he lived and worked, his 'crime', but I refrain from doing so for fear that he might be identified and subjected to reprisals for fraternising with a foreigner.

The paralysed old man, George the prisoner-nurse . . . these strange Chinese people, with whom one has difficulty in establishing any real kind of rapport, nevertheless have a human side. They fall in love; they marry; they mourn. I have often wondered how much difference there really is basically between them and all other people.

10 The Neroni Mystery Solved

ONE afternoon in March, 1969, when I had just completed my first year in prison (how many more, I wondered, would follow?), the guard opened the trap in my cell door. He indicated that I should give him my magazines—all of them. I was upset. If your reading material is limited, you can re-read a dozen times without becoming bored.

A little later, however, to my relief, the trap opened again, and the guard pushed through a fresh supply of magazines. As they were out-of-date issues, I assumed he had exchanged mine for another prisoner's.

I did not look at them all immediately. Reading matter must be rationed to specified hours each day.

Some days passed. I picked up a copy of *China Pictorial*. The coloured picture on the back cover caught my eye, and then I began to flick the pages over backwards. After turning two or three pages I noticed handwriting over the print. I turned another page: two more pages of handwriting, in English. But in the left-hand margin were a few words in Italian. I turned over the next page and came to what proved to be the beginning of a confession. It was a draft. In seconds, I realised it must have been written by Neroni, since it contained certain details of his life which he had told me while we were fellow passengers.

I read the confession through to the end. It was an astonishing document. Neroni confessed to working for the Central Intelligence Agency, and he revealed details of his recruitment in Japan, his assignment, his salary.

If several months had not elapsed since my own case appeared to have been closed, I would have regarded this as a plant.

But as I studied the 'confession' carefully, the faulty English, the deletions, I became convinced of its genuineness. I recognised, too, his handwriting.

It was an amazing slip-up of security that this magazine should have been allowed to fall into my hands. Why had Neroni not destroyed it?

I considered tearing out the pages myself and flushing them down the toilet with water from my bowl, but if I did and the magazine was examined, the missing pages might be noticed. I decided to hide the whole magazine, with one or two others, among my spare clothing. Perhaps when I left the prison I might be allowed to take the magazines with me. (I was not. All the reading matter in my cell was confiscated. I wonder if the Neroni draft confession was discovered?)

By the time I was freed I was convinced that Neroni had been released or transferred to another prison, though I had no certain knowledge. It was a matter of deduction, based on events over a period of twenty-four hours.

One morning, about two months after I discovered Neroni's draft 'confession', I heard the key inserted in the padlock of my door, the bolt pulled back. I got up. The P.L.A. guard entered the cell, indicating that I was to pack up all my belongings, including my bedding. I was transferred to a cell at the far end of the building. It was the most dismal cell in the prison because the window was partially covered by the latrine in the courtyard. It was filthy dirty, the floor and bed covered with thick dust. It had obviously not been occupied for a long while. I was very depressed because I had grown accustomed to the cell from which I was now being removed: I had occupied it for nearly a year all told.

I asked for a broom to clean up the new cell. As I swept, I pondered the reason for my transfer. Were the Chinese making a new attempt to break my spirit? It seemed illogical, for I had been allowed to remain in hospital over Christmas, the New Year and the cold month of January when snow on many days lay on the ground six inches deep.

At 3.00 p.m. the next afternoon I was taken out for exercise —the first time for ten days. On my return to the cell, the guard ordered me to pack up my belongings again. It was infuriating when I had spent all the previous day cleaning the new cell. I was taken back to my old cell.

The whole operation did not seem to make sense. I went over the cell very carefully, examining the walls, under the beds. Nothing seemed to have been disturbed. There was no evidence that a new microphone had been hidden in the wall—I had already been suspicious of two or three patches in the walls that had a hollow sound when tapped, and I assumed that the cell was bugged to tape a prisoner talking to himself.

That night I think I solved the mystery. For the first night since I had moved to the cell I heard no snoring from the adjoining cell. And I never heard it again. (Neroni snored heavily the nights we shared a cabin on the *Hanoi*.)

A few days later the next-door cell was occupied by a prisoner speaking Chinese. I could hear him conversing with the guard. It was additional proof that whoever had been occupying the cell had left.

Why should I have been transferred for a single night? There seemed only one explanation. If Neroni was occupying the next cell, he had been removed during the night. To ensure that I did not see him it would have been necessary for the guard to close the observation trap in my door (these traps were customarily left open at night). This would have awoken me. I should then have heard the door of the next cell being opened, and I might have heard enough to identify the occupant coming out.

On the train journey to Canton I asked my guards: 'Has Mr Anthony Grey been released from house custody in Peking?'

The senior officer hesitated before replying: 'Unofficially, I can say yes.'

'And Captain Neroni?'

Silence.

11 Journey to Freedom

SLEEPILY I sit up on the hard board-bed, automatically checking the time by my friendly star's alignment with the centre bar of the high window. I judge it to be about midnight; I must have been asleep for four hours.

The grey, dreary prison is monastically quiet. Then a warder on the floor above clears his throat, a sound like tearing calico. A sharp, metallic ring as phlegm hits metal tells me his aim is off; he hit the edge. I find it difficult, even after months of imprisonment, not to be revolted by the incessant spitting. It is like living in a tuberculosis sanatorium.

I settle back to seek sleep again, pulling the shabby blue cotton quilt around my ears. The northerly October wind from the open window is chill.

An unexpected noise brings me sharply awake. The observation trap in my door has been closed. The key grates metallically in the padlock. I sit up, suddenly colder than even an autumn wind could make me.

At this hour a few months earlier a prisoner was taken from his cell and shot. After my trap was closed that night, I had heard shuffling feet in the central hall of the prison, the clink of a chain as it dragged along the cement floor. (The chain linked the manacled wrists and ankles of the prisoner; I had seen them hanging on a hook at the entrance of the cell block.) The condemned prisoner passed out of the building; there was an ominous quiet. Then three shots in quick succession, followed by a fourth after an interval of about fifteen seconds. It had presumably been fired by the officer in charge of the firing squad to ensure that the doomed man was dead. A few minutes later the security guard reopened the trap in my cell door.

It is thirteen months since I last faced interrogation, fifty-five weeks of worry and apprehension, 560,240 minutes, most of them awake, of dreariness, deprivation and gnawing uncertainty.

The bolt of the cell door is slammed back with a clang that echoes through the building. The two-inch wooden door opens. The expected warder is not there in the dim light but an officer of the security police, a stranger to me, who, with peremptory gestures, orders me to dress. I stagger to my feet.

Nervously I fumble with the buttons of my silk and polyester shirt. Impatiently the officer indicates that I must hurry. I pull on my trousers, two sizes too big due to a near-starvation diet. I have lost forty pounds in weight in twenty months.

What, I wonder, is to be my fate now? For the first time since my imprisonment, I am thoroughly frightened. My hackles rise.

I walk out into the hall, follow the security officer through the central doorway and across the courtyard to the one-storey 'confessional' building.

Inside the 'confessional' the security officer gestures me to sit down in the wood-and-iron chair. Already seated behind the desk is a young, pleasant-faced officer—also a stranger to me. He is the interpreter.

The officer who has awakened me walks around the desk and sits down on the centre chair. The interpreter hands him a thickly-bound file. The officer begins to flick over the pages. I notice that they are each signed and thumb-printed by me. It is my thirteen-month-old 'confession'. Thousands of words.

There is a long pause while the officer reads passages of the file. I am intrigued. The interrogation, I assume, is beginning all over again. (I recall that after my arrest the officer in charge of my case warned me that unless I confessed all my crimes the interrogation would go on for six months, a year, two years, or longer, and might even be resumed after I was sentenced.) And, yet, if my case is being reopened, why is there no note-taker? These and many other thoughts flash through my mind. Even though it is the early hours of the morning, my mind is fully alert. The sense of danger has vanished; I am calm. I wait expectantly.

The officer stops examining the 'confession'. From his grey tunic pocket he takes out his plastic red-bound volume of *Quotations from Chairman Mao Tse-tung*. Normal procedure. He opens the little book, finds the passage he wants to read. The interpreter, in a stern but respectful voice, intones in English the familiar passage: 'All reactionaries are paper tigers. In appearance, the reactionaries are terrifying, but in reality they are not so powerful. From a long-term point of view, it is not the reactionaries but the people who are really powerful.'

The interrogator looks at me icily. A long minute's silence; then the simple, harsh question: 'What have you been thinking these days?'

I counter with a question: 'When is my case to be settled?'

The officer does not reply but continues: 'What have you been thinking about your crimes?'

'I regret that I infringed the Whangpoo River regulations relating to photography. But I must emphasise, as I did more than a year ago, that no restrictions were imposed upon me with regard to photography. Further, my China Travel Service guide said it was not necessary to have my exposed film developed before I left China.'

'Do you repent your crimes?'

'If you are referring to the photographs I took of the war-ships, the answer is "Yes".' (I remember that only if you profess repentance can you expect mercy.)

The interrogator, a short man with a beak nose, starts to flick over the pages of my 'confession' again. He finds the page he wants. Another question . . . another question . . . another question. An hour passes. But none of the questions relate to espionage—the charge on which I was imprisoned. I still cannot fathom if my case is being reopened. All the questions have been asked a hundred, perhaps a thousand times before. I have answered them all in the greatest detail. It is puzzling.

The mood of the interrogator changes. He speaks softly now.

'How is your health?'

It is an odd question; out of context. Why so solicitous?

'Not very good,' I reply.

'What are your troubles?'

'As you are no doubt aware, I have been suffering from acute stomach and abdominal pains after meals for many months. They are due to a continuous diet of pork. A long while ago the doctor ordered that I must not eat pork, but my diet has remained unchanged. However, I have been prescribed some new medicine, which seems to be helping.'

'Do you think we have taken good care of your health?'

'From the medical point of view, yes. But I am underweight and suffering from malnutrition. I asked to be permitted to buy milk to supplement my low diet. The request was refused.'

By now I am wondering, why this new line of questioning? May I begin to hope? In solitary confinement you examine every nuance of your situation. Certain happenings in recent months take on a new significance; perhaps clues to my early release. There has been an increase in the number of spot-checks of my cell; greater concern about my health, the doctor prescribing vitamins; a perceptible softening in the attitude of the unarmed People's Liberation Army prison guards; frequent visits to my cell by the interpreter, quizzing me about what I write each day with a Chinese-made Hero fountain-pen (copy of a Parker 51) on stiff, brown toilet paper; and on one occasion he even brought me a large tablet of perfumed toilet soap and four sachets of hair shampoo. The warder-barber, I recall, was particularly careful on the last occasion, even neatly trimming my moustache. At the time I did not give it a second thought because he was always considerate, especially about the bone-less section on the right side of my head. I have no idea whether the Chinese journalists detained in Hong Kong without trial since the riots of 1967 have been released; I have always regarded myself as a sort of hostage for them, in spite of the espionage charge made against me.

'What have we done for you medically?' continues the interrogator.

'I have been in hospital five times—three times for a renal infection, and for a long period last winter to investigate a possible recurrence of cancer, for which I had a colon re-section some years ago, and high blood pressure.'

The interrogation is slow because the security officer is writing the questions and answers down in Chinese himself.

'What about the operation we performed?'

I am puzzled. 'What operation?'

'The operation for the soft tumour on your back.'

'I am sorry. I had forgotten it as it was so long ago.'

[The tumour became infected a few weeks after my imprisonment. The surgeon operated on it with a local anaesthetic in the out-patients clinic of the Ward Road prison hospital. The operation was efficiently performed with properly sterilised instruments, though the clinic and its furnishings were very dirty, and the room was full of people who crowded round the doctor, looking over his shoulders as he made the incision. The doctor had seemed quite unconcerned by this audience of female nurses, male prisoner-nurses and a few Chinese prisoners waiting their turn to consult the doctor.

This rubber-necking was consistent with everyday life in Red China—a life in which everyone participates on terms of what they regard as equality. It is this sense of participation which is helping to make Mao's philosophy of a selfless nation begin to work. The doctor who was operating on me would not have dared to have told the onlookers to stand back.

Crowds in the street will gather around to quiz a motor-car that has stopped to permit an official to alight. China is a dictatorship of the proletariat. Everybody interprets this literally. The official's motor-car belongs to the people; they have every right to inspect it, even to opening a door to have a look inside. The official or driver will not demur. It is all very friendly.]

The interrogator goes on writing. A third officer, dressed in the khaki uniform of the People's Liberation Army, enters the room and takes the vacant seat. It is obvious by his demenaour that he is a senior officer, although like all P.L.A. officers there are no badges of rank on his uniform. Without speaking, the interrogator indicates that I should stand up. He pushes the notes across the desk. He speaks to the interpreter, who translates:

'Sign it.'

'It is customary,' I reply, 'to sign the Chinese text only after it has been translated into English.'

'You may accept as accurate my note of the interview.'

There seems no point in pursuing this aspect of what has been an unusual procedure. I am at a loss to understand it.

I pick up his fountain-pen and sign the first five pages. I am signing the sixth and final page as the interrogator says through the interpreter: 'Write, "This is my confession and it is accurate." '

I do not complain, although there was nothing in this statement which could be construed as a 'confession'. No mention had been made of the allegations that I was a spy.

He is pushing a red ink pad across the desk.

'Put your right thumb-print on each page.'

This is normal procedure. The hundreds of pages in Chinese and English I have thumb-printed since my arrest will be stored away by the Chinese Communists in their normal, meticulous fashion. Nothing is forgotten. The spoken or written word, innocent at the time, can be unearthed and used to damn you ten, twenty, thirty or more years later. I was often amazed by the resurrection of statements made by Mao's enemies during the Cultural Revolution. Everything is recorded; you can never escape your past.

I thumb-print the pages.

The officers rise. We leave the room. In the corridor, as I walk back to the cell, I overhear a Chinese prisoner being grilled in another confessional room. Poor devil!

My cell door closes. The bolt clangs. I undress, walk across to the window, check the time by my star. Two hours of the night, I estimate, have slipped away. I lie down on my hard bed, pulling the quilt over me. My brain is still alert. I do not fall asleep immediately. My mind goes back a few days to October 1, China's National Day, and the twentieth anniversary of Mao's takeover.

*   *   *

'Wansui!' ... *'Wansui!'* ... *'Wansui!'* ...

Shouts of adulation burst with ear-splitting noise from the prison loudspeakers. Mao, I assumed, had mounted the rostrum over the gate of Tien An Men Square (the Gate of Heavenly Peace) in Peking. Acclamation continued for fully ten minutes of mass hysteria from the hundreds of thousands of mesmerised soldiers of the People's Liberation Army, industrial workers, peasants from communes and school children assembled below the gate.

Wansui means 'long live'—literally 'ten thousand years'—and is the traditional salute to the Emperor. It is a synonym for Emperor. Today, ever-smiling, hand-clapping Mao, in his cult of personality, is Emperor of China and father of his 750,000,000 (perhaps 800,000,000) subjects, labouring like ants to make their country the most formidable in the world.

Over the loudspeakers came Lin Paio's anniversary address. He spoke with a firm voice, belying western rumours that he is a sick man. I could never obtain a satisfactory explanation as to why Lin makes the National Day speech and not Mao himself. My interpreter's explanation that 'Lin Piao speaks on behalf of Chairman Mao' was not very convincing: to me it would have seemed logical for Mao to choose this important day to address all the people of China. Perhaps his habitual silence—although he is supposed to have delivered two important speeches at the 9th Congress in Peking in the spring of 1969—makes him a more mystical figure in the eyes of China's millions.

But for me, today, the first of the month, had another significance. From its secret hiding place in the second volume of Mao's works I slipped out my toilet-paper pack of playing cards. Jeannine, a young girl from Brittany who had inherited all the superstitions of the Celts, once taught me how to tell fortunes by cards. On the first of every month since my imprisonment, I had played this fortune-telling game. It may sound crazy for an aged journalist to indulge in superstition. But the forecasts for Jeannine always proved accurate; they have done over the years for myself, including predicting some small events during my imprisonment.

Every month to my question: 'Shall I be freed this month?' the answer had been negative. On September 1, it had been the most definite negative under this system—not a single card could be moved. For twenty-four hours I had been very depressed at the thought of another winter in an unheated cell, or even another summer of Shanghai's steaming heat. I had almost decided not to indulge in my superstitious practice again.

On this morning, October 1, however, I could not resist the temptation to entrust my immediate fate to the cards once more.

I played the game while Lin Piao was making his speech. Because the cards were only of paper and too thin to shuffle, I laid them out face down and picked them up one by one at random. My nerves were steady as I played the game. It was going very smoothly. Yet, with every move, I was braced for another negative answer. To my astonishment, it worked out to the most positive 'Yes'. My spirits soared. For the whole day I remained confident that I should be released this month.

I waken at about five o'clock in the morning following my surprise midnight interrogation. It is Thursday, October 9, 1969. Against regulations, I get up, pace the cell floor. I speculate again about the meaning of the curious procedure at midnight. Perhaps because of the forecast by the cards nine days earlier, I have an inner feeling that I am to be released. After being alone for 584 days, I conjecture what it will be like to be with my fellow men again. I have long reached the conclusion that man can only enjoy life when sharing it with someone else.

A warder is looking through the Judas window. He signals me to go back to bed. I do so with reluctance. Nine hours lying on a hard wooden bed is not a luxury, it is a penance. My aging bones have never come to terms with the boards.

A few minutes later the bell to get up echoes through the building. Five-twenty. The warder slams the window shut. I take off my underclothes, standing naked to the chill autumn breeze coming through the window. The temperature is not too bad but I wonder how many more days will pass before it will be freezing from an icy wind blowing across the country from the Himalayas? I give myself my daily cold sponge bath. My morning physical exercises are exhilarating. I dress; kneel and say my morning prayers.

It is seven o'clock. My bottle of ink has not been delivered by the warder. This is unusual. Everything today seems unusual. I eat two *man taus*, which I saved from last evening's meal. Breakfast is an hour off. But this morning I do not feel hungry. My body is tense with an inner excitement. I long for freedom; to travel. I remember how, many months before, while still being grilled, I comforted myself with the thought that one day I should be free to go where I pleased; my interrogators would always have to remain here. They would never know anything of the outside world. Mao would give them three meals a day, moderate homely comforts. But their minds, their bodies, their souls would always be his prisoners.

Again the key grates in my lock; the bolt slams back. I tense even more. It is rare for the cell door to be opened at this early hour. It has happened, so far as I can recollect, only once before: to take a shower.

The P.L.A. warder opens the door, gesticulates with his hands for me to pack up my belongings, but not my two quilts. I then guess I am leaving the prison. On the three previous occasions when I was transferred to another cell I took my bedding with me. The warder leaves me, closing the door, replacing the bolt but not the padlock. But, of course, the Chinese authorities may be transferring me to another prison.

I put all my clothes in a pile; empty the water from my two wash basins and also from my two cups. In one is secreted an enamel spoon which I stole months earlier when in hospital. (To eat you are allowed only bamboo chopsticks, hygienic but impractical when grappling with a piece of pork.) In my haste I pour the spoon with the water down the toilet. Pity. I should have liked it as a souvenir.

Thirty minutes elapse. The door again opens. Outside in the

hall is the security police interrogator of the previous night. He beckons me to follow him. My cell is next to the main entrance to the cell block. To the left is the admittance room with its high desk and an iron-reinforced chair for the prisoner. We enter the room on the right.

On the table is an apparatus for finger-printing. An officer is waiting, together with a photographer using a Nikon F camera (presumably China's copy of a pre-war Leica is not considered good enough for official use).

I am finger-printed, the photographer continually clicking the shutter. The whole operation takes nearly ten minutes because many sets of finger-prints are required as well as prints of my palms. The security officer seems impatient, continuously looking at his wrist watch. My hands are heavily stained with black printers' ink. I try unsuccessfully to wipe them clean on a piece of cloth.

The interrogating officer leads me out into the courtyard, and along to what I long ago dubbed the 'grand committee room'.

In the centre of the room is a small, square table. On one side of the table, facing the prisoner's chair, an officer is sitting; he appears to be an important man. He is wearing P.L.A. uniform, but his demeanour indicates authority. Sitting on his left is the interpreter of the night séance. The interrogator who has brought me from the cell and waited while the finger-printing is done, sits down in the third chair. I am told to sit in the wood-and-iron chair, but the bar which is normally put across the arms is left dangling down the side.

On the table is lying a single document. The senior officer sternly orders me to stand up. 'Bow your head,' he says. He rises, begins to read in Chinese in a solemn voice. The interpreter translates, sentence by sentence.

I am surprised that there is no preliminary reading from the *Quotations from Chairman Mao*. The first words are a clear indication that a decision has been reached in my case. But there is no clue whether I have been found guilty and am to serve a further sentence of imprisonment.

A wave of excitement passes through my body—exhilaration

tempered with apprehension because the officer announces that I have been found guilty of spying, a charge which in China carries with it the death sentence or a long term of imprisonment. Through my mind flashes the recollection that George Watt, a British engineer, is already serving a three-year sentence for espionage.* I do not know if he is in my prison. I have never seen another foreign prisoner, although my interrogator once told me that there were other foreigners, including Englishmen, in the prison on charges of spying. If I am to be transferred to another prison to serve my sentence, it may be to Ward Road, where many Chinese are serving sentences for political crimes. On one of my many visits to see the doctor at the prison hospital, I had deduced that some foreigners were in this prison. My mind is a mass of conjecture.

The officer continues to read the sentence. From his lips come the ominous words: '. . . you have confessed your towering crimes against the People's Republic of China . . . you have confessed to slandering Chairman Mao . . . you have confessed to slandering Chiang Ching . . . you have confessed to collecting military, economic and political information for intelligence purposes . . . you have confessed to photographing military objects.'

Superficially these words may spell disaster for me. But I allow myself to hope, knowing the importance that the Chinese attach to confession.

The officer is saying: 'You have changed your attitude.' This Communist jargon is significant—almost a definite forecast of my release, presumably deportation under armed guard. It had happened to the captain and first officer of British ships a year ago. My spirits soar. Again comes the English interpretation: 'Chairman Mao shows leniency towards those who confess; to those who change their attitude.' I wait only a fraction of a second to have my hopes confirmed. 'You are to be expelled from the People's Republic of China.'

Tears are beginning to well up in my eyes. I steel myself against emotion. I must maintain my dignity, as I have tried to do for these past twenty months. But I cannot quell the

* He was released by the Chinese in August, 1970.

buoyancy of my heart; the inner relief that my ordeal is over. By some strange process of the mind I am straightway able to cast off the feeling of being a prisoner. I feel on terms of equality with the officers in front of me.

As jubilant thoughts and emotions crowd my mind the officer is saying:

'What would you like to do?'

The question surprises me.

'What may I do?' I ask. 'There is the problem of transportation. If I am to proceed to Hong Kong or Singapore, I assume I must travel by ship. You refused me twenty months ago permission to go to Hong Kong by train because, I assume, you did not wish me to see the countryside. A passage by ship will take a few days to arrange. May I stay in the Peace Hotel while this is being fixed up?'

I detect a new confidence in my voice. I feel that I am again master of my own fate. Only a few seconds ago I was a prisoner; now I am a free man.

The officers listen in silence. The senior officer then says to the interpreter: 'You are to be taken immediately to the Hong Kong border.' The previous question was an irrelevant gesture of courtesy without sincerity.

The officer is pushing the document across the table: 'Sign it,' he commands. I do so with my Hero fountain-pen—the pen with which I have signed my name hundreds of times on the bottom of pages of 'confessions'.

The interrogating officer of the previous night is looking nervously at his watch.

'When do we leave?' I ask.

'We are going immediately to Shanghai railway station,' he replies.

Into the room guards come carrying my belongings from the cell and two suitcases which have been in store. As I am trying to pack my things there is the utmost confusion. Everyone is trying to help me. As I have been forced to buy many things while in prison, I appreciate that I am not going to get them all in my suitcases. There is the problem of two enamel basins and two enamel cups. Where do I pack these?

'I have no more use for these articles,' I say. 'Please give them to someone who needs them.'

The security officer says I must take them with me, presumably because I have paid for them.

(I recall a curious incident over my bowls and cups only a fortnight ago. A warder came to my cell and tried to take a bowl and a cup away from me. He could not speak English but with hand gestures I indicated that they were my own property, that I had paid for them. I took from my jacket pocket the prison account for my money on which was recorded all my purchases. The warder studied it carefully for several minutes and then, I thought, left the cell rather crestfallen. Had the decision to release me already been taken?)

I take a blue canvas cover with a zip fastener off one of my suitcases and put the bowls and cups in it. I pick up my toilet paper and try to hand it to a warder. I must take this too. I have paid for it.

To the relief of the security officer and the interpreter who are to accompany me, everything at last is packed. Actually, it has taken only a few minutes, but it has seemed longer, partly because the officer every minute or so looks impatiently at his wrist watch.

The interpreter explains that my cameras—three Leicas, a telephoto lens and a wide-angle lens—have been confiscated. So, too, have all my papers—letter files, carbon copies of articles written over the past several years, the research material for two books that for several years I have been planning to write, a folder containing personal photographs, including my father and mother—long since dead—and my daughter, through her childhood years. It is sad. They are irreplaceable.

I examine the contents of my briefcase. I am told that my money will be returned at the frontier. I enquire about my return K.L.M. air ticket to Europe. It has been confiscated.

'Where is my portable typewriter?'

'What do you use it for?'

'I am a writer. I use it for my work.'

'You use it, too, to write your intelligence reports. You cannot have it back.'

It is futile to argue. But I bought that small Corona type-writer nearly fifty years ago when I began my career as a journalist; and one of my Leica cameras—a model ɪɪ—was nearly forty years old, a museum piece, which I had always regarded as a lucky talisman.

Warders pick up my suitcases and the canvas cover containing my washing bowls and cups, towels and Chinese cotton-fleece underclothes. We cross the courtyard and through the first gateway. Overhead I notice that the time is nine-fifteen. I have not had an opportunity to wind and set my gold wrist watch (this had been returned to me, together with my gold heirloom ring and the gilt Royal Air Force buttons of my blazer).

In the next courtyard is the 1948 Oldsmobile, waiting to take us to the Shanghai railway station. I have grown to have an affection for this car.

The off-duty warders, wives and children excitedly follow. They surround the car, gesticulating, talking animatedly. My departure on this beautiful, sunny morning makes an exciting diversion in their humdrum lives.

My belongings are stowed in the boot of the car. Holding open a rear door for me to enter is a warder who came to the prison about three months ago. He is about forty-eight years of age, short, with closely cropped, crinkly grey hair. There was little within the regulations which he could do to alleviate the harshness of my prison regime, and yet he did display some friendliness towards me, even if he never spoke a single word. His demeanour was different from that of the younger P.L.A. guards, though he was obviously a staunch Communist in the Maoist sense.

I step into the car. The warder looks into my eyes. There is not a flicker in them and yet his eyes seem to be congratulating me on going home. (Perhaps I am being sentimental. I have always had an affection for the Chinese; I have always got on well with them, and they with me.) This gesture of kindness touches a chord. Any bitterness in my heart vanishes. To forgive washes away resentment.

The security officer gets into the back of the car with me,

and a third officer climbs in on my left. I have never seen him before but he is obviously the senior officer. The interpreter sits beside the driver. The crowd of warders, wives and children stand back. It is almost a royal send-off. The car begins to move. We drive through the inner gate and along the tree-lined avenue to the outer gate. An armed P.L.A. guard—the only man other than the exercise-watcher in the prison to carry a gun— opens the green iron gates. I glance back for my last view of the grim, grey-brick prison. We pass out into the street. As usual, there are a crowd of children by the prison gate who press their snub noses against the windows as the car pauses for traffic. Their eyes light up when they see that one of the occupants is a 'long nose'. The driver blows his horn to clear them away. We turn left and speed off down the crowded narrow street of shops, with trees on each side, leading out of the former French concession.

I enquire from the interpreter what time the train is due to leave for Canton. He replies: 'Nine-fifty.'

'It is strange,' I add, 'that when I applied twenty months ago for a visa to travel by train from Shanghai to Hong Kong it was refused. Why did you not take me by air today? Then I should have seen nothing of the country.'

'We considered taking you by air,' replied the interpreter, 'but the doctors advised against it because of your high blood pressure.'

'But the cabins of aircraft are pressurised.'

'We thought it safer to take you by train.'

At the station there is an orderly bustle. I am taken to a large waiting room with leather upholstered armchairs. It is obviously reserved for foreign visitors and perhaps high-level Chinese officials. The senior officer of my guard goes off with my passport and the identity cards of the other two officers. He returns with four small documents, presumably our travel permits. It is now nine-forty. We walk to the platform. There is nothing in the attitude of the three guards to indicate that I am a prisoner. In a sense, I am walking alone, the guards being a courtesy escort.

A long, three-deep, orderly queue is passing through the

platform gate. They stop to allow us to pass through, but no one appears to show much interest in me. Perhaps they recognise my guards, who are wearing very ill-fitting khaki P.L.A. uniforms, as members of the Secret Police.

We pass down the platform. I recall walking down this same platform forty-five years ago to the strains of a Chinese warlord's army band which followed behind me playing the Japanese national anthem.

[I had an appointment with Chang Chung-chang, a general who had just captured Shanghai on behalf of the notorious General Chang Tso-lin, the ruler in those days of Manchuria and much of Northern China. On that morning, Chang Chung-chang had an appointment too, with the Japanese Consul-General. When I arrived at the gate of the platform the Chinese officer in charge of the guard of honour and the band mistook me for the Japanese Consul, although I did not remotely resemble a Japanese diplomat, being only twenty-four years of age. The guard presented arms, the band struck up the national anthem. Ceremoniously, I was escorted to General Chang Chung-chang's Pullman coach. What happened when the Japanese Consul-General arrived an hour later I shall never know. The only thing I can recall from the interview was that the general was accompanied by four of his wives, including his first wife. 'But she is old now,' said the general. 'I never sleep with her.']

We are walking nearly to the head of the train. The hard-seat carriages in which the proletariat are travelling are speedily filling up. We pass the dining-car and get into the next carriage along. A four-berth sleeping compartment is reserved for us. It is made up for day travel, the two upper berths being folded back against the wall. The compartment is immaculately clean, snow-white antimacassars protecting the blue upholstery. A porter stows my luggage under the seat. My guards each have only a small, grey cloth bag. These bags are part of the security police uniform equipment, used to carry files of cases and interrogation notes. I have never seen a member of the Public Security Bureau without one.

As soon as we are seated, I take off my gold wrist watch,

wind it and check the time with the watch of the interpreter. It is nine forty-nine.

The interpreter enquires the make of my watch—a Japanese Seiko.

'Japanese watches do not keep accurate time,' he comments. 'Chinese watches are very accurate.'

He takes his own off his wrist and hands it to me to inspect. It has a stainless steel case and expanding strap. The design is not very aesthetic. But China has been making watches for the masses for only a few years; the day will come when she will compete with Switzerland and Japan.

[Until recently, China could only repair or rebuild old ships. Today, she is building 10,000 and 15,000-ton cargo ships with speeds of up to 17 knots. The first of these ships, the *Dong Fong* (East Wind), took nearly four years to build in Shanghai to a Chinese design. Even the 8,500 horse-power, oil-burning engine was built in China (the Chinese did consider building an engine under licence from a Swiss company, but so many restrictive conditions were demanded that the Chinese broke off the negotiations).

The hull of the sister ship to the *Dong Fong* was constructed in three months, while I was in prison. The Chinese plan a cargo fleet of 100 ships to make the country independent of foreign lines, and the time will assuredly come when Peking will insist that all goods exported to foreign buyers are carried in Chinese vessels.]

The train is pulling slowly out of the station. I check the time with my watch. It is nine-fifty. The train is leaving punctually to the minute. The interpreter tells me we are due to arrive in Canton at 7.00 p.m. tomorrow.

I settle in my corner of the carriage and look out of the panoramic window. The train, drawn by a coal-burning locomotive, is gathering speed. Shanghai is left behind. I suppose I shall never see it again. Momentarily the thought makes me feel sad.

I have a feeling that the guards do not wish it to be known to other passengers that I am a prisoner. Ten minutes after the train has left Shanghai, the senior guard addresses me: 'I am sure you would like to go to the toilet and have a wash and shave.' (My long, unbrushed hair and unshaven face are certainly rough-looking.)

If the same suggestion had been made in prison I should have jumped at the opportunity. But at this moment it is not important. I know that within forty-eight hours I shall be able to do what I wish. To refuse to accept the guard's suggestion is a pleasure. (Also, I do not wish to leave the window at that moment: I want a close look at the environs of Shanghai and the semi-urban communes that feed the city's millions.)

I reply: 'I have not had a haircut or shave for many weeks or combed my hair for many months. To wait a little longer is no hardship. I will do it later.'

This reply disconcerts the guard, but he does not press the point. An hour later, however, he makes the same suggestion.

'Am I to be allowed to eat my meals in the dining car?' I ask.

'Yes.'

'Then I will wash and shave before lunch.'

The guards smile, look relieved.

At eleven-thirty I finally announce I will go and spruce up. I take my hairbrush and comb, razor, soap and towel along the corridor to the toilet. I have not seen my face in a mirror since I entered prison. I am almost afraid to look at myself. When I was arrested I had only a little grey hair at the temples, but when my hair and beard were trimmed in the prison I noticed on the cloth around my neck some almost white hair. I expect to find my hair has turned grey, but to my astonishment I find it has hardly changed colour, though my shaggy beard is almost white. I present a revolting sight. I look like a beatnik.

When I return to the compartment the guards eye me with pleasure. The interpreter says: 'It is nearly time to eat. What would you like?'

'As I have been on a very low diet,' I reply, 'I had better not eat a heavy meal. I should like a little clear soup and some chicken.'

'I will go and talk to the cook,' says the interpreter, immediately leaving the compartment and vanishing down the corridor. He is back again in a few minutes.

'The cook is very sorry,' he says, 'that he cannot give you chicken at this meal but he will prepare it for you this evening. He will make a dish of pork for you now.'

I smile. There is no escape from pork. The meal, however, is excellently cooked and served; the dining car spotlessly clean. The three guards eat at one table; I alone at another. Every few minutes the interpreter turns and enquires if there is anything I want. I ask for bread and butter; he tells the waiter. It is produced immediately. It tastes delicious.

At dinner in the evening, the cook keeps his promise by preparing chicken for me. And throughout the two-day journey to Canton, any food I ask for is cooked for me.

On the morning of the second day I have diarrhoea, which I assume has been brought on by the change of food. (In Hong Kong two days later, it was diagnosed as dysentery.) The guards are very concerned. I tell them not to worry.

As I finish my lunch, the train stops at the station of a small town. The interpreter and one of the guards leave the dining car. In a few minutes they return with a doctor, carrying a first-aid kit.

He is a grey-haired man of between fifty and sixty years of age. He speaks fluent English. He enquires my symptoms, checks my temperature and blood pressure, puts the stethoscope on my chest to listen to my heart action. He prescribes antibiotic tablets, advising me to see a doctor when I arrive in Hong Kong. All this transpires in the dining car. I thank him and he leaves.

Back in our compartment, I enquire from the interpreter: 'Did you call the doctor especially for me?'

'Yes,' he replies. 'We called the hospital by radiotelephone.' I express my appreciation. But I assume I am a great responsibility to them: they do not wish me to leave China unwell.

It is suggested that I lie down and sleep—the custom of all Chinese after a meal. I say I am not tired. The truth is, I want to see every inch of the journey during the daylight hours. The everchanging scene is fascinating; the countryside often beautiful.

The harvest is good. As we travel farther south it has already been garnered.

China is still a poor country. Many houses on the communes (and many on the outskirts of towns) have mud walls and earth floors; water is obtained from an outside communal tap. The houses are barely furnished, the family sleeping on *kangs* —brick beds with charcoal fires underneath to keep the sleepers warm on cold winter nights.

But if the surroundings are squalid, there is constant vitality. Children play lustily, excitedly, in spite of the way they (and their parents) are regimented—they march in crocodiles to school, each with his Mao Thought red book carried in a small red satchel with a red strap over his shoulder.

Roads and spaces between houses are clean and free of rubbish. The only smells come from cooking or manure on the fields. Cleanliness is a virtue. Flies were eliminated in a nation-wide campaign during which everybody swatted flies until there were virtually none left.

China is poverty and vitality. Children and laughter. Shrill revolutionary martial music belching from loudspeakers on the streets. Mao Thought meetings. Self-criticism.

And looking down on the scene from every wall and building, the fat, ever-smiling, benevolent face of beloved Chairman Mao, with a background of sunrays, or huge sunflowers.

(The train stopped on the first evening at a small station. The senior guard left the train and I saw him with a crowd of other passengers making a purchase at a kiosk. I assumed it was food. But when he returned to the compartment he opened a small parcel to reveal about a dozen Mao badges. They all portrayed Mao as a young man in the Red Army. The guards examined them excitedly, each making their selection. The interpreter then left the compartment and bought some more. When he returned I asked if I could have one too.

'Why did you buy so many?' I asked.

'These badges are made only in this town,' was the reply. 'We are buying them to give our friends.')

It is Friday evening. I look at my watch. The time is 6.50 p.m.

'What time shall we arrive in Canton?' I ask the interpreter, assuming that the train was probably running late.

'At seven o'clock,' he replies.

Ten minutes later the train draws into Canton station—dead on time after a thirty-one-hour journey.

Three officers of the Canton Security Bureau are at the station to meet us but we have to wait fifteen minutes for a car to arrive to take us to the East Wind Hotel, built only ten years ago. In architecture it might have been opened at the beginning of the century. And it is furnished in the same style.

We have not been in the hotel more than a few minutes when it is suggested that I might like to visit the Friendship Shop and buy some souvenirs. They are anxious for me to spend some of my foreign currency. Even in Mao's utopia the Chinese have not lost their business instinct.

To please the guards I agree. It will give me a chance to buy a present for my daughter, Anne, to add to the painting I bought in Shanghai the day before I was arrested.

I decide to buy a piece of carved ivory. I choose a model of a river junk—the husband at the tiller, the wife helping with the foresail. But the assistant who serves me is disappointed. She has used her best sales technique to sell me a miniature carved ivory screen. The price, £30, however, was more foreign currency than I felt prepared to give China.

In the hotel we have two adjoining bedrooms, each with three beds and a bathroom. The three guards who have escorted me from Shanghai are to sleep in one and I with the three security officers from Canton in the other.

We have returned from the Friendship Shop. I inform the interpreter I should like to take a bath before I have my dinner. It is nine months since I had my last bath—the only one during my imprisonment—in the hospital.

While I take my bath, the three officers from Shanghai and the Canton police confer in one of the bedrooms. I am standing alone in my own bedroom drying myself with a large bath-towel. The young interpreter, whom I like very much, comes into the room.

'Tomorrow you will be free,' he says. He puts his hand on my bare shoulder and continues: 'I hope you are secure?' He says these words with emotion. A tear trickles down his cheek.

'If you mean by the word "secure" that I do not intend to harm your country, the answer is "Yes". As I have told you during our long talks on the train, I have always liked China, I have always liked the Chinese people. It made me sad that an innocent act on my part should be misconstrued. I have no intention of trying to do China harm. I wish your country and your fellow citizens well. I would like to see a better understanding between China and the western countries. Maybe, we have made mistakes. But so has your government, too. If there is to be a better understanding, the initiative must come from Peking. And there cannot be a *rapprochement* while your government preaches armed violence; interference in the internal affairs of other countries.'

He takes his hand off my shoulder. He looks me straight in the eyes. And then puts out his right hand and shakes mine. Without another word he turns and walks out of the room.

It is 9.00 a.m., Saturday, October 11—a day that I shall never forget. A four-man Pakistani delegation, which has travelled in the same coach with us from Shanghai, are at the Canton station bound for Hong Kong.

The platform is lined eight-deep with girl and boy students, of all ages. They give a performance of the picturesque hip drum dance as we board the train. The accompaniment is played on small cylindrical drums with sticks to which are attached long red sashes. As the drum is beaten the sticks are raised above the head, the red sashes streaming out like pennants.

To the interpreter, I say jokingly: 'You are giving me a joyful send-off.' He smiles.

Two hours later, the train, with seats adjustable like a dentist's chair, and foot rests, stops at the village of Shumchin. Although the railway line crosses the frontier, there is no through train to Hong Kong.

'You will be free in ten minutes,' says the interpreter.

'I hope so,' I reply.

176

But his ten minutes turns out to be half an hour.

The Immigration officer stamps my passport: 'Expelled.'

We proceed to the customs. The officer hands me a form. I have to declare all my money—which is then still in the possession of the senior security officer who has escorted me from Shanghai. I even have to record my cheque book.

The customs officer demands my money entry form in English. I explain that I was arrested aboard ship. In consequence, I was not given a money entry form. But he cannot accept this. I must have the form. Without it I cannot take my money out of the country.

The interpreter is explaining the situation in Chinese to the other security officers. They look embarrassed. There has been a slip-up. They have lost face.

They talk to the customs officer for several minutes, and then they retire to an office together, leaving me alone. They are gone for twenty minutes. On their return the customs officer says I may take my money.

He searches my luggage meticulously, examining the antique stamp on the Chinese painting I have bought for my daughter.

We walk downstairs to the Chinese side of the frontier—a hundred-yard, metal covered bridge. We sit down on a wooden seat. The interpreter takes from me the receipt for my money which was given to me when I entered the prison. He, too, produces receipts for everything for which he has paid on the journey from Shanghai—meals on the train, the overnight stay in Canton's East Wind Hotel, the ivory junk bought in the Friendship Shop the night before. He insists that I check his addition. He then gives me the receipts. I say I do not want them. I trust his accountancy. But he insists on my taking them.

He then hands me the remainder of my money to count. I find that since my arrest and imprisonment I have spent £56 on food from the Peace Hotel during the first ten days of my detention, winter clothing, washing bowls, cups, toothpaste, soap for washing and laundry, toilet paper, towels, straw mats for my low, wooden bed, Mao's works.

We all stand up. The senior officer gives me a short lecture. ' "Lifting a rock only to drop it on one's own feet" is a

Chinese folk saying to describe the behaviour of certain fools. The reactionaries in all countries are fools of this kind. . . .'

My luggage is piled beside me. They want me to carry it. I put my foot down and demand a porter. A porter is called.

Without any formal farewell, I turn round and walk across the bridge to freedom. I look back; wave my hand. The security officers are standing immobile, watching me.

Surely they do not expect me to retrace my footsteps into Red China?

Part Three

12   The Red Mushroom

As I sat at my desk on Sunday, April 26, 1970, writing this story of my imprisonment in China, the short-wave radio beside me blared out *Dong Fang Hong* (The East is Red), a revolutionary song in praise of Chairman Mao. The broadcast came from Communist China's first man-made satellite, launched the day before, and then orbiting immediately above my home on Hong Kong island.

The 380-lb satellite circled the earth every 114 minutes, passing over the United States, Britain and the Soviet Union. Ninety cities around the world were told by Peking exactly when the satellite would pass overhead, with repeated renderings of 'The East is Red', followed by telemetric code signals.

The wavelength on which the satellite broadcast, 20.009-mega Hertz, was the same as used by some Russian satellites—the first example of 'space jamming' of radio communications from earth to orbit.

This launching not only marked the beginning of China's journey into space, but, more ominously, emphasised that Peking is obsessed with nuclear status and is determined, at whatever cost to its economy, to go ahead with the production of nuclear weapons. Launching of a single satellite does not in itself indicate the existence of an operational missile force. But the fact that Peking is pressing ahead with its nuclear-weapons programme can only complicate the endeavours of the rest of the world to reach an agreement on the non-proliferation of nuclear weapons. And China is expanding her nuclear capability at an alarmingly rapid rate. Her potential is tremendous.

Estimates are that China has more than two hundred nuclear weapons on order and possesses 100 H-bombs. By the time this book is published, or shortly afterwards, she is expected by western intelligence experts to have tested an intercontinental ballistic missile (I.C.B.M.) with a range of 6,000 miles—probably by adding a third stage to the two-stage rocket used to launch the satellite. U.S. intelligence photographs have pinpointed considerable activity at a new launch complex in Manchuria, from which a missile could be fired down range more than 2,000 miles into Western Sinkiang province. The pace of development is being maintained with a native genius for natural sciences now applied to a centralised, high priority programme using both local and imported talent. Peking, too, has a vast pool of science students to draw on.

Chien San-chiang, director of the Institute of Atomic Energy of the Chinese Academy of Sciences,* in a *People's Daily* article of October 11, 1959, reviewed the progress in the peaceful uses of atomic energy made by China since the Communists came to power ten years before. Chien attributed the emergence of a 'strong scientific and technological force' in this field to the 'leadership and fostering' of the Chinese Communist Party and to the 'warm assistance of the Soviet Union'. He claimed that even before 1949 China had begun research work in nuclear science, though on a minute scale.

In 1950 China and the Soviet Union set up a joint body to exploit non-ferrous and rare metals, which included deposits of fissionable minerals in Sinkiang. Chien San-chiang and his wife, Dr Ho Che-hui, were said to have carried out a survey that year in various parts of China, especially Sinkiang and the north-east, to assess the extent of deposits of uranium and other radioactive minerals. The exploitation of uranium from mines near Urumchi in Sinkiang began in 1951 under Russian control. By 1954 various agreements were providing for the

---

* The Institute was founded in 1955. In 1964 it could boast 1,000 employees and 256 researchers.

'guided missile-nuclear weapon' test. The missile 'flew normally' and the warhead 'accurately hit the target at the appointed distance, effecting a nuclear explosion'. The test was carried out at Lop Nor in Sinkiang's Taklamakan Desert. This main testing site in a security area of 116 square miles is guarded by a special People's Liberation Army regiment known as the Black Eagles. It is one of six sites scattered around a huge marshy salt lake (though five may be dummy installations to deceive American and Russian spy-in-the-sky photography). Lop Nor is connected to Urumchi, the Sinkiang capital, near the uranium mines, by a canal built with forced labour.

China's principal source of nuclear weapons is at Lanchow, in Kansu province.* It is serviced by the city highway built by the People's Liberation Army, but it is forbidden to all vehicles except those connected with the nuclear plant, a complex of research buildings, underground workshops and deep shelters. It has a capacity to produce 100 kilogrammes of uranium 235 a year. Most of the ordinary work at Lanchow is done by political prisoners undergoing rectification through labour.

China's nuclear development is probably basically controlled by the army. The existence of a Scientific and Technological Commission for National Defence of the Army is known from Chinese sources; but its relationship to the State Council's similarly-named organisation is far from clear. The army's Commission may be in charge of studying and developing a nuclear weapons system. The Second Artillery Corps is possibly supervising the rocket unit.

* There are several other plants concerned with producing nuclear energy for military purposes. The Yumen plant, also in Kansu province, began working in 1968; it has a high-powered reactor which will eventually turn out more than 200 kilogrammes of pluton-239 annually. In the adjoining province of Chinghai, the underground thermo-nuclear bomb and missile assembly unit located between Haiyen and Huang Yuan on the eastern side of Koko Nor (Lake Tsinghai) also went into production in 1968. The plant is covered with grass to look like a playing field, and is serviced by a branch of the Lanchow-Sining railway. Other missile producing and assembly plants are located at Sian in Shensi province; Shenyang in Liaoning province; and Peking—where a two-stage liquid fuel missile with a range of 1,500–2,000 miles, similar to the rocket which launched China's satellite, is due to be tested in the near future.

It was reported more than a year ago that the Chinese Academy of Sciences had been put under the control of the Ministry of National Defence. The intention behind this move was said to have been to speed up the nuclear weapons programme because the defence planners had been frustrated by a series of delays caused by the Academy. The army had already had connections with work at the Academy since the autumn of 1967 when the army helped to set up Mao-study courses there. Peking radio spoke, on November 8, 1968, of the activities of worker-army Mao-propaganda teams at the Academy and its various institutes.

Our knowledge of the Chinese nuclear programme must remain inadequate. But there is ample evidence that the emphasis is on ballistic missiles rather than on H-bombs.

The rocket which fired China's satellite into space had sufficient thrust to fire a missile with a nuclear warhead several thousand miles, and a three-megaton warhead having a weight suitable for delivery by an I.C.B.M. has already been exploded. Western Intelligence estimates that China may have, by the end of 1972, 20 such missiles, rising to 500 by 1978, and 1,000 by the end of the decade—sufficient to overwhelm the defences of the United States and the Soviet Union (at present the United States' Sentinel system is designed to stop 40 to 50 missiles). Mr Melvin Laird, the U.S. Defence Secretary, has predicted that China will site the direction of its first nuclear missiles at the east or west coasts of America where there will be no anti-ballistic missiles to intercept them (the north-central area of America is protected by the Safeguard anti-ballistic missile system).

China has already deployed a small number of nuclear-tipped missiles with a range of 600–1,000 miles for use in an emergency against the Soviet Union.

China's satellite will have significant repercussions on the East-West balance of power in the next few years. The United States and the Soviet Union will have to perfect their anti-ballistic missile systems, as well as the multiple, independently-targeting missiles such as the Russians launched into space the day after China sent her satellite into orbit.

The Chinese ability to overtake western estimates of the pace of its technical development gives its satellite an additional psychological significance. The gap between the missile capability of the Americans and the Russians on the one hand and the Chinese on the other may seem particularly large, but it is one which even in technical terms is likely to be narrowed more quickly than one might think. In psychological terms this closing of the gap is also likely to occur much more rapidly.

While I was in prison the Chinese made their second and third H-bomb tests—the first was on June 17, 1967. The communiqués after the test were broadcast, as was usual with important announcements, at midnight; on the first occasion I was in hospital and so was able to witness the interest and excitement of the Chinese prisoners as they heard of their country's achievement.

The first H-bomb was dropped from an aircraft and was the seventh in China's nuclear bomb test series. While it took the United States eight years to progress from atomic to hydrogen bombs and the Soviet Union four years, China had made the leap in development in only two years and eight months.

The full significance of the launching of China's first man-made satellite will be felt in the long term. The occasion was exploited by Peking as an excuse for massive militant propaganda. Both North Vietnam and North Korea linked the satellite with China's development of nuclear weapons—hailing the combination as 'a potent force against imperialist aggression'. The Viet Cong and Hanoi congratulated China's army for its part in the 'glorious achievements in nuclear and space technology which build and strengthen the defence of Socialism throughout the world'.

That Communist China has every intention of trying to achieve some sort of military balance with the United States and the Soviet Union constitutes a serious complication for the strategic arms limitation talks (S.A.L.T.) between America and Russia. These talks aim at halting the spread of nuclear weapons and thus contributing to world-wide and general disarmament, and must take some account of China's achievement.

It is no longer realistic for these two powers to arrive at an agreement on a freeze or even a cutback of nuclear arms without considering China's potential.

Fears for future world security are founded on the irresponsibility shown in the past by the Communist Chinese in their development of nuclear arms. Totally indifferent to world opinion, China refused in 1963 to sign the partial nuclear test ban treaty which nearly every country in the world signed. Nor is China a signatory to the outer space treaty, which came into force on October 10, 1967, and in which ninety-three nations, including the United States and the Soviet Union, agreed not to put nuclear bombs into orbit or to appropriate the moon.

All this poses the question: for what purpose is China engaged on a military nuclear and rocketry programme? It strengthens the morale and unity of the nation; it acts as a deterrent against possible American or Russian attack; it gives China power and prestige in the world, especially with those countries where China is encouraging armed rebellion; it enhances China's possibilities of blackmailing neighbours.

Both Mao and Chou En-lai have said that China's main object is to break the nuclear monopoly held by the western 'imperialists' and Russian 'revisionists' so that these would be obliged to agree to 'the complete prohibition and thorough destruction of all nuclear weapons'.

Mao and Chou have also stressed that China will 'at no time and in no circumstances' be the first to use the bomb. But in reading this pledge one must remember Mao's statement in 1957 that in an atomic war 'if half of mankind died, the other half would remain: while imperialism would be razed to the ground and the whole world would become socialist'.

supply of Soviet research, equipment, specialists and operation manuals, and for the training of Chinese personnel at Soviet installations. In the following year at least one atomic pile was under construction in Sinkiang, and the Soviet Union signed agreements on the peaceful application of atomic energy with Poland, Czechoslovakia, Rumania and East Germany as well. Under the agreement with China plans were made for the installation of an experimental heavy water reactor near Peking, burning enriched uranium.

The year 1955 was also marked by the return to China of Dr Chien Hsueh-sen from the United States after nearly twenty years of studying, teaching and doing research work. This brilliant Kiangsu-born rocket expert was for six years head of the Guggenheim Jet Propulsion Laboratory at the California Institute of Technology—a space laboratory responsible for the Ranger, Mariner, Surveyor and Lunar orbit spacecraft.

Dr Chien tried to leave the United States in 1950 with eight large packing cases of scientific equipment, but was forced to remain for a further five years until the American security services considered that his science and technology was sufficiently out of date!*

China's first satellite orbiting the earth is probably Dr Chien's brain-child. But China has had the help of other foreign experts as well as Russians and repatriated Chinese, notably the Italian physicist, Pontecorvo, who defected from Harwell, Britain's atomic centre, to Russia; he spent a long time in China as a 'Soviet' expert.

Sino-Soviet co-operation reached a new stage with the foundation of the Joint Nuclear Research Institute at Dubna near Moscow. China contributed 20 per cent of the costs, providing a third of the research workers. This co-operation probably reached its height in the years 1956–58. Certainly Russia signed an agreement with China on October 15, 1957, to supply a 'sample of an atomic bomb and technical data

* Of the twenty-two senior men in the China Academy of Science, at least ten were educated in leading American universities. Others studied nuclear physics, astrophysics, ultrasonics, mathematics, computers and other expertise necessary to build nuclear bombs and rockets, in Britain, France and Russia.

concerning its manufacture'. And it has been suggested, but not confirmed, that work on a Chinese missile system began at about this time.

The Chinese leaders were considering the military possibilities of nuclear development. In June, 1958, Mao thought it entirely possible for 'some atom bombs and hydrogen bombs to be made in ten years'. These words were recalled when China's first hydrogen bomb was tested nine years later.

By 1959 the Chinese nuclear programme showed clear signs of expansion. On April 19 Peking University added an Atomic Energy Department and that year Tsinghua University, Peking, was building a 2,000 kilowatt atomic reactor. Other projects included the construction of a 2,500,000 electron-volt proton electrostatic accelerator and a high tension multiplier; the development of spectographs and detecting instruments; work in the field of nuclear electronics; the building of a cosmic ray laboratory in southern China; and research into the theory of atomic nuclei and fundamental particles, and into the chemistry and application of isotopes.

Work started in 1959 on the construction of an isotopic separation plant at Manchow in Kansu province, powered by hydro-electricity from the Yellow River and capable of producing the enriched uranium necessary for the manufacture of A-bombs. The plant is a gaseous diffusion plant capable of separating fissionable uranium 235 (used to trigger China's H-bombs) from uranium 238 (used for their jacket, covering a lithium core).

As new techniques were developed, an increasing number of Chinese scientists specialised in various branches of atomic research, and there was a corresponding increase in the number of young scientific workers.

With the intensification of the Sino-Soviet dispute, China became increasingly loud in her assertions of independence of foreign assistance in its nuclear programme. Russia, on June 20, 1959, abrogated the short-lived 'agreement on new technology for national defence' concluded in October, 1957.

In 1960 Soviet technicians were withdrawn. Chinese participation in work at the Joint Nuclear Research Institute at

Dubna continued, but on a decreasing scale. On March 25, 1960, the New China News Agency (N.C.N.A.) reported the discovery of a new nuclear particle at Dubna by a group of scientists led by Wang Kan-chang, the Institute's deputy director. At the end of 1962 there were possibly still about 70 Chinese there. But on June 23, 1965, N.C.N.A. reported the return to Peking of the '47 Chinese scientists' who had been working there. Their withdrawal may have been accompanied by the stopping of China's financial support.

In spite of the Soviet withdrawal, the Chinese continued to enlarge their nuclear resources. Further small experimental reactors were said to have been built at Wuhan, Hupeh province and in Shensi and Kirin provinces, and by the end of 1962 more than forty chemical plants had been built for the extraction of uranium and thorium, of which large deposits exist in Sinkiang and Tibet, and for the separation of plutonium from spent uranium from reactors.

On June 20, 1964, the *People's Daily* carried an article entitled: 'What is fissionable material?' It discussed in simple terms chain reactions, uranium, etc., and was presumably intended to familiarise its readers with the processes of releasing atomic energy. The article stressed the peaceful potential of nuclear force.

Four months later, on October 16, China exploded its first atom bomb. N.C.N.A. asserted China's right to defend itself, and denounced the partial nuclear test ban treaty of 1963. It said that China would never be the first to use nuclear weapons, and proposed the convening of a summit conference to discuss the question of the 'complete prohibition and thorough destruction of nuclear weapons'.

After this first Chinese explosion, the United States collected samples of the radioactive dust from the stratosphere and brought them down to earth. An examination showed that the Chinese bomb had been made from the isotope of uranium 235. The Americans, and probably the Russians, too, had hoped that the first Chinese bomb would be a plutonium bomb.

Plutonium bombs are in fact 'advanced' and were developed in America and Russia after the U-235 type, but they are what are called 'dirty' bombs—producing huge quantities of radio-active fall-out and therefore unsuitable for use in support of ground troops. Further, the manufacture of plutonium bombs does not require a particularly large industrial infrastructure. France made only plutonium bombs at the beginning of her atomic programme. But any country that can manufacture a U-235 bomb proves that it has a large atomic industry and armaments capacity.

Some physicists have advanced the theory that China has developed a completely new process for the manufacture of nuclear bombs. Theoretically there are fission processes which require considerably less electrical energy and a great deal less industrial plant than those at present used in the United States and the Soviet Union. But western physicists have so far found no way of putting these theoretical methods into practice.

Have the Chinese made a break-through? In the course of their history they have often demonstrated original and inventive genius. (China, after all, invented the rocket—for military purposes. During the siege of the city of Kai Fung-fu by the Mongols in A.D. 1232 a new weapon called an 'arrow of flying fire' was used by the Chinese to drive away their besiegers. It is agreed that the arrows were the first primitive rockets. China, too, invented gunpowder, though not for use in military weapons.) It may sound improbable that the relatively backward Chinese might be capable of making bombs more quickly and cheaply than the West, but the possibility is dis-turbing for American defence experts—and, no doubt, the Kremlin is worried too.

The third nuclear test, it is understood, was perturbing because the device contained elements which western scientists could not precisely define.

The first Chinese atomic-propelled submarine was probably launched at Dairen, Liaoning province, in the spring of 1965 and it was later reported that other submarines had been equipped to launch rockets from under-water, but the first real indication that China had made progress in missile development came on October 27, 1966 (in spite of the upheaval of the early stages of the Cultural Revolution), when N.C.N.A. announced a 'guided missile-nuclear weapon' test. The missile 'flew normally' and the warhead 'accurately hit the target at the appointed distance, effecting a nuclear explosion'. The test was carried out at Lop Nor in Sinkiang's Taklamakan Desert. This main testing site in a security area of 116 square miles is guarded by a special People's Liberation Army regiment known as the Black Eagles. It is one of six sites scattered around a huge marshy salt lake (though five may be dummy installations to deceive American and Russian spy-in-the-sky photography). Lop Nor is connected to Urumchi, the Sinkiang capital, near the uranium mines, by a canal built with forced labour.

China's principal source of nuclear weapons is at Lanchow, in Kansu province.* It is serviced by the city highway built by the People's Liberation Army, but it is forbidden to all vehicles except those connected with the nuclear plant, a complex of research buildings, underground workshops and deep shelters. It has a capacity to produce 100 kilogrammes of uranium 235 a year. Most of the ordinary work at Lanchow is done by political prisoners undergoing rectification through labour.

China's nuclear development is probably basically controlled by the army. The existence of a Scientific and Technological Commission for National Defence of the Army is known from Chinese sources; but its relationship to the State Council's similarly-named organisation is far from clear. The army's Commission may be in charge of studying and developing a nuclear weapons system. The Second Artillery Corps is possibly supervising the rocket unit.

* There are several other plants concerned with producing nuclear energy for military purposes. The Yumen plant, also in Kansu province, began working in 1968; it has a high-powered reactor which will eventually turn out more than 200 kilogrammes of pluton-239 annually. In the adjoining province of Chinghai, the underground thermo-nuclear bomb and missile assembly unit located between Haiyen and Huang Yuan on the eastern side of Koko Nor (Lake Tsinghai) also went into production in 1968. The plant is covered with grass to look like a playing field, and is serviced by a branch of the Lanchow-Sining railway. Other missile producing and assembly plants are located at Sian in Shensi province; Shenyang in Liaoning province; and Peking—where a two-stage liquid fuel missile with a range of 1,500–2,000 miles, similar to the rocket which launched China's satellite, is due to be tested in the near future.

It was reported more than a year ago that the Chinese Academy of Sciences had been put under the control of the Ministry of National Defence. The intention behind this move was said to have been to speed up the nuclear weapons programme because the defence planners had been frustrated by a series of delays caused by the Academy. The army had already had connections with work at the Academy since the autumn of 1967 when the army helped to set up Mao-study courses there. Peking radio spoke, on November 8, 1968, of the activities of worker-army Mao-propaganda teams at the Academy and its various institutes.

Our knowledge of the Chinese nuclear programme must remain inadequate. But there is ample evidence that the emphasis is on ballistic missiles rather than on H-bombs.

The rocket which fired China's satellite into space had sufficient thrust to fire a missile with a nuclear warhead several thousand miles, and a three-megaton warhead having a weight suitable for delivery by an I.C.B.M. has already been exploded. Western Intelligence estimates that China may have, by the end of 1972, 20 such missiles, rising to 500 by 1978, and 1,000 by the end of the decade—sufficient to overwhelm the defences of the United States and the Soviet Union (at present the United States' Sentinel system is designed to stop 40 to 50 missiles). Mr Melvin Laird, the U.S. Defence Secretary, has predicted that China will site the direction of its first nuclear missiles at the east or west coasts of America where there will be no anti-ballistic missiles to intercept them (the north-central area of America is protected by the Safeguard anti-ballistic missile system).

China has already deployed a small number of nuclear-tipped missiles with a range of 600–1,000 miles for use in an emergency against the Soviet Union.

China's satellite will have significant repercussions on the East-West balance of power in the next few years. The United States and the Soviet Union will have to perfect their anti-ballistic missile systems, as well as the multiple, independently-targeting missiles such as the Russians launched into space the day after China sent her satellite into orbit.

The Chinese ability to overtake western estimates of the pace of its technical development gives its satellite an additional psychological significance. The gap between the missile capability of the Americans and the Russians on the one hand and the Chinese on the other may seem particularly large, but it is one which even in technical terms is likely to be narrowed more quickly than one might think. In psychological terms this closing of the gap is also likely to occur much more rapidly.

While I was in prison the Chinese made their second and third H-bomb tests—the first was on June 17, 1967. The communiqués after the test were broadcast, as was usual with important announcements, at midnight; on the first occasion I was in hospital and so was able to witness the interest and excitement of the Chinese prisoners as they heard of their country's achievement.

The first H-bomb was dropped from an aircraft and was the seventh in China's nuclear bomb test series. While it took the United States eight years to progress from atomic to hydrogen bombs and the Soviet Union four years, China had made the leap in development in only two years and eight months.

The full significance of the launching of China's first man-made satellite will be felt in the long term. The occasion was exploited by Peking as an excuse for massive militant propaganda. Both North Vietnam and North Korea linked the satellite with China's development of nuclear weapons—hailing the combination as 'a potent force against imperialist aggression'. The Viet Cong and Hanoi congratulated China's army for its part in the 'glorious achievements in nuclear and space technology which build and strengthen the defence of Socialism throughout the world'.

That Communist China has every intention of trying to achieve some sort of military balance with the United States and the Soviet Union constitutes a serious complication for the strategic arms limitation talks (S.A.L.T.) between America and Russia. These talks aim at halting the spread of nuclear weapons and thus contributing to world-wide and general disarmament, and must take some account of China's achievement.

It is no longer realistic for these two powers to arrive at an agreement on a freeze or even a cutback of nuclear arms without considering China's potential.

Fears for future world security are founded on the irresponsibility shown in the past by the Communist Chinese in their development of nuclear arms. Totally indifferent to world opinion, China refused in 1963 to sign the partial nuclear test ban treaty which nearly every country in the world signed. Nor is China a signatory to the outer space treaty, which came into force on October 10, 1967, and in which ninety-three nations, including the United States and the Soviet Union, agreed not to put nuclear bombs into orbit or to appropriate the moon.

All this poses the question: for what purpose is China engaged on a military nuclear and rocketry programme? It strengthens the morale and unity of the nation; it acts as a deterrent against possible American or Russian attack; it gives China power and prestige in the world, especially with those countries where China is encouraging armed rebellion; it enhances China's possibilities of blackmailing neighbours.

Both Mao and Chou En-lai have said that China's main object is to break the nuclear monopoly held by the western 'imperialists' and Russian 'revisionists' so that these would be obliged to agree to 'the complete prohibition and thorough destruction of all nuclear weapons'.

Mao and Chou have also stressed that China will 'at no time and in no circumstances' be the first to use the bomb. But in reading this pledge one must remember Mao's statement in 1957 that in an atomic war 'if half of mankind died, the other half would remain: while imperialism would be razed to the ground and the whole world would become socialist'.

13 Expansionist China

THE Chinese call it Chen Pao (Treasure). The Russians call it Damansky. Both claim the 6,200 square-yard, uninhabited island, located in the midst of the frozen Ussuri River that forms the common border of Russia and China.

Precisely what happened in the first week of March, 1969, in this bleak, snow-swept wilderness of eastern Asia, while I was still in prison, may never be known. Tension between Russia and China boiled over in two small but fierce battles—the second more serious than the official accounts from both sides allowed.

Doubtless to serve her own purpose, Russia offered more details than the Chinese. The violence lasted for several hours on each occasion and both sides agreed that the situation came as close to war as the two countries have come in the long succession of border incidents and shoot-outs since their ideological split in 1960.

At least the equivalent of a battalion of men were engaged on either side, and armour, field artillery, mortars and heavy machine-guns were employed before the battles were over. Along any other frontier in the world, the scale of the battles would almost certainly have caused immediate large-scale mobilisation.

Moscow was the first to report the actions. Peking immediately countered it was a case of 'thief crying thief' (a favourite Chinese cliché) and that the incidents revealed 'the fiendish features of social imperialism'—a new epithet in the already lengthy and inventive lexicon that China employs against Russia.

According to the Russian version, the fighting was a coolly calculated aggression on the part of the Chinese. Under cover of wintry darkness, some 300 Chinese soldiers camouflaged in white uniforms crept across the river ice to the tiny island. Taking advantage of cover provided by a low hill and the island's trees and shrubs, the troops dispersed. A second unit concentrated mortars, grenade throwers and heavy machine-guns on the Chinese side of the river. They strung field telephones between the two units.

At dawn thirty armed Chinese appeared on the river-bank and crossed over to the island in full view of the Russian border guards. It was a type of mild intrusion that had happened frequently before. Senior Second Lieutenant Strelnikov, the Russian station commander for the area, took seven men and walked out to meet the Chinese. If the lieutenant's intention was to protest, he did not get the chance. As the two groups neared each other, the Chinese opened fire. Strelnikov and his men were killed—'literally killed at point-blank range by the Chinese provocateurs', according to the Soviet communiqué. At the same time the Chinese gunners across the river opened fire at the Russian border guards covering Strelnikov. The Russians rushed up reinforcements. The fight raged for four hours until the Chinese broke off the engagement with an orderly withdrawal, taking their dead and wounded as they fell back.

The Russians claimed that the Chinese inflicted 'blood-curdling brutalities' before they withdrew. Russian wounded soldiers were shot at point-blank range or bayoneted, some so mutilated as to be almost unrecognisable. The Chinese insisted that it was the Russians who opened fire first, that Soviet armoured vehicles had crossed the frozen Ussuri. But Peking offered scant details except photographs of captured Russian weapons and radio equipment.

What China did offer was an orchestrated but nonetheless astonishing display of country-wide protest. From my cell I could hear the noise of marching people for days on end. In Peking a million demonstrators jammed the streets around the Soviet Embassy shouting anti-Soviet slogans and carrying placards, HANG KOSYGIN! and FRY BREZHNEV! At least 150 million Chinese men, women and children all across the country frenziedly displayed their hatred of the 'new czars'.

China's Foreign Ministry assailed the 'Soviet revisionist renegade clique' for donning the 'mantle of czarist Russian imperialism'. In return, Moscow accused Peking of deliberately manufacturing the incident for the sake of arousing 'extreme chauvinism'. Although Soviet mass demonstrations failed to match the Chinese ones in size, 50,000 Russians stormed past the Chinese Embassy in Moscow, hurling rocks and inkpots that shattered 104 windows in the residence buildings, and left ugly, multi-coloured stains on their façades. Next day still more Russians marched, but violence was curbed. One poster read: 'BLOOD FOR BLOOD, DEATH FOR DEATH, DOWN WITH MAO.'

Considering the scrap of territory at issue, all the bloodshed and passion seemed scarcely worth while.

Chen Pao was originally a peninsula jutting out from the Chinese side of the Ussuri River. In the course of time, the river's shifting currents changed it into an island, which both nations then claimed. But the most spectacular provocations have been taking place further to the north, in the Amur–Ussuri area near Khabarovsk, the 'bread-basket' of the Soviet Far East. On several occasions the Chinese have marched prisoners to the centre of the river, accusing them of being pro-Soviet traitors, and then beheading them. Another favourite habit was forming up on the river ice, sticking tongues out in unison at the Soviet troops, then turning round and dropping trousers to the Russians in an ancient gesture of contempt. That tactic stopped when Soviet soldiers took refuge behind large portraits of Chairman Mao!

The territorial quarrels of China and Russia are by no means confined to this area, however. Continuing border disputes arise from the fact that since the Chinese Communists came to power in 1949, no boundary agreement with the Soviet Union has been finalised. The frontiers remain governed by treaties drawn up in the nineteenth century when Russia's Czar Alexander II took advantage of the faltering Manchu Empire to seize pieces of territory all along the two nations' 4,500-mile joint frontier.

Since around 1880, successive Chinese regimes have regarded these treaties as invalid and 'unequal'. Lenin described czarist policy in China as 'criminal' and in the first flush of the Russian revolution in 1917 proclaimed the principle of restoration of lands seized by the czars and national determination by subject peoples. Then on July 25, 1919, Leo Karakhan, Assistant Commissar of Foreign Affairs, stated: 'The Government of the Russian Socialist Federated Soviet Republics declares as void all the treaties concluded by the former Government of Russia with China, renounces all the annexations of Chinese territory, all the concessions in China and returns to China free of charge, and for ever, all that was ravenously taken from her by the Czarist Government and by the Russian bourgeoisie.'

This Declaration had a great impact on Chinese opinion and played a considerable part in China's conversion to Marxism. It was followed up in 1924 by a Sino-Soviet agreement providing for a conference, within a month, to 're-demarcate national boundaries' and to annul 'all conventions, treaties, agreements, protocols, contracts, etc., between the Government of China and the Soviet Government' and replace them with new treaties on the basis of equality, reciprocity and justice in the spirit of the Karakhan Declaration. The conference was never convened, but so long as Sino-Soviet relations remained amicable there seemed no need to face the issue of demarcation.

Today China can no longer afford to ignore it. Talks in Peking which arose from the March 1969 border battles have made no progress—at least not at the time of writing. The reasons for the deadlock are probably twofold: Russia's refusal now to accept the principle that something approaching 600,000 square miles of 'lost territories' were wrenched from China when she was weak; and Russia's refusal to withdraw her troops until the Chinese stop insisting on a complete Soviet renunciation of the czarist treaties.

The border problem is not exactly at the root of the Sino-Soviet dispute however. The Russians are pondering whether they should take action to prevent China from acquiring nuclear weapons in sufficient numbers to threaten Moscow. They have to decide whether China's pro-Russian elements can 'save' their country or whether Peking is setting up a naked military dictatorship, abandoning 'socialism' and even laying the groundwork for an alliance with the United States to encircle the Soviet Union.

In my submission China is already a military dictatorship. It is the most important development arising from the Cultural Revolution. It has been brought about by the country-wide setting up at all levels of the 'three-in-one' committees on which the People's Liberation Army representatives play the major role. This fragmentation of the P.L.A. is also an important factor in the country's preparedness for nuclear war. Because the P.L.A. is in effect governing China at every level, it means that in spite of widespread devastation from H-bombs, government in small units would still go on.

When Mao describes the H-bomb as a 'paper tiger' it is not quite a meaningless, rhetorical statement. Because of the vastness of China, her tremendous population, and the control exercised by the P.L.A., she is perhaps less vulnerable to nuclear attack than most countries.

However, from my own experience in China and from recent evidence, I think Peking today is genuinely nervous at the prospects of war. On July 31, 1970, to mark the forty-third anniversary of the Chinese People's Liberation Army, a joint editorial was published in the *People's Daily*, the *Red Flag* and the *Liberation Army Daily* and was specially broadcast as an 'important announcement' by Radio Peking. It called on the Chinese army to build up their ranks, heighten their vigilance and defend the motherland against a 'surprise attack' by social imperialism (the Soviet Union). The editorial was the strongest denunciation of Soviet troop deployments along its frontiers since the Sino-Soviet border talks began in Peking in October, 1969.

The editorial accused the Soviet Union of despatching troops to a neighbouring country (apparently Mongolia, which is wedged between China and Russia). 'She has not for a single day relaxed her preparations to attack China,' said the editorial. 'In words, she claims that she poses no threat to China. Why then does she mass her troops in areas close to the Chinese frontier? . . . Why has she despatched large numbers of troops into another country which borders on China? Why does she frenziedly undertake military deployments to direct her spearhead against China?

'It is clear that social imperialism says that she poses no threat to China only to weaken our vigilance and to fool the people of her own country and the world.'

The editorial then quotes Chairman Mao as saying that China would not attack unless it was attacked, and points out that: 'The people throughout the world know that it is imperialism and social imperialism which have conducted aggression and posed threats against China and that China does not have a single soldier stationed in any foreign land.'

Russia has created a new Central Asian Command along the border and is pouring out propaganda attacks in Mandarin Chinese broadcasts. During 1970, she deployed hundreds of tactical nuclear missiles and rockets in this area, including a new, solid-fuel mobile missile known to western Intelligence as Scaleboard. This missile, which is mounted on a tank chassis, has a range of 500 miles and carries a warhead of over one megaton (equivalent to 1,000,000 tons of T.N.T.). Conventional Soviet forces in the area now number at least 35 combat-ready divisions, with a rapid-reinforcement capability of 25 additional divisions.

The Russians are facing 50 Chinese divisions in Manchuria alone and another 8 divisions in Sinkiang. And it is believed that China has increased five-fold—to nearly 2,000,000 men—her armed production and construction para-military units along the entire northern border. The arms and training of border militia units have also been upgraded.

Inner Mongolia and the bordering Lanchow, Peking and Shenyang regions, which form natural invasion corridors, have been divided into three parts for the purposes of military control and civil administration. Instead of a shallow, elongated defensive position, the Chinese are thereby enabled to defend these areas in depth. China has also established a new military headquarters in the Wuhan region to co-ordinate country-wide defence in the event of invasion.

Although the Soviet Union and China have avoided overtly provocative military moves since the winter of 1969, Russia's military build-up has passed the point of merely being able to defend herself against a Chinese thrust. The military posture provides a clear offensive option, either conventional or nuclear. And the Russian build-up is continuing without any evidence of stopping.

In addition to the deployment of the potent Scaleboard missile along the China front, the Russians have added a fourth company to each of their Frog nuclear rocket battalions —in Europe, such battalions have only three companies. The Frog is a tactical rocket with a range of about thirty miles.

Existing Soviet border airbases have been expanded and dozens of new landing strips have been constructed, although they remain unoccupied. These strips could be used for a speedy logistics build-up, as well as serving as dispersed emergency strips for jet fighters and bombers. A massive airlift, such as was employed in the invasion of Czechoslovakia in August, 1968, could deposit upward of sixty divisions on the Sino-Soviet border within a few weeks.

On this evidence, it would be rash to assume that Russia would under no circumstances consider either a strike to destroy China's nuclear weapons capability, or a more extensive thrust against Peking aimed not at occupying China, but at installing a more amenable regime.

Although Russia could destroy China's nuclear installations, she would thereby earn the undying enmity of the numerous and increasingly powerful Chinese people.

As well as pressing ahead with her nuclear weapons development programme, China is also improving her conventional forces. She is now producing about 400 MiG-19 jets a year; tank and artillery production have also been stepped up. The regular army, which has been helping to run factories, communes, schools and government services since the Cultural

Revolution, is now devoting more time to military training. Large-scale field exercises are taking place.

But China's military capability is small compared with that of the Soviet Union, whose strength is even challenging that of the United States. Any analysis of the comparative nuclear strengths of the United States and the Soviet Union brings into sharp focus the weakness of China while she is building up her own capability.

Given her growing strength, the temptation for Russia to launch a pre-emptive nuclear strike against China within the next three years must be very great. If the Russians fear a possible *détente* between Peking and Washington, the Chinese are equally apprehensive of a better understanding between the United States and the Soviet Union.

Mao Tse-tung has bitterly criticised the Soviet Union for its territorial ambitions in Europe and Asia. She is seeking to gain control of the Middle East and its oil and establish a foothold in Africa.

Since the Cuban crisis revealed Russian naval weakness in supporting overseas political ventures, the Soviet Union has pursued an expansionist naval policy. She now has a powerful fleet in the Mediterranean (rarely less than fifty ships and sometimes as many as eighty: almost double the strength of the U.S. 6th Fleet) and she has gradually increased her strength in the Indian Ocean, the Persian Gulf and the Pacific. Bases to service the Russian fleet are being built at the eastern and western ends of the Mediterranean, and she also has the use of Alexandria. Since, under the Montreux Convention, Russia has to give ten days' notice to the Turkish Government to pass her ships through the Dardanelles, she makes daily applications although often not making use of the passage rights when granted. By this means she always has 'free passage' facilities through the Dardanelles for more than twenty ships.

The Arab-Israeli conflict has altered significantly the strategic balance in the eastern Mediterranean in favour of Russia. An effective air defence system is working over the air-bases in Egypt west of the Canal Zone, and about 10,000 Russian troops are stationed in Egypt in addition to about 4,000 technicians and advisers. This means that the Russian fleet, largely based on Alexandria, can be given cover by aircraft operating from well-known land bases. Although Soviet aircraft in Egypt at present do not have sufficient range to cover the fleet effectively, longer range aircraft could be flown in within a few hours.

To thwart Russia's Middle East aims, China is backing the Palestine Liberation Army with arms, money and training in guerilla warfare, in the hopes of bringing pro-Chinese Communist revolution to the area. As Chou En-lai said on February 21, 1970, in a letter to the late Gamal Abdel Nasser, then President of the United Arab Republic: 'Although this struggle is very arduous, I believe that through protracted struggle the Arab people will certainly overcome all kinds of difficulties.'

Mao has long recognized that Palestine is a ready-made people's liberation war. The 1967 Arab-Israeli war aggravated the position of both the United States and Russia by giving the Palestinians a sense of national entity, prodding them into taking the first steps down Chairman Mao's classical path of 'protracted' war.

Palestinians of all political shades have clearly indicated that Soviet policies in the Middle East are unacceptable. Russia helped establish the State of Israel. Any peace proposals which she might make and which would be acceptable to the United States and other western powers must call upon all Middle East states to acknowledge the sovereign independence of Israel. That the Palestinians will not accept. And this attitude will continue to have the political and material support (money and arms) of China.

After the lightning Arab-Israeli war in 1967, China stepped up its activities in the Middle East, urging the Arab nations to settle the Middle East question by military means. General Huang Yung-sheng, Chief of the General Staff of the Chinese People's Liberation Army, has on repeated occasions denounced all efforts of peaceful settlement of the Arab-Israeli crisis as 'a sheer plot for a Middle East Munich aimed at selling out the interests of the Arab people'. Peking's *People's Daily* has also published editorials harping on the theme that 'armed struggle is the only way to the national liberation of the Arab people'.

When Yasser Arafat, Chairman of the Executive Committee of the Palestine Liberation Organisation, arrived in Peking in March, 1970, as leader of a delegation of the Palestine Liberation Movement (Al Fatah), he was welcomed at the airport by Vice-Premier Li Hsien-nien and other high-ranking Chinese officials. At a banquet later given in his honour, amid mutual declarations of admiration, Arafat said: 'It is no secret if I say that the Al Fatah, initiator of the Palestine Revolution, received aid first from Peking.'

At the time of writing all Palestinian elements have rejected the United States' ninety-day 'cease fire' plan in the war between Israel and the Arab states. Although the plan has the backing of the Soviet Union and has been accepted by Egypt and Jordan, it has been rejected by Iraq. This is of the utmost importance in the Sino-Russian confrontation. It is through Basra, the port of Iraq at the head of the Persian Gulf, that China is supplying arms to the Palestinian guerillas. Funds from Peking are being transmitted via Baghdad.

Following the visit of Yasser Arafat, two deliveries of arms from China have been made to the Palestinians. The P.L.O., the moderate guerilla movement, has had diplomatic relations with Peking since 1965, although Chinese aid has been channelled principally through the two main Marxist-Leninist groups, the Popular Front for the Liberation of Palestine and the Popular Democratic Front.

But the Arab moves for a peaceful settlement of the Middle East is forcing the moderate guerillas to align themselves with the Marxists, otherwise they may face extinction. Their only Arab ally is the extremist Baath regime in Iraq, upon which the guerillas have relied for the safe passage of arms and material supplies from China.

The political base of China in the Arab world is Damascus where it has an embassy with an over-large staff of 100 diplomats, propagandists and spies. Here Chinese aid has not stopped at arms. Her instructors are at training bases in Jordan, probably smuggled into the country through the medium of several delegations of journalists and 'observers' which visited Jordan and Syria during 1969 and 1970.

Aden has been chosen by Chou En-lai for increased revolution in the Middle East. The choice is wise. Not only is South Yemen the base of operations for the Chinese-directed revolution movement in the neighbouring Dhofar jungle of Muscat and Oman, but the radical regime is poverty stricken and has suffered heavily by the closure of the Suez Canal. In August 1970 the Chinese announced an £18 million interest-free loan to South Yemen in addition to medical teams and experts in other fields. They are also building the Sanaa-Sada road, a technical school and a textile mill.

To strengthen her position in Africa, China, after prolonged negotiations, has signed an agreement with Zambia and Tanzania for the construction of the strategic 1,060-mile Tanzania-Zambia railway.

China has undertaken to lend the two African countries £168 million to cover the cost of the railway, which will take five years to build. The loan is interest-free and repayable over thirty years, starting in 1973.

The railway will run from Dar-es-Salaam to the Zambian village of Kapiri Mposhi on the existing railway network.

China's prime purpose in building the railway may be ferrying African guerilla armies to the borders of Rhodesia and South West Africa. However, for Zambia the main strategic significance of the railway is economic. Its construction will fulfil President Kaunda's dream of severing Zambia's dependence—because of trade and transport links—on the white south. Two-thirds of Zambia's vital copper exports are at present taken through Rhodesia or Portuguese territories, and an even higher proportion of imports travels the same way.

The Zambians at first had worries about the ultimate intention of the Chinese, and both the Zambians and Tanzanians had doubts about the financing of the railway. Apart from the loan—shared equally by Zambia and Tanzania—local costs of construction, such as the payroll of thousands of Chinese workers and the purchase of equipment obtainable locally, will be paid for under a plan which enables China to avoid having to spend scarce foreign currency. Local costs will be paid from the proceeds of selling Chinese goods on credit, to state-owned trading corporations in Tanzania and Zambia. This is by far China's biggest aid project (much bigger than the £14.5 million loan to Sudan in August, 1970).

China is also planning a long-range international air service linking China with Tanzania. It is to be inaugurated in 1971. She has purchased from Pakistan International Airlines four second-hand British-built Hawker Siddeley Tridents. Though smaller than the Boeing 707 and Douglas DC-8, the 100-seat Trident would be ideally suited for the service. Two of them have been delivered and are already being flown by Chinese civil air crews to familiarise them with performance.

China's latest move in Africa is to help Tanzania establish an air force using Chinese-built Russian-designed MiG fighters. Russia, anxious to break the increasing stranglehold on Tanzania, is pressing the Dar-es-Salaam-Tirana Government to build an up-to-date air force and supply it with weapons and missiles. But the Chinese grip on Tanzania is so strong, particularly since the Tanzania-Zambian railway agreement— a project turned down by the World Bank and several western nations—that Russia is likely to be excluded.

Further to strengthen her lines of communication to the Indian Ocean and the African continent, China has built a road through Pakistan which links up with one into Sinkiang.* She thus has an outlet through the important port of Karachi, which could be used by her fast-growing cargo fleet. The day may not be far distant when a Chinese naval fleet also enters the Indian Ocean, but it will be an insignificant force compared to that of the Russians.

Firmly entrenched in the Mediterranean and the Middle East, Russian strategy looks to the Indian Ocean as a focal point for strengthening her encirclement of China, with the Suez Canal as the essential route, once it is reopened. Already a Soviet flotilla of ten to fourteen warships of various types,

---

* When the Pakistan President, General Yahya Khan, was in Peking on a five-day State visit in November 1970, an agreement was signed whereby China is to loan Pakistan £83 million.

and submarines, is regularly sailing the Indian Ocean. By arrangement with the Indian Government, Russia has *de facto* bases in the Andaman and Nicobar Islands. Moscow also has 'advisers' at the port of Vishakapatnam on the east coast of India for training Indian submariners (Russia is giving India submarines).

Russia has an agreement with the small strategic Indian Ocean island nation of Mauritius, with a population of 850,000, which gained independence in 1968 after 175 years of British rule. Officially called a 'fisheries agreement', it offers Russia a range of facilities for so-called civilian planes and fishing vessels (whose additional role as 'spy ships' is well known to western governments). The island is ripe for a Communist takeover. All the ingredients for subversion are there: limited resources (the island is dependent on sugar-cane production and fishing), with accompanying poverty and unemployment; a rapidly increasing population, who are more interested in feeding themselves than in killing each other; and racial tension between the Indians, who make up 45 per cent of the population, and the other races—Creoles of mixed French and African blood, Arab Muslims, Africans and some Chinese.

Chinese Communist influence on the island comes from the Movement Mauricien Militant, which seeks its inspiration from Chairman Mao. Within its ranks are some 20,000 unemployed high-school graduates and teachers. To show them that they are not alone in their struggle, the Chinese have successfully smuggled rifles and other arms to the Movement—and the Russians, not to be outdone by Peking, are contributing financial support for the dissidents.

While the new British Government is committed to a 'presence' east of Suez, there are also indications that the United States will increase its naval strength in the Indian Ocean. At present the 7th Fleet—150 ships, 500 aircraft and 65,000 men—has an area of responsibility from Guam in the Pacific Ocean to the central Indian Ocean. Vice-Admiral Maurice Weisner, Commander of the 7th Fleet, has stated that he hopes for greater freedom, with the end of the United States' involvement in Vietnam, to commit American warships to the Indian

Ocean in numbers 'more than we have recently had'. He admitted that this commitment would be related to Russian activities in the area, though his desire for more U.S. ships in the Indian Ocean did not presage a new Washington policy.

Vice-Admiral Weisner said that to the best of his knowledge there had so far been no substantial Chinese units in the Indian Ocean. But this did not mean China had no significant naval capability. 'That would be far out of line,' he said. 'However, compared to what the Soviets are doing on the seas, the Chinese Communists have done very little.'

China has nevertheless declared her intention to emulate her former Communist ally and present-day rival, who built up her naval strength in less than twenty-five years to become the world's second largest naval force. Peking's *People's Daily* says: 'Whether or not we vigorously strive to develop the ship-building industry and build a powerful navy as well as a mighty maritime fleet is an important issue depending on whether or not we want to consolidate our national defence, strengthen the dictatorship of the proletariat, liberate Taiwan and finally unify our motherland, develop the freight business and marine products enterprises, build socialism and support world revolution.'

To this implied question, the answer is obviously yes. Although China's shipbuilding yards at Shanghai, Dairen and Canton are not impressive, one cannot dismiss her pretensions as absurd. She has certainly embarked on a big naval building programme to meet Soviet naval expansion in the Pacific and Indian Oceans.

The underlying motive of this new move was made plain by an earlier statement by the New China News Agency, which said: 'The Soviet Revisionist clique has time and again sent its fleets to South-east Asia and grabbed the right to set up naval bases in India, thus extending its military power to the Indian Ocean' in order to 'build a ring of encirclement against China'.

The *People's Daily* also insisted: 'We must work harder to develop our shipbuilding industry more quickly in order to build a strong navy and consolidate our national defence, when Soviet revisionism and U.S. imperialism are preparing to unleash a war of aggression against China.'

The seriousness of these preparations can no longer be denied. The thesis expounded by some experts that the war hysteria in China was being inflamed to reunite the country after the Cultural Revolution can be dismissed. The country is being mobilised because the Chinese perceive a real and deadly threat.

In South-east Asia, China is intensifying her involvement. Thailand, Malaya and Singapore are threatened. In Indonesia, General Suharto, the President, is still grappling with Communist guerillas, in spite of the massacre of some 300,000 in the abortive *coup* of 1966. China's position in Indo-China has been greatly enhanced since the overthrow of former Cambodian Head of State Prince Norodom Sihanouk and the subsequent American invasion of Cambodia. The Chinese have definitely scored off the Russians by supporting Sihanouk. On August 17, 1970, in Peking, China and Sihanouk's Royal National Union Government signed an agreement for free military aid. And it was disclosed on the same day by the New China News Agency that an agreement granting a loan to Sihanouk's government had been signed in May. The disclosure of the two agreements came only two days after a sharp warning from Peking to Thailand against 'increasing intervention in Cambodian affairs'.

It is obvious why Sihanouk turned to Peking for help instead of Moscow. He realised China's 'claim' to all the regions in South-east Asia, and he chose to back what he considers to be the power house for military and political dominance in the region. At the moment of writing, a third of Cambodia is under Communist control and so is half of Laos. The setting-up of a Liberation Front at a secret Peking-sponsored meeting of all Communist forces in Indo-China has welded these insurgent elements together under China's influence. All have agreed to fight until the Americans are driven out of the region and until 'running dog' leaders are overthrown.

China's foreign policy in Asia is easily understood. It is to wipe out United States influence from Indo-China and other areas. And to do so, she will support any force to wage a 'war of liberation' without necessarily becoming involved in the fighting.

The military stalemate in Vietnam and the American phased withdrawal is interpreted in Peking as a defeat for the United States. It has increased Peking's confidence that wars of liberation can be won.

Mr William Rogers, the United States Secretary of State, has said that a peace settlement could be quickly worked out if China would co-operate. British and French governments have toyed with the idea of new Indo-China negotiations at a conference similar to that in Geneva in 1964. The Soviet Government, too, might favour such a meeting as it has lost influence in the area since the U.S. military operations in Cambodia.

China today is in a far better position than she was before the fall of Sihanouk to exert her influence in Indo-China and make sure that a peace conference is meaningless. Also, she can see the day will come when her influence will cover wide areas and, without being complacent, she can afford to sit back and wait for these areas to be 'liberated' with her assistance.

Logically she feels that any negotiated settlement would mean settlement with some concessions being made to the opposing side. Why, then, negotiate and concede when victory can be won on the battlefields (or by the actions of the American people) without going through the indignity of making concessions at the conference table? She will not allow interference in Indo-China which has provided her with a valuable springboard for launching future wars of 'liberation' in South-east Asia. In my submission, it is not in China's interests while she is building up her nuclear strength, for wars in the Middle East and Indo-China to end.

During 1970 she made a major foreign policy effort. Whereas during 1969 five countries sent delegations to Peking and Chinese teams visited four countries between the months of April and July, in 1970 during these months fifteen countries sent delegations to Peking, many being granted audiences by Mao, and Chinese teams were sent to nine foreign countries. The main emphasis in 1970 was to demonstrate China's solidarity with North Korea and the 'united front' of Indo-China. It is too early to say what this re-emergence on the diplomatic scene means. But one would have to be a great optimist to assume that China wishes to 'normalise' relations with the rest of the world. Peking goes on preaching Mao's gospel of armed revolution in all countries.

War between the Soviet Union and China may be drawing steadily closer. Russia has advised Moscow-oriented Communist parties: 'Naturally the Soviet Union cannot permit events to develop in such a way as to bring about protracted frontier wars, and we will undertake additional measures to safeguard the interests of the Soviet people and the frontiers . . .' What China expects those 'additional measures' to be is shown by the huge scope and intensity of her defence preparations.

The army has divested itself of some of its usual civilian roles. There have been heavy troop movements towards the frontier provinces. Militia training has been geared to combat conditions. The communes are preparing to continue resistance when cut off from the centre, even after enemy occupation. Trenches and deep shelters have been dug in the cities and towns against air raids.

On the political level Russia has been conditioning other Communist governments to believe that Chinese actions might leave Russia no alternative but to carry out an 'invasion' on the Czechoslovak model in defence of the socialist world. The Soviet government could, in fact, claim they were freeing the Chinese people from the tyranny of Mao.

For the Russians, China is a historical enemy. To liken Mao to Genghis Khan is credible to the Russian people. China is regarded by Moscow as expansionist (ignoring that Communist Russia, too, is expansionist) and daily growing stronger. Moscow can visualise the day when China is militarily and economically as powerful as Russia, or even stronger. This decade must see every Russian city open to nuclear attack by China. And as China appears to disregard the threat of nuclear war, she might not be susceptible to deterrents.

The temptation for the Soviet hawks to undertake a short, ruthless and conclusive offensive, either by a combination of air and land forces or by missile strike alone, must be very great. In the case of the latter, Russian troops might not be committed. Russia has broadcast to China in Mandarin Chinese that 'in a nuclear war an enemy can deliver very powerful strikes against the most densely populated areas of a target country at the outbreak of the war without sending troops to invade it'. And the Russians have declared that if they fight, it will be with nuclear weapons.

On paper, the military strength of Soviet Russia is superior to that of China. The Institute of Strategic Studies puts the Russian armed forces at 3,300,000 men, with 250,000 para-military troops and 2,100,000 trained reservists. The Chinese are estimated at 2,820,000 with 300,000 para-military troops. I am inclined to the belief that the People's Liberation Army is stronger. Recruiting was going on while I was in prison. Because of its immense responsibilities, military as well as civil, I would put the figure at 3,250,000. The duties of the P.L.A. are numerous. They are responsible for telecommunications, road building in remote areas, medical clinics in the country-side and the over-all supervision of local government at all levels.

Chinese reserves are more difficult to calculate. In 1958 Mao announced a people's army and the 'everyone a soldier' movement. In this period a figure of over 200 million was spoken of. At that time there were not sufficient arms or training facilities to maintain such a vast force. But the idea must not be dismissed as ludicrous. In Switzerland every man is a trained soldier. Israel's trained reserves total a tenth of the population. Mao's ambitions are not impossible. The Russian threat has provided the nation-wide incentive.

In terms of fire-power and mobility, the Russians are far superior to the Chinese. Their motorised rifle divisions and tank divisions are designed for rapid movement. Russia, too, has a substantial airborne force. Out of a total organisation of 150 divisions, she has about 35 deployed on the borders maintaining her confrontation with China.

The latter is adequately equipped with standard range infantry weapons—all produced in China. She also has light and medium artillery and is manufacturing 75-mm recoilless rifles, machine guns, light and medium mortars (up to 122 mm) and 90 mm rocket launchers. Although she has been short of vehicles, heavy and self-propelled artillery and tanks, these deficiencies are being made good by a drive of self-sufficiency. (The supply of modern tanks to Pakistan is significant.) By preaching a philosophy of 'frugality', Mao is persuading the Chinese to accept 'guns before butter'. Nor is it difficult to convince his people that they are in dire peril from attack from outside.

The Russians have declared that they will not hesitate to use nuclear weapons. But would they attack Chinese cities? Robert McNamara, when U.S. Defence Secretary, suggested that the destruction of fifty Chinese cities would knock out the industry and leadership capability of China. Russia is certainly powerful enough to carry out such an attack, either using bombers or rockets, but to forecast what effect this would have on the remainder of the country is impossible. It is a contingency, as I have said, that Peking has already taken into consideration and for which nation-wide preparations have been made.

The truth is that no one can hazard a guess at what degree of nuclear devastation would be needed to bring China to her knees. The Chinese say that nuclear attacks on 1,000 towns would wipe out no more than 11 per cent of the population. It is impossible to know if Chinese leaders who traditionally place a rather low value on human life would be ready to accept these losses.

Russia is confronted with a China daily growing more powerful. So long as the country is led by Mao, seeking to dominate the Communist world and plotting to overthrow by force of arms the capitalist world, the problem for Moscow remains. Only a political disintegration of China can free Russia from painful decisions in the near future. Not even the death of Mao, and the accession of Lin Piao to the leadership, would necessarily change the present policy of China. In his foreword to the second edition of *Quotations from Chairman Mao Tse-tung*, Lin Piao wrote: '. . . the most fundamental task in our Party's political and ideological work is at all times to hold high the great red banner of Mao Tse-tung's thought, to arm the minds of the people throughout the country with it and to persist in using it to command every field of activity . . . to build our country into a great socialist state with modern agriculture, modern industry, modern science and culture and modern national defence.'

The Russian invasion of Czechoslovakia and the Ussuri River battles transformed Chinese thinking. To Japanese visitors in 1964, before Krushchev fell, Mao said he was fighting a paper war with Russia and it could go on for twenty-five years. But it is no longer entirely a paper war. In consequence, while China builds up her military might, Mao and the group with which he is surrounded, including the indispensable Chou En-lai, are exercising an extremely cautious approach to the threatened conflict.

It is just possible that the danger point of Russia attacking China has passed. But this does not mean that the crisis in Asia is over. By the middle of this decade—certainly by the end of it —China will be sufficiently powerful in the military field—(and politically, too, perhaps) to blackmail Russia.

Although China is the fourth largest country in the world— 3,768,726 square miles—it has to feed today a population rapidly approaching 1,000 million. While I was in prison I made many calculations to reach an estimate of China's population, based on official figures. Like Harrison Salisbury, I reached the conclusion that if the figure was not already 1,000 million, it would most certainly be so within the next few years.

When I lived in China in the 'twenties the population problem was solved by floods, famines, disease, and civil wars, as it had been for countless centuries. Today, because of modern medicine and hygiene, life expectancy is longer. Birth control has made little advance, even though male members of the Party are not permitted to marry until thirty, nor women until twenty-eight, and early marriage for all young people is discouraged. Further, married couples have to keep their families to three children; if they have more, the additional children are denied ration cards.

In other words, China may one day be faced with a critical

food situation. Harvests during recent years have been
including those during the Cultural Revolution, and pe
are being urged to produce bigger and better harvests, but h
more than two-thirds of China's lands are under cultivation—
mainly because vast areas are sparsely populated mountainous
and desert regions. (To overcome the problem of drought,
three major water-conservancy projects, employing 1,750,000
workers, were completed in 1970.) Already, for the past
decade, China has had to import large quantities of food,
largely grain from Canada, Australia, New Zealand and
France. Wheat imports have risen to six million tons a year.
To earn the necessary foreign currency to pay for these food
imports, China sells food to Hong Kong—high-value meat, pigs,
eggs, butter, milk, fruit and vegetables.

China will not starve in the next few years. But there is harsh
logic in Peking's territorial demands on Russia. And beyond the
territories lost to the czars are the virgin lands of Siberia. If
famine can be perceived, then Mao's polite suggestion to
Krushchev in 1954 for 'rectification of frontiers' will make a
lot of sense.

Today, we are talking about a population of 1,000 million.
In the next century, the twenty-first, it may be almost doubled.

If war comes in the next year or so, the aggressor will be
Russia. But if war is avoided now and if, at some future date,
a China able to compete on equal nuclear terms with Russia
is confronted with the problem of whether to starve or fight
for the 'lost territories', she will undoubtedly choose the latter.

Either way the world watches, with a growing sense of
apprehension.

INDEX

Acupuncture, 66
Aden, Chinese influence in, 199
Alexander II, Czar, 191
Andaman Islands, Russian base, 201
Anti-British campaign and propaganda, 1–2, 112
Arab-Israeli conflict, 196, 197
Army Day message (August, 1966), 15
Atomic energy and weapons in China, 177–88:
    exploitation of uranium, 180; I.C.B.M., 180, 186; Sino-Soviet co-operation, 180–2; Soviet with-drawal, 182–3; first atom bomb exploded, 183; plutonium bombs, 183–4; atomic-propelled submarine, 184; guided missile test, 184–5; development controlled by army, 185; further H-bomb tests, 187; launching of satellite (1970), 179, 187; China's nuclear policy, 187–8

Baath regime, Iraq, 198
Barker, Garry, 37
Barrymaine, Norman:
    incident in Shanghai (November, 1967), 2–8; attempt to enter North Korea (January, 1968), 36–47, 88; detained off Chungjin, 42–7, 52–3, 56; and Pueblo 'confessions', 46, 52; sails to Shanghai in Hanoi, 55; off Shanghai, 56–61, 68; on shore in Shanghai, 61–8; questioning and searches on Hanoi, 72–85; inter-rogated in Frontier Station, 85–101; attempts to obtain confession from him, 87, 89, 91, 98, 101; made to write life history, 94–7; and photo-graphy of warships, 98–101, 120–1; accepts responsibility for three rolls of film, 101, 102, 124; medical ex-amination in hospital, 103–6; further interrogation at Security headquar-ters, 107–13; and ritual observance to Mao, 109–10; charged with espion-age, 113; imprisonment, 1, 2, 38, 114–68; interrogations in prison, 118–31; 'confessional' block and 'confessional' sessions, 122–4; draft 'confession', 130–1, 156–7; life in prison, 132–41; cleanliness routine, 132–4; bugs and ants, 134; reading matter, 135–6; exercise and exercise yards, 136–7; food, 137–8; prayer, 138; reaction to solitary confinement, 138–41; illness, 142–51, 157–9; taken

to Ward Road prison, 142–3; in prison hospital, 144–6; discharged and readmitted, 146–7; types state-ment in hospital, 147; life in hospital, 147–51; final interrogation, 157–60; ordered to be expelled from China, 165; taken by train to Canton, 168–176; journey on to Hong Kong, 176–8
Bevin, Ernest, 139
Blake, George, Russian spy, 136
Boxer rising (1900), 2
British Consulate, Shanghai, 3, 62
Bucher, Commander Lloyd M., captain of the Pueblo, 46, 48–52; 'con-fession', 46
Burgess, Guy, 97

Cambodia:
    China and, 203–4; U.S. invasion, 203, 204
Canton, 175–6:
    East Wind Hotel, 175, 177; Friend-ship Shop, 175, 177
Censorship and distortion of news, 139–140
Central Asia Council, Soviet, 194
Central Committee of the Communist Party of China, 22, 25–6, 34:
    meeting (August, 1966), 14–15; sixteen-point decision, 15; new public security regulations, 32
Central Intelligence Agency (C.I.A.), 80, 108, 152
Central Military Committee, Urgent Directive (October, 1966), 22
Chang Chun-chiao, Vice-President of Cultural Revolution Group, sup-ports Shanghai Rebels, 25, 30–2
Chang Chung-chang, General, 170
Chang, Dr, Shanghai surgeon, 105, 142
Chang Tso-lin, General, 170
'Change of attitude,' 31, 87, 165
'Character posters,' 12, 16
Chen Pao island, 189, 191
Chen Po-ta, head of Cultural Revolu-tion Group, 11, 13, 16, 24:
    compiler of Mao quotations, 11
Cheng, China Travel Service guide, 2, 6–8
Cheong, China Travel Service guide, 56–7, 61, 64, 65, 67
Chiang Ching (Mao's wife), 12, 13, 16, 34, 122, 123, 141, 165:
    in charge of Chinese culture, 12
Chiang Kai-shek, General, 49n., 79

212

16; Red Guard activities, 17–18; nuclear energy plant, 185n.

Peking Review, propaganda magazine, 135, 140

Peking University:
purge, 13; Atomic Energy Department, 182

Peng Chen, 12–13:
purged, 13; publicly humiliated, 19

Peng Teh-huai, 13

People's Daily, 17, 19, 140, 183, 193, 197–8, 202

People's Liberation Army (P.L.A.), 159, 161, 163:
mobilised by Mao against workers' violence, 32–3; becomes dominant power in China, 32, 193; Cultural Revolution Group, 32; Mao's reliance on it, 33; prison guards, 114, 115, 118, 136, 137, 144, 147, 153, 158, 168, 169; Black Eagles regiment, 185; estimated strength, 206

Plutonium bombs, 183–4

Poland and China, 111

Polish Ocean Line, 37, 38, 76, 90, 108, 111:
and Chinese authorities, 111

Politburo, Chinese, 13

Pontecorvo, defects to Russia, 181

Popular Democratic Front, 198

Popular Front for the Liberation of Palestine, 198

Population of China, estimates of, 208

Press, *see* Official press

Propaganda machine of Communist regime, 139–40

Public Security Bureau headquarters, Shanghai, 106

Pueblo incident, 36, 41–3, 46–54, 88, 108:
'confessions' of officers, 46, 52; involvement of Soviet navy, 47–8, 50–1

Quemoy, 79

Quotations from Chairman Mao Tse-tung, *see* Mao Thought

Radio Peking, 193

Ramage, Rear-Admiral James, 78–80

Red Flag, Peking newspaper, 30, 193

Red Guard Despatch, 26

Red Guards, 33, 59–60:
recruitment of two million students, 9, 16; activities in Peking, 17–18; purges of Party workers, 17–19; Peking Red Guards in Shanghai, 20–2

Red Lantern, The, Peking opera, 141

Richardson, Admiral David, 79, 80

Rogers, William, 204

Salisbury, Harrison, 208

Sanpietro, Nando, 83

Sassoon, Sir Victor, 61n.

Scaleboard missile, 194, 195

Scarlet Guards:
set up in Shanghai, 27–8; fighting with Rebels at Kunshan, 28–30; discredited, 30

Schools, closure of, 14

Scientific and Technological Commission for National Defence of the Army, 185

Seamen's Club, Shanghai, 63–4, 68

Shanghai, 3–6, 8:
university purges, 13–14; Red Guards, 20, 22; arrival of Peking Red Guards, 20–2; ferment among workers, 23–4; Rebels, 23–9; Scarlet Guards, 27–30

Shanghai General Hospital, 103–6, 142

Shanghai Institute of Foreign Languages, 6, 57

Shanghai Municipal Party Committee, 20–9:
headquarters attacked by Peking Red Guards, 21; and the Rebels, 23–7; reorganisation required by Rebels, 31

Shanghai prison for foreign and political offenders, 1, 114–41, 152–68

Shanghai Workers' Headquarters (the Rebels), 23–33:
hijacking of train, 23–4; *Liberation Daily* building taken over, 26–7; fighting with Scarlet Guards at Kunshan, 28–30; 'Message to all the People of Shanghai', 30; infiltration in factories, 32

Shenyang, nuclear energy plant, 185n.

Sian, nuclear energy plant, 185n.

Sihanouk, Prince Norodom, 203, 204; Chinese support for, 203

Sinkiang, 185:
fissionable minerals, 180, 181

Sino-Soviet co-operation on atomic development, 180–1

Sino-Soviet dispute, 44, 45, 193–4, 205–9:
border disputes, 189–91; fighting on Ussuri river, 189–90; Russian propaganda attacks, 194; Russian military build-up, 194–5; Chinese conventional forces, 195; Soviet expansionist naval policy, 196; estimates of Russian and Chinese strength, 206–7

South Yemen, Chinese influence in, 199

Stalin, 16–18

Strategic arms limitation talks (S.A.L.T.) between U.S.A. and Russia, 187

Strelnikov, Senior Second Lieut., 190

Strong, Anna Louise, 80